D1570633

NOURISHING WORDS

SUNY SERIES IN FEMINIST THEORY IN EDUCATION
MADELEINE GRUMET, EDITOR

NOURISHING WORDS

*Bridging Private Reading
and Public Teaching*

WENDY ATWELL-VASEY

STATE UNIVERSITY OF NEW YORK PRESS

Cover Art: *A Reader* by Albert Joseph Moore, 1877, oil on canvas. © Manchester City Art Galleries, Manchester, England. Reproduced by permission.

Poem on p. 111, "Dream Deferred" ("Harlem") from *The Panther and the Lash* by Langston Hughes, © 1951, is reprinted by permission of Alfred A. Knopf, Inc.

Passage on p. 116 excerpted with permission of Scribner, a division of Simon and Schuster, from *A Farewell to Arms* by Ernest Hemingway. Copyright 1929 Charles Scribner's Sons. Copyright renewed © 1957 by Ernest Hemingway.

Published by
State University of New York Press, Albany

© 1998 State University of New York

All rights reserved

Printed in the United States of America

LB
1576
.A797
1998

For information, address State University of New York Press, State University Plaza, Albany, NY 12246

Marketing by Dana Yanulavich
Production by Bernadine Dawes

Library of Congress Cataloging-in-Publication Data

Atwell-Vasey, Wendy, 1952–
    Nourishing words : bridging private reading and public teaching / Wendy Atwell-Vasey.
        p.   cm. — (SUNY series in feminist theory in education)
    Includes bibliographical references and index.
    ISBN 0-7914-3631-4 (hc : alk. paper). — ISBN 0-7914-3632-2 (pbk. : alk. paper)
    1. Language arts. 2. Language and languages—Sex differences. 3. Feminism and education. 4. English teachers—Biography. 5. Curriculum change. I. Title. II. Series: SUNY series, feminist theory in education.
LB1576.A797 1997
428'.007—dc21   97-45757
                                                                                                          CIP

10 9 8 7 6 5 4 3 2 1

For Craig—

whose love and labor have sustained me;

and

for Bridget, Adam, and Dylan—

who have inspired me to try harder for all children.

CONTENTS

PART III
Regenerating the Curriculum

APPENDICES
The Teachers' Autobiographies

FOREWORD

Many of us in educational theory and research were drawn to the field of education by the expectation that we would act on what we knew. Implicit in curriculum studies was the promise that we would gather together what we understood about learning, the disciplines, the institutions of schooling, and our own insights on educational experience to construct learning experiences for students that were engaging and enlightening. Rightly, we recognized that in order to understand the experience of education, we needed to grasp its fullness. We needed to understand its social history, relationships to economy production and media, and we needed to understand the social construction and epistemology of the academic disciplines. We needed to understand the motives that draw us to study literature, or geology, or anthropology, as well as the motives that direct our interest in teaching little kids, or administering school districts. Curriculum theory invited us to study all these things and to bring our understanding to bear on what happens at ten o'clock in a tenth grade classroom in Sioux City or a head start program in Philadelphia.

In the past twenty years we have developed some sophistication in these studies and we have found company among postmodern theorists of gender, culture, epistemology as they, as well, have studied the motives that draw us to learning and teaching as well as the social histories and meanings of the disciplines and the institutions of knowledge that shelter them. Distinguished by its creativity, range, and liveliness, our scholarship has made curriculum theory a vital and provocative field of inquiry.

Nevertheless, as the field has stretched its scope and imagination, making its view larger and its tools of analysis more varied, it has sought to capture educational experience in a larger mesh, and too often what goes on in schools and classrooms has fallen through our sieve. As we have worked our way out from what Paulo Freire called the "limit situations" of schools and lessons to what he called the "generative themes" that addressed the social, historical, material, political, and psychological influences on our concrete problems, we have lost our mooring in curriculum, unable or unwilling to tie what we understand about education to what we do, day after day, in schools.

Wendy Atwell-Vasey's powerful study of literacy, *Nourishing Words: Bridging Private Reading and Public Teaching*, realizes the promise of curriculum theory by gathering together what we know and what we do with what we feel and what we want. In this study of three teacher's reading experiences and teaching practices, Atwell-Vasey, using object relations theory, offers ways for us to understand how limits on learning are both imposed and sustained by the resistance that teachers feel about engaging students in the profoundly emotional and personal experiences that they associate with their own experiences of reading. The method of this work has required her to engage both narrative and ethnography, combining what people say about their experience with an observer's account of what they do in the classroom. It has involved weaving together narrative texts, classroom texts—reading assignments, syllabi and mid-term exams—and the professional discourse of the field of English education.

The thread that Atwell-Vasey pulls through these texts is her conviction that teaching and reading are both acts of communion, grounded in love and relation. But love is not easy, she recognizes, and instead of falling into a sentimental evocation that makes us all feel as if only we have failed to love, to read, to teach well enough, she explores, carefully and persistently, the reasons for our half-hearted renditions of deeply beloved experiences. By bringing the work of Kristeva, and of object relations theory which situates language development within the dramas of attachment and separation that shape identity, to a reading of autobiographical narrative of reading, Atwell-Vasey *uses* narratives and theory to make something new. She is able to use the autobiographies of April, Jane, and Phillip without exploiting them because she has located them within a theoretical discourse that is rich and complex enough to embrace them without diminishing them. She is able to use them without exploiting them because she sustains her own interest and connection to these writers, maintaining her recognition of their independence and the dignity of the conflicts and issues they present.

Finally, she is able to use these materials because instead of merely presenting them to us in a display of ambivalent motives and inadequate pedagogies, she uses this material to create curriculum, nourishing us.

MADELEINE GRUMET

ACKNOWLEDGMENTS

I would especially like to thank Madeleine Grumet whose brilliance, courage, hard work and kindness come in equal and great measure and who taught me and cared for me.

Thank you to my mother, Julia Herrmann, my late father, Robert Herrmann, and my siblings, Bob, Laurie, and Alan Herrmann for their love and the language they gave me growing up.

Also thanks to Charlotte Itoh, Laurie Watkins, Steve Watkins, Linda LaFave, Diane Wood, Paula Salvio, and Maynard Mack for their help, interest, ideas, support and friendship.

Thank you to Bernadine Dawes and Lois Patton at State University of New York Press.

Special thanks to April, Jane, and Philip.

INTRODUCTION:
RELATIONSHIPS AMONG LANGUAGE ARTS,
AUTOBIOGRAPHY, AND FEMINISM

> Like music, the patterns of melody, rhythm, and quality of
> voice become templates against which we judge the sweet-
> ness and justness of new patterns and rhythms; and the pat-
> terns laid down in our memories create expectations and
> hungers for fulfillment again. . . . I picture each of those lay-
> ers of experience and language gradually accumulating and
> thickening to form a kind of living matrix, nourishing like a
> placenta.
>
> —Robert MacNeil, *Wordstruck*

Words have always been nourishment. We fill our bodies with them to
comfort ourselves; we send them into the air to join us to other people.
Words stand for us on the page—they push themselves on the page,
indenting, imprinting, impressing the sheet and impressing others. We
want people to live by our words as they would live by us, and we
want to be helped by what we hear and read. These are our objectives
as language users.

They come to us from everywhere. Words float gently around us,
at hand, to be plucked like plums. Or they strike us suddenly like birds
sweeping down from an unseen perch. They course through our veins,
waiting to be called for service, and we search them out on the lips of
other bodies. To not have any words in life is rare: cooing with mother
at the breast, crying at being left alone, whispering in bed with a sibling, laughing in the bathtub with Dad, haggling with playmates over

a toy, joking in the streets of the neighborhood, arguing over the dinner table or in court, singing in the church choir, in a rap group, in a rock band, hollering our pain, whooping our joy, making our case.

But a hush falls over the school classroom. The lush word climate that sustains students and teachers in private life somehow turns into a thin and rarified school air. Children find themselves in classrooms in which only a very few and certain words are wanted and it is a puzzle as to which ones they might be. Children learn to leave their words outside, in the hall, on the bus, at home, removing them like muddy boots. Words stick in their throats. And they are surprised to find that just as they are no longer understood by others, they do not understand. They stare at unyielding marks on a page, at blank lines on the ditto. They strain for meaning in primers that are not about anything. They feel dulled by textbooks and lectures that do not ask them anything. Even teachers do not know what to say to the class, what to write to the parents, whether to talk at faculty meetings. Used to finding words whenever and wherever they wanted or needed them in daily life, people crossing the bridge to school, experience the wind being knocked out of them and often find themselves silent, or wanly imitative.

To be sure, in public society, words are regulated, and specialized vocabularies prevail. But I would argue that the inventive and organic use of language by participants in the daily business of our public and private institutions is more welcome and more counted on than it is in schools. I think this is true even in law courts, hospitals, and corporations. In those places, we may have official forms, documents, and language protocols, but we still deeply appreciate and seek out the particular talker or writer who speaks from the heart, from wide experience and diverse seasoning. Think of the trial lawyer who, after all the depositions, and affidavits, and indictments, has the last word with the jurors. Think of the doctor with the good bedside manner. There is a premium in corporations on advertising and public relations people; it is they who are relied on to relate to other people, to use inventive and touching language to connect. In journalism, it is not the reporter or writer who knows the formula who makes a good story or a great paper, but the one for whom the rules are just scaffolding, just background, for a fresh effort to show us a new world or new way of looking at the world.

If the flow and vitality of words are so prized in daily life, why are they constrained so harshly at school so that there results a kind of deafening silence?

I think it is that students are resocialized at school into thinking that language is a generalized map of words, and a system of signs and rules established and owned by others elsewhere. That which drives language in all walks of life, intention and desire, is neglected and defended against in school. Instead, teachers rely on structuralist grammars and formalist literary criticisms, curriculum choices that do not include human relations or motives as objects of concern.

In her book, *Verbal Hygiene*, Deborah Cameron discusses how traditional grammar and traditional pedagogy are related in content and form by beliefs, values, and goals selected to order and fix a language that seemed chaotic, vulgar, and liable to degeneration (1995, 104). Cameron, a British linguist, writes,

> If it was intended either to enhance pupils' actual linguistic performance or to give them a metalinguistic understanding of English structure, traditional grammar teaching was a conspicuous failure. Studies conducted when grammar was still a formal part of the English language syllabus at GCE 'O' level [upper ability level at age 16], found that instruction in grammatical analysis had no discernible effect on reading comprehension or writing skills, while in addition many examination candidates had failed to master the techniques of grammatical analysis itself despite many hours of instruction . . . preference for methods that do not work must be seen in the light of the moral significance they accord to grammar. If the lesson is less about language than about order, good behavior and respect for authority, the value of drilling becomes much clearer . . . the issue of grammar was persistently linked to a nostalgic yearning for grammar schools. . . . And the logic of the connection is once again not difficult to see. There is the linguistic coincidence ('grammar'/'grammar school'), the historical link (according to popular belief, grammar schools taught grammar whereas secondary modern and comprehensive schools did not), but most of all there is the underlying value system based on order, tradition, authority, hierarchy and rules. (1995, 105)

In rendering a scene from the sociologist Mary Evans's study of traditional grammar schools, Cameron reviews Evans's memory that she and her classmates "passed their time underlining nouns in red and verbs in green—a procedure which left them with the vague impression that 'grammar is rather like traffic lights'" (p. 106). Cameron reports from a research project of her own, "Most people remembered grammar lessons as scenes of failure and humiliation. 'I could never do it,' and 'I never got the hang of it,' were recurring comments, . . . but they waxed sentimental about the good old days of order and certainty." Grammar was something "you could get 100 per-

cent for" (p. 107). Cameron concludes that worries about the lawless-
ness of lower classes and immigrants made people pin their hopes on
grammar. Linguistic law and order, she concludes, are discernible not
only as grammar, but as hyperstandardization as practiced by stylistic
authorities, for instance, "where orderliness takes the form of an endless quest to make the rules exhaustive and absolute" (p. 219). "Messi-
ness, fuzziness, uncertainty and relativism may be part of life, but if
we try we can banish them from the more tractable sphere of language" (p. 218).

But I think to use language well, students need to stay close to
the way they use words in life—as a way to sustain themselves and
other people. Educators would be better off, I think, to focus on this
signifying process of students, that is, what students mean and want
from language. The grammars, structures, and stylistic forms so preva-
lent in the language curriculum should be treated as ancillary to the
larger function of language as a signifying practice, and resituated to
help students shape what they want.

This book is about how language arts teaching, or English education, as it is called in higher education, can be realigned to acknowledge that linguistic structure comes from within ourselves, and
between ourselves, and not from outside ourselves.

Julia Kristeva, the French linguist and psychoanalyst, reconcep-
tualizes language as a signifying process. Interested in language as a
relation between bodies, she focuses on "biophysiological processes
(themselves already inescapably part of signifying practices, what
Freud labeled 'drives,')," and "social constraints (family structures,
modes of production, etc.)" (Kristeva 1986, 28).

Kristeva is not the first to write about the connection between language and desire—the link between what people want and what they
write, read, and say. Jacques Lacan, another psychoanalyst, asserted
that the psyche is structured like a language, emphasizing that language and symbolic activity absorb what we want into their structure,
shaping and determining what we feel, think, and strive for.[1] Lacan
conceded that there is always a gap between what we want and what
can be said, but that it is the structure of language that allows us to
know at all what our experience in the world is *like*, if not, what it *is*.

Lacan's ideas, although situated in desire and psychoanalysis,
are still compatible with those of structuralist linguists, like Chomsky,
and a history of teaching language as a structure to be imposed. However, unlike Chomsky, Lacan's emphasis is on how linguistic structure
is internalized through unconscious early relations with parents and
other significant others (Wilden in Lacan, especially pp. 160–177). For

Lacan, the signifying *system*, stands ready to engross a fragile, dispersed psychotic existence into a structured and symbolic one.

But Kristeva disagrees that language's structural qualities deserve the credit for all this shaping. Kristeva sees the structures of language—rhythms, grammars, syntaxes, and symbols as extensions of existing *body and relational experiences* that have linguistic qualities. For teachers, I believe, this alternative view makes all the difference. Kristeva helps us see that schools ought to be making use of how students experience language in their bodies and in their social relations so that they can better generate and control its courses. She sees this not as a paternal function, as Lacan and Freud did, but as a maternal one.

THE RULE OF THE FATHER

But to back up a little, how did the structured and symbolic ordering capacities of language come to be associated with a paternal ordering capacity in the first place? A cornerstone in the accumulated and prevailing philosophical account of human development is the need for "natural" material, like human bodies, to be civilized by culture. Such a dualism is familiar in Plato, Rousseau, and Descartes (see Bordo, Flax, Keller). It was not Freud who first associated the two elements, nature and culture, with women and men respectively (we will see such references later in Plato), but Freud did make the associations between nature and culture more explicitly female and male and more explicitly part of family relations. For Freud, the super-ego was paternal. He wrote, "The super-ego arises, as we know, from an identification with the father taken as a model" (Gay 1989, 655), and did nothing less than "represent the ethical standards of mankind" (Gay 1989, 37).

It was hard for Freud to prove or count the presence and influence of the father as the authority figure in our families and our institutions. But, of course, we noticed that very father in our laws, customs, religions, and moral codes. He dominates how we name our children, our ideas about what a conscience is; his presence is there in the judge and the priest, the one who owns property first and votes first. He is the one at whom Freud asked us to look harder; to consider who this father was to us in ways we had not thought about before. For Freud, it is the paternal function that is law-bearing, and among the first laws to which the child submits, are the laws of language. Thus, we see the connection between psychoanalysis and language and the association between authoritative, paternalistic law and language, an association quite meaningful, we shall see, to schooling.

Lacan, a Freud revisionist, went on to link language to the father much more explicitly than Freud. He carried on Freud's line of vision that the structuring capacity of fathers was civilizing, but he especially saw language as the medium by which paternal authority structured the psyche (Lacan 1968, 165).

Given the disputes among major psychoanalytic theorists, and its speculative basis, how can a psychoanalytic understanding of language enrich our options? As the history of psychoanalysis has proven, speculation has its costs and benefits. The results mean we can imagine both more and less. Freud's visions, both researched and speculative, put us on a track that ignored other paths. But it opened new courses as well. The images of significant others in our lives are drawn more sharply now, so that we can study them. If some believe more than ever in the myth of the authoritative father, others more actively wonder or worry about this doctrine. Although it is crucial to critique paternalism, I think it is vital to study language development from the domain of our early relations with parents and other significant others, a context that is often neglected in our thinking about language arts teaching. In my prologue, Robert McNeil's quote is a reminder of what we intuit about a language environment in which we are embedded in "a living matrix." This living matrix is composed of bodies and relations. But without psychoanalytic theory, we are left with the *mystery* of language as a force or network surrounding us, and we are left confounded as to its pedagogical implications. Although we want to keep the link between parental care and language, the problem is that Lacan linked the signifying system with the *paternal* order, and the emphasis on domination, law, and deferment associated with it.

In contrast, Kristeva found it inescapable to look at she who most frequently brought language to the child, the mother,[2] and she shows that a corporeal and social relationship to her, was prototypical of language experience. She also warned that because the mother is female in a patriarchal society, her contribution to language experience will have been severely neglected and distorted in linguistics. As Kelly Oliver observed in her book, *Reading Kristeva,* for Kristeva,

> social problems always have their core in representation: and she argues that our representations of maternity are not only detrimental to women but, since the first relation is with the mother, to all human relations. To reconceive of this relation is to reconceive of human relations. (1993, 7)

In their pioneering work, Kristeva, Nancy Chodorow, and Dorothy Dinnerstein made motherhood more visible as an institution, as a sociology of cultural reproduction with a history pertinent to teaching. These writers focus on how what is maternal is masked and distorted in patriarchy. Kristeva's work in maternal theory opens up this history and sociology of nurturance and teaching to questions of representation. How has the historical mother been represented in art, language, and professional practice? Unimpressed by the naming of biology and culture as foundational distinctions in the representation of self-formation, Kristeva finds constructed *gender* to be foundational in the re-production of human beings. For Kristeva, that we as bodies and as symbolic actors, form and represent ourselves as male and female, girls and boys, mothers and fathers, daughters and sons, sisters and brothers, is the germinal problem to be studied in how we reproduce ourselves. These categories are not essential for Kristeva; they are, rather, representations that are currently foundational, and represent original divisivenesses in body and self formation.

DIVISIVENESS AND GENDER

Feminist interpretation has sought to question and undo gender divisiveness, as it ought. But Kristeva is warning us that the inevitable pain and unpredictability of divisiveness itself in self-formation as body and psyche, will not disappear with the jettisoning of gender. Worse, she is warning, particular social practices born of divisiveness that have been genderized historically and oppressively, may nevertheless be valuable and lost to representation when they lose their gender representation. Such, she suggests, may be the social practices we represent as maternal. Kristeva traces self-formation as beginning in bodily processes regulated by social caring practices, both characterized by divisiveness—the intake and expulsion of material, the holding and unholding of the body related to psychic holding, the stops and starts of body fluid, changes in temperature and light, and so on. She turns our attention to how mothers, as transhistorical caretakers, nurtured and taught human beings through mutuality, involving physical actions like touching, holding, and releasing, and psychic mechanisms like projections and reduplications of experiences.

Maternal practices are often unacknowledged or distorted in patriarchies, those societies that live by the dominance of masculine strategies and power. We are aptly warned by feminist educator, Madeleine Grumet, that school is the place in patriarchies where children are delivered from the mother's private and nurturing world to the father's public and demanding one.[3] What has traditionally come to be associated with women (nature, biology, body, sexuality, desire, nurturing) is often exiled off from mainstream linguistic theory's reliance on maps of general cognitive development or structural syntactics. In this scheme of things, language learning in school is conformity and little pleasure. It means teaching writing and reading to students whose histories as language users are to be ignored and whose need for language is irrelevant. But I believe that Kristeva's maternal theory brings back to the center of language learning theory, the need to nourish the speaking, reading, and writing student as a subject who was brought to reality and language by others through love.

A MATERNAL MODEL

Kristeva, a linguistic scholar and practicing psychoanalyst, writes a theory of a powerful and nourishing parent, which is a representation or model that dissents from both Freud and Lacan. In this newly configured standard, the primary Other to us children, often a mother, first fed our bodies and held our bodies, setting up the regulation of drives that is transformed into speech. She also loved us into language by allowing us to imagine ourselves in her place, as speaking subjects, not by our understanding of the words or referents she used, but by our knowledge of the position she occupied and the functions she performed. Third, by turning her attention to the attractions of the world, and staying close to us at the same time, she made it possible for us to identify with her desire and enterprise, and thus to be enterprising and hopeful that words lead us out to the world in order to act on it. These are three maternal legacies for language use (which I introduce in Part I) from which we can draw a new way of looking at teaching language arts.

When we turn to maternal theory, not only are we challenged by sexism, but by the fact that we are unconscious of many aspects of the biophysiological and sociofamilial relations through which language comes to us. We do not remember crisply, clearly, and discretely, the circumstances in which we uttered our first words (How did my body move and how did it feel? Who was there? Who was not? What did I want? Whom did I want? What were the stakes? What did I lose? What did I gain?). The event must have been saturated with biological and environmental processes and limitations. Psychoanalysis, especially the branch of it known as object relations theory, seeks to help us recover some of these unconscious experiences by naming, shaping, and researching these processes and limitations, and to locate the desires, losses, pleasures, and efforts that we constantly ask language to carry. Psychoanalytic discourse challenges the talk we are used to in education, which funnels meaning into static and controlled positions beyond the reach of the projections, introjections, reversals, repressions, and fantasies of real humans who strive with and against the limitations of biology and culture.

USING FEMINIST OBJECT RELATIONS THEORY
AS AN INTERPRETIVE LENS FOR ENGLISH TEACHING

The critical theorist, Jurgen Habermas, made a case for how interpretations of experiences can help people take new action. Here, I am offering feminist object relations theory, with an emphasis on the maternal, as an alternative perspective for interpreting language arts and English teaching. Teaching is a self-formative process, and in his book, *Knowledge and Human Interests*, Habermas describes how the interpretation of self-formative processes, works as a method to promote new action. He writes:

> Here we are dealing not with an empirical theory, but a metatheory, or better, metahermeneutics, which explicates the conditions of the possibility of psychoanalytic knowledge. Metapsychology unfolds the logic of interpretation in the analytic situation of dialogue. In this respect it is on the same level as the methodology of the natural and cultural sciences. It, too, reflects on the transcendental framework of analytic knowledge as an objective structure of organized processes of inquiry, which here include processes of self-knowledge. However, in contrast to the logic of the natural and cultural sciences, methodology cannot exist detached from material content at the level of self-reflection. For here the structure of the cognitive situation is identical with the object of knowledge. (1968, 254)

Teaching, as a self-formative process, can only reflect on itself *in self-reflection*. This stance is a significant departure from the action research paradigms currently in vogue in education, which ask participants to reflect on themselves in action. Reflection on action or reflection in action, extends the logic of the natural and cultural sciences as it requires a subject who studies not how she or he thinks, but the objects of her or his actions, supposedly abstracted from thought. These objects are not much different from the objects that empirical educational researchers have made of children's activity abstracted from *their* thought. In contrast, for studying self-formative processes like teaching and learning, Habermas sets the standard that basic metahermeneutical assumptions derive from subsequent reflection on the conditions of the inquiry. The use of autobiographical narratives by teachers in the study of teaching in recent years has provided a form for the language and thought of teachers about their own teaching. Narratives of teaching display conditions of thinking, action and feeling for the purpose of study for teachers who want to change. In my view, they are most valuable as records of conditions of inquiry on which teachers reflect, subsequent to adopting an interpretive framework. For the purposes of self-formation, they are not to be regarded in themselves as empirical objects of science. The narratives, rather, ought to be used as indicators for the teachers who wrote them of the life-world (including consciousness and action) of the same teachers' inquiry.

Complementary to a record of the history of the conditions of the teacher's inquiry located in the narrative, in Habermas's words, are self-processes represented *schematically* as a "*systematic generalization* of what otherwise would remain pure history" (1968, 259). Here, psychoanalytic object relations theory is used as such a schema. In psychoanalytic theory, individual history "is represented schematically as a self-formative process that goes through various stages of self-objectivation and has its telos in the self-consciousness of a reflectively appropriated life history" (p. 259). If this feminist interpretation of self-formation comes to mean something to teachers, it will take shape as a meaning that changes how they would narrate their teaching stories, thus opening up new possibilities for their action. Habermas stipulates, that

> In the final instance, the meaning of the process itself must be capable of becoming part of our consciousness in a critical manner, entangled as we are in the drama of life history. The subject must be able to relate his own history and have comprehended the inhibitions that blocked the path of self-reflection. For the final state of a self-formative process is attained only if the subject remembers its identifications and alienations, the objectivations forced upon it and the reflection it arrived at, as the oath on which it constituted itself. (1968, 260)

A recognizable general interpretation like this feminist one (or any other) is necessary in interpretive scholarly inquiry. Habermas writes:

> A general interpretation . . . must break the spell of the historical without departing from the level of the narrative representation. It has the

form of a narrative, because it is to aid subjects in reconstructing their own life history in narrative form. But it can serve as the background of many such narrations only because it does not hold merely for an individual case. It is a *systematically generalized history*, because it provides a scheme for many histories with foreseeable alternative courses. . . . Here the concept of type designates a quality of translatability: a history or story is typical in a given situation and for a specific public, if the "action" can be easily taken out of its context and transferred to other life situations that are just as individuated. We can apply the typical case to our own. It is we ourselves who undertake the application, abstract the comparable from the differences, and concretize the derived model under the specific life circumstances of our own case. (1968, 263)

The psychoanalytic, feminist, object relations framework is an interpretive scheme that I narrate in this book. It is a story about human development, especially with regard to language, desire, and attachments to parents and primary others. In order to meet the criteria Habermas rightly outlines for hermeneutic interpretation, it is a systematically generalized history and it remains in narrative form. The action of the story's characters, who are children, parents, and significant others, can be transferred to the stories of teachers. This translation is what I set out to accomplish in this book.

PRELIMINARIES FOR READING PSYCHOANALYTIC NARRATIVE AS AN INTERPRETIVE SCHEME

To gather diverse and elusive human activities into its discourse, psychoanalysis is not only abstract and metonymic—it not only names things in order to generalize and handle them—it is also metaphorical, in that it relies on the imagination of its users to see that we can only include some elusive phenomena in our talk by letting other things, more sensible to us, stand in the position of the more elusive phenomena. For example, Kristeva uses words like the Greek "chora" meaning "womb" to help us imagine our own sensual receptacle of experience. Her use of "chora" reminded me of Robert MacNeil's use of the "nourishing placenta," which binds together templates and patterns of language experience. We find other metaphors in psychoanalysis such as "ego," that Latin word for "I," related to forms of "I" in Greek, Teutonic, and Old English cultures used to speak of the self. "I" is also a Roman numeral for one and so "ego" and "I" can be compared to an expression of experience unified. Ego helps us see mind when it is consciously unified, in relation to "Id," a word meaning a more dispersed energy source, according to the *Oxford English Dictionary*. We know that the metaphorical position in which we put elusive phenomena is not a perfect fit, but we come closer to these phenomena by trying them out in the new position. For example, our language experience is not a placenta, but thinking of language in the position of one, helps us focus on how language surrounds and fulfills us. By contrast, in the field of education we are used to relying on the orderliness of the labels and categories we posit to define experiences. We rely on this positivism to such an extent that we replace experience with the names chosen for them, and forget the slack between phenomenon and name. But metaphors invite comparison, not complete identification. With their visceral, sensual, dimensional quality, they do not easily replace the experiences to which they refer. This mind set of comparison, leaving spaces for reflection and conversation, is the one I hope readers will adopt in dealing with the psychoanalytic theory in this book.

Letting one thing stand for another, but never completely believing that it can, is the theme for this book. Child and mother stand for one another; words stand for people, wishes, things, and each other; theories and stories stand for experiences—but we are conscious of the incomplete comparisons.

AUTOBIOGRAPHY AS REFLECTION
ON THE CONDITIONS OF INQUIRY

I asked three English teachers to write multiple narratives of both their personal and school reading experiences because I think their texts can stand provisionally for an American culture of English teaching in today's schools. In these texts I find questions and problems that suggest a familiar discrepancy between how teachers are moved by language and literature in their personal lives and what they do in their classrooms, and I look at these problems in the light of feminist psychoanalytic theory. I also find in them the kernels of ideas for curriculum choices that more vividly connect language to the worlds they adjoin—ideas for using theater, dialogues with other students, journals, and community enterprises.

My request was for the teachers to write at least three separate autobiographical narratives about reading literature or learning to read literature, to write a reflection on this process, and to show me some curriculum samples illustrating how they teach literature. I asked that the narratives be separate reminiscences written at separate sittings so that it be clear that none of these was the definitive objectification of their experience, but all were provisional, open, and only alternatives. The teachers, called Philip, Jane, and April, wrote four to five narratives each, over the course of about five months, and offered me a number of curriculum samples to look at. The complete autobiographical narratives as submitted to me, are located in the Appendix.

Jane has taught secondary English for many years in a large suburban school system near a metropolitan area. She is a poet and painter, has five grown daughters, and has written about her American Literature class in her autobiography. Philip is also a veteran teacher of high school English who teaches in a magnet high school for boys in a large city public school system. He was a pioneer in computer work and writing initiatives at his school. He has written about his ninth grade English class in his autobiography. Both Jane and Philip have, and are continuing to work on advanced graduate degrees and have taught in diverse settings. Robin is newer at teaching, having taught in a private high school for girls in a large city for three years at this writing. She has lived abroad as a child and travels extensively. She has written about her eighth grade English class.

Autobiographical narrative is a technique on which I have come to rely. In the classes I taught at George Mason University, near Washington D.C., I asked participants to write autobiographical narratives related to the topic we are exploring in class. In the Master's of Education program which focuses on curriculum development and teacher reflection and research, teachers write about their own educational experiences. In an interdisciplinary course on the self as citizen, first-year undergraduates write about personal experiences they associate with course topics: forming communities; work and family; leadership; welfare and homelessness. Methodologically, there are strong benefits to this autobiographical practice. First, by bringing material to the academic table, class members experience their participation *explicitly and in relief*, so that their efforts, investments, responsibility and freedom are demanded and not taken for granted. They experience themselves in conversation and partnership with theory and research because the narratives provide material throughout the course for dialogue with what they read, view, and discuss in class.[4] As the teachers' coursework progresses in the foundations of education, such as philosophy, psychology, sociology, and history, and as they prepare to design and conduct their scholarly inquiry and research projects, they revisit their narratives to flesh out theory spread too thin or to reinterpret what has happened to them. Often their reflections suggest gaps in theory and then remedies, and often theory offers them a chance to invest their experiences with new meaning.

This pedagogical use of autobiographical writing is not meant to unite subjectivity—it is meant to lay out its dimensions and the dimensions of the worldly settings in which we locate them. Thus autobiographical narratives used in the reflective process, including the entries I submit here, are not always dramatic, nor do they stand on their own as comprehensive stories. They are meant to be studied, like research data might be studied for their usefulness in treatments. Sometimes it is necessary to repeat parts of the narratives in this text in order to bring them into a position of alignment with critical theoretical perspectives that bring more meaning to them. Thus the narratives are more like raw data than explanatory evidence, but they are not raw in the sense that they are objective or "uncooked."

The autobiographical narrative of a teacher often triggers both a liberation and a conflict for him or her. Teachers' reminiscences of being students allow them to break away from the preeminence of the standardized and well-organized curriculum to acknowledge how this curriculum might have let them down in the past. Unlike essay forms that are purely propositional, the discursive narrative form the teacher uses stimulates vivid imagery—"A scene I see in my head is standing right in the face . . . nose to nose with the students . . . cramming my curriculum down their throat." At the same time, the teachers' own stories threaten the decisions he or she is making today as a teacher. The narratives provide tensions between him- or herself as student and as teacher, and between his or her understanding of the phenomenological reality of the inner life of a reader and the leathery political climate that demands that readers prove themselves to parents and the public quickly and definitively. The narratives provoke tensions among the teachers' personal feelings, theoretical reading, relations with the community and his or her political will.

Because the autobiographies are written fairly quickly, and rather unselfconsciously in class or at home in a few sittings, one cannot expect or demand the aesthetic cohesiveness or drama one demands of short stories. But we find something different and perhaps even more important: teachers representing themselves in multiple and competing situations. They write in one paragraph about something as ambitious as wanting to save a child's life or change the way reading is taught in the United States. In the next, they write about how risky it would be to change a vocabulary worksheet or face parents with a new grading scheme or how they still feel a minor humiliation of childhood. Here is an example from a teacher's autobiography written for a class assignment:

> At the time I had no clue that my autobiographies were even remotely related to each other, and I certainly never fathomed that the issues they raised were haunting me today, in my seventh grade Language Arts classroom.
>
> . . . I am amazed that I often put my students in the position I, myself, was once in. . . . Dewey says that, "Teachers have an obligation to support, anticipate, evaluate, and encourage worthwhile activities, and students have a right to pursue projects mutually constructed and approved."
>
> . . . I began to panic because I could not find "the perfect lesson plan" that would encompass what I wanted. . . . I then proceeded to evaluate my teaching of grammar, vocabulary, and writing, against what I said I believed about teaching and learning. I found that I teach much as I had been taught.
>
> . . . A scene I see in my head as I picture this situation is my standing right in the face . . . nose-to-nose with the students, literally cramming my curriculum down their throats while wondering why they don't seem to talk to me. Obviously I'm too close. They are literally choking on what I want them to learn.

What is exciting about these pieces, unlike short stories, case studies, or even many fine published accounts of school problems by teachers, is that an individual and real person's divided subjectivity, unfinished thoughts, and contradictions are sought, tolerated, valued, and used to find space for change.

Similar tensions arise when undergraduates write about their experiences of "home" and then juxtapose these reminiscences with public policy statements on welfare and homelessness, archival data from welfare service centers, and novels and histories on the subject. Their concrete memories of home, and how and who provided them with it, often suggest that the boundaries we think we can draw among personal, private and public help are messier than we thought, and the solutions more complex.

I hope this autobiographical method is an entry point for teachers reading this book. Here, teachers have written about their educational experiences with reading and literature, and I construct a bridge between their images and a feminist and psychoanalytic view of the culture of language arts teaching, so that the teachers will see *themselves* in the larger cultural issues of our day. In turn, the narratives of the three teachers' reflections invite readers who are teachers, and anyone else who has spent a good deal of time in schools, to look more carefully and creatively at everyday educational experience. I invite readers to compare their own stories with these teachers', and with the histories of literary theory and practice I provide.

AN INVITATION TO READERS

A writer never really knows who will want to read his or her book. Like any author, I can only imagine the contexts to which its frames might be applied. By way of invitation to potential readers, I can suggest some of the sites from which its motifs got their moorings and to which readers might bring them to bear: They are English education, teacher education, reader response, and literary theory. I have also found the bridging of language arts to psychoanalytic feminism interesting for gender studies and cultural studies work, psycholinguistics, and for graduate education classes in research, foundations, and curriculum theory.

The narratives of the three teachers were written over the course of several months at my request after our meeting at a National Endowment for the Humanities Summer Shakespeare Institute for secondary teachers. I found the narratives to present the story of a gap between how teachers are inspired by language and literature in "private life" and what they do in school. One teacher writes that literature has "a living meaning" for her and yet she does not remember anything she read in school. Another writes about school teaching as chronic missed opportunities: He feels "pressure to cover the required curriculum and personal discomfort with contrary and unreconciled feelings of student readers." A third worries that "there was much [in a novel] I was responding to that my students did not or could not respond to."

The book is structured so that Part I lays out history and theory of English teaching as we find it, and offers an alternative theoretical base for English teaching from psychoanalytic maternal theory. Part II shows how English teaching practices could change, and Part III applies both theory and practice to the specific teaching problems raised by the three teachers who wrote narratives. Again, the appendix includes the complete texts of the teachers' autobiographies.

Although the contact I had with these three teachers was limited to about one year, and to commentary on about a dozen of their written narratives, I hope that the kind of conversation we raise about these narratives in the terms of psychoanalytic and literary theory, will help to carry these conflicts over from the realm of individual teaching and reading lives to the public realm of culture and curriculum policy.

PART ONE

UNDERSTANDING A LIVING MATRIX
OF WORDS AND EXPERIENCE

ONE

THE CONFLICT BETWEEN
PRIVATE READING AND PUBLIC READING

> My parents introduced me to reading the word at a certain moment in this experience of understanding my immediate world. Deciphering the word flowed naturally from *reading* my particular world; it was not something superimposed on it. I learned to read and write on the ground of the backyard of my house, in the shade of the mango trees, with words from my world rather than from the wider world of my parents. The earth was my blackboard, the sticks my chalk.
>
> When I arrived at Eunice Vascancello's private school, I was already literate. . . . Eunice continued and deepened my parents' work. With her, reading the word, the phrase, and the sentence never entailed a break with reading the world. . . .
>
> Not long ago, with deep emotion, I visited the home where I was born. I stepped on the same ground on which I first stood up, on which I first walked, began to talk, and learned to read. It was that same world that first presented itself to my understanding through reading it. . . . I left the house content, feeling the joy of someone who has reencountered loved ones.
>
> —Paulo Freire, *Literacy: Reading the Word and the World*

When the English teachers I worked with wrote about reading, they wrote about love. They grieved for dying friends in novels and they named their own children after characters in books. Jane doesn't know why, but she took *Moby Dick* with her to the hospital for the birth of her child. Philip used Hemingway's *A Farewell to Arms* to meditate on his own experiences of love and death. As a teenager, April became pre-occupied with reading about missing prisoners of war in Vietnam, and kept it secret.

A veteran English teacher, artist, writer, and graduate student, Jane wrote that from earliest childhood, "I was always reading." Of her family, including four daughters, she wrote, "We all talk about books when we are together, comparing our reactions and memories." Yet she also admits, "I didn't learn anything about reading in school, so I don't really know how to teach others what no one taught me."

> My own reading experience is no guide. I do not remember anything I read in school. I have no idea how texts were taught at the High School of Music and Art in the years 1946–1950, because I either had read the things already or I simply didn't do anything with them in any personal way. I know, for instance, that we read *Silas Marner* and *Ivanhoe*—and yet I came to George Eliot [recently as an adult] with delighted discovery and still am telling myself I want to read Scott. Reading in school just wasn't reading, that's all. And maybe it shouldn't try to be—maybe it should just be the material from which we teach skills. The trouble with that is, that it denies everything I believe in about literature, everything I have formed myself around.

Philip, an English teacher at a selective college preparatory school that emphasizes science and technology, wrote,

> I must have been reading before first grade. Reading was a mystical adventure of discovery, joy. Getting a story, people, feelings, ideas, from page to mind. A simple miracle—human. In first grade—Miss Jarvis—I learned phonics; I could do that. I learned to read—one word at a time. Still do. I remember anxiety and stress. I couldn't name the feelings. I could perform. The fun was gone. Reading for school was usually work. Reading for me was always pleasure . . . school assignments were tedious; in college and even in grad school the first time—I remember mostly not reading the books. Instead of feeling involved . . . I felt distracted.

April, a fairly new teacher in a private girls' school, wrote about a rich personal life with books:

> Books and bookstores have always been a special, magical attraction for me—My parents were always buying new books to read to us—it may be that in living overseas, we read and were read to more often than my peers who grew up with television—My sister and I devoured Nancy

Drew, the Hardy Boys, and a whole series of English boarding-school stories by Enid Blyton. When we read Blyton's "Adventures of the Famous Five," about four cousins and their dog, we assumed the characters' personalities, speech patterns, and quirks.

. . . I always reach a point in my reading when I look anxiously to see how many pages remain and I wonder if I should "save" the book, space it out over a few days—I look at the clock, and debate whether I should be prudent—one more hour? two? There is a satisfaction that feels slightly illicit when I decide no, this is my indulgence—I'm going to go for it.

On that night, with Antonia White's *Frost in May*, I read until seven in the morning, until my eyes ached and I had to close and rest them at times—but there was nothing about feeling tired, only a wistfulness as I watched the story coming closer to its end. During the next few days I carried the book about with me, picking it up again to reread—not quite ready to let it go. . . . That is my reading as a luxury and indulgence, a huge, fat chocolate candy bar. It frustrates me that I seldom have time to read like that—that it is so difficult to read an entire book through. I listen to my students with envy and disbelief—these voracious adolescent readers who can devour a book over the weekend, who casually hand back *The Europeans*, *Pride and Prejudice*, *Rebecca*, *Brave New World*, and ask "so what else do you have?"

But April has doubts about school reading too:

High school reading. A few reading experiences stand out vividly. My first high school class was a chilling introduction to the American system; but then the entire school—with a student body of three thousand, as opposed to my eighth grade class of eight students—was something of a shock. That [high school English] class was dominated by unruly, loud boys, and kept in shaky control by a mousy middle-aged woman, who broke down and wept in class the second week of school. . . . I don't remember the full reading list, though I think it included *The Diary of Anne Frank*, *The Catcher in the Rye*, *Brave New World*, and *Lord of the Flies*. I do remember *Lord of the Flies*, and the feeling of despair—repulsion—I remember slumped low in the back of the room, watching the boys in front of me rolling a joint, thinking that my worst nightmare would be to be trapped on an island with that English class—wondering who would be killed first.

It is not comfortable for the teachers to see the same disappointment they experienced as students in their own students. Philip wrote about one experience teaching a novel, "Most students' written responses state: 'boring,' 'dull,' or 'uninteresting.' . . . I missed significant opportunities." In fact in writing about their teaching, the teachers continue to emphasize that reading in private is a world apart from reading in school. They assume it to be an occupational hazard that private reading has an authentic quality that cannot be matched in a public setting like school. Jane wrote,

> Since school isn't all of life, and since English isn't all of school, I have made some choices. One of them is to acknowledge the realm in which literature can touch one's own personality while concentrating on the more analytical, perhaps more appropriate and fruitful realm of language—how do words work? What choices does a writer make? What can one do with words that can't be done in other media? To do that even a little bit is enough; let unconscious activities go on in decent privacy.
>
> Since many of my kids don't seem to know how to engage with their reading at the personal level, I try to make them do it, (or pretend to do it) in their early journals and in many of their ongoing assignments: write a diary entry or a letter, etc.

In this last paragraph, Jane seems to prize private reading, but it is interesting that she exiles it to the unconscious or to a private diary. We can pick up this theme of exile in April's narrative as she makes plans to attend more to what is read *outside* of the classroom:

> Is there any doubt that reading is personal? That readers develop opinions about a text, and try to guide others to those views? . . . As I began to perceive that my students did a good amount of reading outside the classroom, and that perhaps that might be one area in which I could contribute, I began to look for ways to do this—hence the book talks and occasional journeys up to the library. (I make it a habit to read the middle school overdue lists, which are posted on the bulletin boards, to see what kinds of books they are reading.) The book-sharing of this year has been well-received and I am looking for different ways to expand it next year.

While April makes private reading more social by providing an opportunity for students to share their readings with peers through book talks, she too, sees private reading as different from public reading as she explains,

> My aunt, [a veteran teacher] again, has also greatly influenced the way I think of books, pointing out to me that it is not enough to simply give

students books—that you have to show them how to read them. Judy rejects the idea that teaching students how to read books stops after grade school—it's an on-going process, particularly as students approach more difficult texts. She feels that it is important to help students make transitions in their reading—from the personal, intimate family readings to public readings, away from picture books and so forth.

And Philip openly expresses conflict between the worlds of school reading and private reading. He remembers,

> During my elementary school years, I loved to go to the library to check out books. Especially in the summer, just for fun . . . I would read for hours. Time would suspend. I'd read at bedtime—especially at bedtime—long into the morning. My imagination would reach and gather and grow. School assigned readings were had to's, not want to's—a horrifying thought for a teacher.

Philip's concerns remind us that whatever our successes as individual readers outside of school, as teachers, our interests extend to large groups of students in school. We work at how we could bring reading to those who might not otherwise have it, and what we can do to make reading more meaningful to those who do.

WHAT DO WE DO IN ENGLISH CLASS?

These concerns have been most difficult for public school teachers who live with the knowledge every year that some students leave their care able to function as readers and some do not. Worried and even remorseful, they hope that the mandates that take up most of their professional development space—the directives for preparing students for standardized exams, the curriculum guides, and the "content" courses they take from college English teachers—are somehow addressing these problems. In many ways the culture of the secondary school English classroom comes to us through the pedagogies of college English departments and we find the same themes in higher education that plague the public school teacher. The individual reader is acknowledged, but hard to reach in a group, and certainly hard to negotiate with in class. Often, in theory and in practice, the professor has tried to address the collective quality of the classroom by focusing on those aspects of texts that are common to all. And like school teachers, he or she has been tempted to rationalize the omission of the reader's viewpoint by characterizing individual response as private and irrelevant to public life.

Throughout the history of English teaching we see how the literary theorists' interests, the college teacher's interests, and the secondary teacher's interests intersect. William Cain reports that at the beginning of the twentieth century, prior to the advent of what is known as the "New Criticism," the study of literature was kept out of most academic departments because reading or appreciating texts did not employ rigorous scientific analysis, and reading was something people could do on their own (1984, 89). A stern discipline and training in the "scientific" study of literature was permitted in a few departments that primarily consisted of careful excavation of medieval facts. Cain reports that an editor of *The Nation*, Stuart Sherman, wrote a scathing attack on such academic source-hunting in 1913, which he claimed "divorced philology from general ideas" (p. 90). But along with such rebukes against sterile scholarship, were attacks against undergraduate English departments whose curricula consisted of only "a potpourri of 'facts,' spiced with impressionistic asides" (p. 92). Facts are still important in most literature classes. April taught etymologies and definitions of archaic words. The thirty or so teachers at the summer Shakespeare Institute where I met Jane, April, and Philip, eagerly anticipated sharing with their students the scholarship on the Court of King James. There is however, less wholehearted acceptance of "impressionistic asides," as Philip acknowledges:

> Central to my curriculum is students' making inferences and predictions. With responses [from me] such as, "That's a possibility," I encourage students to speculate; then I require students to support their hypotheses with evidence from the text. I am not as clear about how to respond when students go beyond the text to support their hypotheses with personal experiences.

THE INFLUENCE OF NEW CRITICISM

As Philip's comment illustrates, impressions that seem to come from the internal order of the text are legitimate, while impressions from experiential knowledge are suspect. Likewise, skepticism and dissatisfaction with the condition of both undergraduate and graduate English studies persisted well into the 1940s, preparing the field for an approach that did not emphasize ancient or medieval allusions, nor the emotions of the reader, but focused on the structures of texts. Defending itself from attacks of both pedantry and shapelessness, the field welcomed a fresh approach in the "New Criticism." In "New Criticism," the literary work had autonomy, a solid and ideally penetrable structure that demanded from ideal readers a suspension of their own personalities and interests. "New Criticism" transformed literature into a very public commodity in two ways. First, it shifted focus away from individual, "private" subjectivities, and second, it located the text, not in its exotic, philological roots, but in its universality. Text became something "out here" for anyone to see and work on if they possessed the right tools.

New Criticism cultivated ideal readers who suspend their own beliefs, hopes, and intentions to better notice textual cues revealed through scrutiny of the structures of a literary work. Such tenets of formal integrity in New Criticism had been building and were sown in the fertile ground worked on by nineteenth-century theorists, like the novelist, Henry James, who envisioned the self-abdication of the reader. Slatoff articulates James' position:

> Like Henry James' ideal critic, he [the ideal reader] would seek to be the "real helper of the artist, a torch-bearing outrider, the interpreter, the brother . . . armed cap-a-pie in curiosity and sympathy . . . to lend himself, to project himself and steep himself, to feel and feel till he understands . . . to be infinitely curious and incorrigibly patient, and yet plastic and flammable and determinable." (1970, 59–60)

John Crowe Ransom, Cleanth Brooks, Northrup Frye, and Allen Tate are among the best known of the New Critics. Kaplan paraphrases Ransom's view of the ideal reading of a poem:

> As an autonomous object, a poem is a special kind of nondiscursive verbal structure that must be read closely for the complex meaning that is there only because it is inherent in style, technique, and form. (1986, 451)

Kaplan quotes Ransom,

> The poem was not a mere moment in time, nor a mere point in space. It was sizable, like a house. Apparently it had a "plan," or a central frame of logic, but it also had a huge frame wealth of local detail, which sometimes fitted the plan functionally or served it, and sometimes only subsisted comfortably under it; in either case, the house stood up. (1986, 461).

In his book about literary response, Slatoff writes of Bradley's similar ideas about the text becoming a public commodity with a general appeal:

> Enter that world [of the poem], conform to its laws, and ignore for the time the beliefs, aims, and particular conditions which belong to you in the other world of reality. (1970, 65–66)

Thus structural analysis was revered as a closed system that stood apart from reality, which gave the text more integrity as a form, but disconnected it from its past contexts and diluted its potential to help readers reconceptualize their present and future worlds. Practicing public school teachers rely on structural analysis as a closed system. For example, when Philip had students study Langston Hughes's "Dream Deferred," he asked them to define the word deferred, to list seven unpleasant verbs that refer to a dream deferred in the poem, and to identify five similes in the poem and one metaphor. When teaching Steinbeck's *Of Mice and Men*, an objective is to have students know that by the end of chapter 2, Steinbeck has "created suspense through exposition and the introduction of conflict and complication." Complication is defined as "a person, event, or situation which tends to thwart the will of the main character or make the solution of the problem difficult." To get at the objective, students "discuss why Curley's jealousy over his new wife and why Curley's liking to fight bigger men could create a situation which makes the solution to Lennie and George's problem more difficult." One can see that in this type of analysis, plot events are selected for their ability to illustrate the terminology of literary structure students are supposed to learn. Students may never return to these events to study them in any kind of social context near to them today (violence in our public places) or far from them (the economy of the Great Depression).

Northrup Frye pushed the text out even further into the arena of objectivity—away from the subjectivities of not only readers, but of authors:

> The preliminary effort of criticism [is] the structural analysis of the work of art. . . . The poet's task is to deliver the poem in as uninjured a state as possible, and if the poem is alive, it is equally anxious to be rid of him, and screams to be cut loose from his private memories and associations, his desire for self-expression. (Kaplan 1986, 505–506)

The teachers who wrote about their classes carry out the exile of personal reading associations Frye dreamed of. They provide private reading experiences through independent reading and writing in journals, but they rely on standard, public forms of objective analysis for the bulk of their literary activities that count in the classroom. Their lesson plans often stress the convergent aspects of vocabulary study or structural analysis, what everyone can agree on about the text. They feel that they don't want to disturb personal readings by addressing them in school. Philip wrote,

> When students' personal experiences seem related to an idiosyncratic interpretation (not clearly based on the text), I feel ambivalence about affirming students' experiences while interpreting the text. Are the "facts" of the text negotiable? Does an individual have the right to an interpretation? Who controls the interpretation(s)? The teacher (authority)? Is the teacher (text) open to interpretation(s)?

READER RESPONSE, SUBJECTIVE CRITICISM, AND POSTMODERNISM

These are the same questions Postmodernism and subjective criticism have recently posed as they criticize the pedagogical value of the object New Criticism had made of the text. Murray Schwartz argues the case against the objective status of the text in claiming that a responsible pedagogical position "cannot come from any methodology that avoids or denies the personal origin of the criticism it makes possible" (Schwartz 1975, 758). He rejects Frye's dualist, idealist critical methodology as an intellectualization removed from "the effective source of our organizing powers themselves" (p. 757). Feminist and historicist literary criticism argue the same point, that traditional literary theory has hidden the intentions of privileged interests by projecting them onto the texts themselves. In current literary theory, the New Critic's view of the text as "out there" as an autonomous object that is radically public, is challenged by subjective critics like Bleich, Holland, Fish, and Barthes (see Leverenz 1982).

In one of the earliest research projects on reader subjectivity, a study of five college readers reading, Norman Holland set out the means by which he thought readers came to interpret literary works:

> A reader responds to a literary work by assimilating it to his own psychological processes, that is, to his search for successful solutions within his identity theme to the multiple demands, both inner and outer, on his ego. (Holland 1975, 209)

Holland showed that readers experience a literary work so as to recreate their personal style, and that this personal style or identity is a fixed term of subjectivity (p. 214). He allows that subjectivity is unlimited, but that it will express itself within the confines of an unchanging identity theme or personality complex that is fairly stable. To analyze the readers in his study, Holland named four phases of reading response that reflect the reader's personal style or identity theme: (1) the way the reader makes what is read match the reader's defensive and adaptive capacities; (2) the way the reader uses the literary work as a source of pleasure, projecting onto it kinds of fantasy that unconsciously gratify the reader; (3) the way a reader transforms fantasies to themes that are of particular concern to the reader; and (4) the characteristic expectations the reader has of texts based on the reader's identity theme (p. 209). Subsequently Holland studied the reading responses of five college students to three short stories, and found evidence of these processes in responses to the stories. He concluded that a student is likely to demonstrate patterns of responses characteristic of the preoccupations of the reader's personality. Mauro (1980) found that in interviews, secondary students who articulated identity themes in response to the idea of death exhibited the same themes in their responses to death in literary works.

Subjective criticism progressed from the rather static categorizing of reader types and themes that tried to predict response. David Bleich (1978) asserted the primary importance of subjective responses by individuals, but advocated that they be negotiated by a community, like a class, or a group of critics, so that alienated subjectivities might be influenced by others, and so that collective interests can be scrutinized as well (p. 280). Bleich has developed a curriculum that provides readers the opportunity to resymbolize their responses to texts. He writes that resymbolization occurs "when the first acts of perception and identification produce in us a need, desire, or demand for explanation" (p. 39). In his work with undergraduates he has found that even distorted and banal responses can be negotiated into knowledge through dialogue with other members of a class and the teacher. He offers examples of the development of student response statements in which readers gradually reduce gross projections of their own fears and desires onto heros in texts, or reduce the tendency to identify themselves as just like fictional characters (p. 254). In starting with very subjective responses, the readers in Bleich's classes have material to offer teachers and class members as a basis for interpretation. Through negotiations about their interpretations, the readers develop knowledge about both texts and themselves.

Although the National Council of Teachers of English has published one of Bleich's books, called *Readings and Feelings,* and teachers interested in reader response respect his ideas, it is still difficult for them to justify the time taken away from structural analysis to focus on reader response, and to feel comfortable learning how to help students resymbolize their responses. Jane wrote,

> If there were not a county-wide final examination at the end of the year, I would diverge spaciously indeed from Butler County's requirements. I should at least stop complaining about the county's requirements, because mine are much more demanding, at least for my honors-level students. I teach a dual vocabulary, SAT preparation, a systematic language and usage program, a program in expository writing, and a program in literature. It is no wonder that I feel that nothing is done completely. (I should say here, however, that there is an unwritten curriculum guide behind that fat book, and that the message English teachers get from the county is that there is no limit to what we should be doing and doing thoroughly.)

Jane goes on to discuss how she chooses which works to include in her syllabus, and the message seems to be that an appropriate canon and preparation for objective exams leave the typical English teacher with little chance to develop response statements. She wrote,

> You ask about their individual responses, to what degree are these at the center of the curriculum, to what degree are they marginal? I guess the answer is both. The journals are preparatory; I believe you have to engage with the text first before you can analyze it. I suppose I am recapitulating my own reading history, a long period of unsupervised encounters at the level of emotion and fantasy, overlaid with the kind of analytical thinking I am now doing in graduate school.

Jane's experience illustrates that teachers find it difficult to guide the rich and often emotional responses individual readers bring to texts.

Another reader response theorist, Stanley Fish, is more interested in interpretive communities than in individual readers. He claims that "the meanings and texts produced by an interpretive community are not subjective because they do not proceed from an isolated individual but from a public and conventional point of view" (Kaplan 1986, 624). Fish seeks to highlight the purposes and goals, structures and assumptions which comprise the situation in which reading response occurs.

He stresses that meanings are made in contexts which are not idiosyncratic, but communal and conventional. His view suggests that readers are embedded in social situations that are public and shared and
that determine their understanding of texts. If they have had experiences to which the text refers, they will understand it; if they lack the
relevant experience, they will not be able to understand the text. In his
scenario, the text activates a response that is typical of a conventional,
situational context of the reader. An example he cites is that the question, "Is there a text in this class," can only be intelligible to those who
are familiar with certain conventions of schooling, and that they will
interpret the word "text" in a way that can only be called typical of the
school community they represent.

Fish's insistence that texts and reading communities be histori-
cized is compatible with the "whole language" philosophy in elementary schools that attempt to undo decades of decontextualized reading
pedagogy. April recognizes this communal and historical context in
her reading and teaching. But her experience shows us that communities' tastes are problematic and complicated as she finds herself
wedged between different generations who seem to her to read *The
Good Earth* uncritically:

> The curriculum I inherited seemed to be a hodge-podge of readings.
> When questioned, the members of the department admitted that these
> books were left over from various eighth grade courses, which had been
> organized around themes such as Mystery, Adventure, Fantasy. Some-
> how, these texts remained, but they didn't "hang together" in any way.
> I particularly objected to *The Good Earth*, which I consider poorly written
> and racist. . . . It fascinates me how many people in their late fifties extol
> the virtues of this book—and I have to wonder if their view is not col-
> ored by their memory of Louise Rainer in the film. But I have also con-
> sidered how thirteen year-old girls respond to the book (—especially
> because I remember reading it when I was an adolescent, and loving it;
> for weeks my sister and I imitated the heavy and sorrowful tones of
> these characters . . .). In the first two years, the department implored me
> to "at least try it." so I gave in, assigning *The Good Earth* as summer read-
> ing. Most students responded to it with enthusiasm—they enjoyed the
> foreign setting, the elemental-ness of the living—life and death, starva-
> tion, floods. Only a few were disturbed by the portrayal of the Chinese
> and the women.

As a reader of *The Good Earth*, April feels alienated from the community of fellow teachers and from her students, and finding no way

to reconcile with them, she decided not to teach this text anymore.

Jane finds communal reading problematic since and she and her students come from different worlds:

> But, lord help me, I have read all of Ngaio Marsh and Dorothy Sayers and John Dickson Carr and Raymond Chandler and so on and on. I forgot to mention *Dracula* and Mark Twain. I read *Tom Sawyer* and *Huck Finn* before I was thirteen, then discovered a whole set of Twain in the attic Down South and read most of them. (How did I know they were funny, long before I was old enough to understand or explain their humor? How did a child understand Twain's laughter at childhood? These kinds of questions make me feel that there is an impassable gulf between me and my students. . . . Can a woman who remembers a time before there was frozen orange juice or instant coffee speak to sixteen-year-olds in any meaningful way? What questions could I ask to find out if their experiences were like mine?)

Identifying the historicity and conventionality of readers does not free us of the complexity of negotiation among groups and the work the individual must do to abstract conventional meanings from total contexts. Elizabeth Bates insists that symbols emerge for the individual reader in "the selection process, the choice of one aspect of a complex array to serve as the top of the iceberg, a lightweight token" that can stand for the whole 'mental file drawer' of associations" (Rosenblatt 1976, 11).

This look at the reader response theories of the New Critics, of Bleich, Bates and Fish, and so forth, and of the teachers' misgivings, reminds us that we swing wildly from focus on text to focus on reader, yet we have a hard time deciding what to teach. April describes the aimlessness and anxiety of composing the book list for the eighth-grade curriculum:

> Last spring I sat down with my department head for two hours, trying to discover the overall SENSE of the reading program, of the books chosen. And though, at the end of the session she had broken the books down into units and categories of "fantasy and exploration," "language and structure," and "exploration of the self," etc., it still seem/ed/s like artificial and arbitrary categorization.

Language and structure are separated from exploration of the self, and exploration of the self is separated from fantasy. Likewise, high school literature anthologies frequently use thematic categories separating the individual from the social. April sees the categories as arbitrary, but do they reflect a bias in epistemology toward separation of the inside from the outside, and of interior and exterior life? Do they reflect the same sense of the self as exiled, asocial and not reliable?

We continue to get the same warnings from literary theorists. David Leverenz warns us that a desiring unconscious, an alienated phenomenological subjectivity, or a persistent idiosyncratic theme can dissolve into "mindless pleasure to derive similar insights again and again from different texts" (1982, 455). Grant Holly is concerned about subjectivist readings being too much like a stimulus-response situation in which the text activates readers' fantasies and desires which he or she fulfills through the text. He prefers a more Postmodern view such as those put forth by Roland Barthes or Jacques Derrida, in which we look for discord and incoherence within texts. Holly suggests that an appropriate reader response is not harmonious with the text. A text should shatter our placid beliefs (Holly 1980, 255). Furthermore, to "deconstruct texts" is to show that elements in texts are often in opposition to each other, and that meanings diverge so that multiple realities must be maintained.

MAKING SENSE OF LIFE THROUGH READING

However, while acknowledging that texts do not reflect uncomplicated and coherent purposes of authors or readers, Richard Rorty brings the focus of literary theory back to how humans read texts to get on better in the world. He insists that human beings want to identify with the struggles of finite men and women who have made sense of life through literature throughout history, and that this is purposeful. He critiques deconstruction as a process that throws into relief the vulnerability of texts. He points out that in contrast, New Criticism boasts the integrity of texts. What both have in common though, according to Rorty, is contempt for human finitude (1982, 158), and lack of interest in the human purposefulness of reading literary works.

In the autobiographical narratives of the teachers, I see them caught between the values of the child-centered, reader-response approaches, and the objective, more standardized approaches. We teachers vacillate wildly from the pole of objectivity to the pole of subjectivity, trying to protect both ends, by switching frantically from journal entries to multiple choice tests. In classroom life, we have drawn boundaries around subjectivity and called it private and drawn boundaries around objectivity and called it public. The availability and widespread use of guide books like *Cliff's Notes* attest to the temptation to commodify the public text. The marginalization of students' interests and hopes for the text attests to the embarrassment we feel for our private thoughts. It is the contempt for human finitude that Rorty identified. I think Rorty is correct in his assessment that people want to read for a purpose, and that is, to get on in the world. They are not satisfied to be sold the beautiful and coherent, but untouchable, text of the New Critics, nor are they satisfied to notice how easily texts can be dismantled through deconstruction. Readers may be attracted to reader response as a critical approach that does not treat texts as concrete, but as functions of reader subjectivity, but teachers need to know how to negotiate reader subjectivity in the very social setting of a classroom. Reifying a particular critic's response or a particular student's response is as abhorrent as "solidifying" the text. As reading theorist Murray Schwartz suggests, concretizing subjectivity outside the world or outside the text is as false as concretizing the text as an autonomous object (Schwartz 1975, 60).

All three teachers who wrote about their pedagogy try to honor the thoughts, feelings and interests of their students. But their curricula are dominated by facts, information, literary terms and vocabulary drill, and tests and assignments focusing on how authors make texts and how critics evaluate them. They try to provide space in private journals for students' perceptions, but these are often left unread, ungraded, and underdeveloped. These private forms are usually marginalized from mainstream curriculum activities that are "counted" for grades. Students' personal responses are written as exercises and facts about literature are learned for grades, but reading literature is rarely brought to bear on the reality and future of the world. The teachers recognize a sad irony in that they remember how important books have been in helping them imagine their futures, but they do not know how to bridge the gap between students' private reading and the public classroom.

What I have come to question from reflecting on their work and my own, and from reading feminist theory, is whether the nurturance and protection of what we call the private and its separation from public life, is hurting our chances to do meaningful classroom work with literature. In her autobiographical writing, Jane thinks it important to pair what she knows about literature "with everything she has formed herself around." Actually I believe that we come to know something *as* we form ourselves around it. Therefore we cannot separate what is to be known, from ourselves. In bringing relationships back into the picture of how we know, feminist theorists also show that we cannot separate what is to be known from *those* around whom we have formed ourselves. Feminist theory shows us how the dichotomies of objectivity/subjectivity and public/private are in the way. Even more exciting, feminist theory's epistemologies founded on relationships present a guide for practice. How we provide the relationships and experiences for students to form themselves in our classrooms is the curriculum question this book addresses.

TWO

OBJECTIVITY AS A RETREAT
FROM MATERNAL LIFE

> Experientially the first body we escape (physically, then emotionally) is that of our mother. . . . The eternal, unchanging forms [which are pure, abstract, eternal, universal objects of thought, but invisible] assure freedom from the cave, the womb, the unending cycle of birth and death, the realm of necessity and of women (mothers).
>
> —Jane Flax, "Political Philosophy
> and the Patriarchal Unconscious"

TALES OUT OF SCHOOL

Jane, April, and Philip face a disturbing commonality in their narratives: the school reading they experienced in the past, built on structural analysis cleansed of personal meaning, does not sustain them today as readers or as teachers. As teachers, it is not easy to accept that they do not remember anything special about their school reading experiences, or worse, that their school reading experiences were alienating or detrimental. It is the suspicion aroused by their autobiographies that school reading was inferior to almost any other reading experience, that diverts their attention to the features of reading experiences out of school. Reading out of school was both physical and imaginative, both individual and social, and both playful and constructive. Outside of school the teachers remember both merging effortlessly with literature and constructing new understandings of the world through them:

April:

> My sister and I devoured Nancy Drew, the Hardy Boys and a whole series of English boarding-school stories by Enid Blyton. When we read Blyton's "Adventures of the Famous Five," about four cousins and their dog, we assumed the characters' personalities, speech patterns, and quirks. We created our own stories about Nancy Drew and her boyfriend, Ned, and we made dolls to represent characters from different stories. . . . From ayahs [babysitters in Nepal] I learned folk tales, ghost tales, tales of village life and superstition.

Philip:

> Babaar—colorful hot air balloons. Hefalumps floating with the breeze. . . . Floating free-imagination. Tiny people, miniature villages, vast horizons. There and here together. See yourself floating up there into nothing. See our house sitting down there shrinking away. . . . I loved to go to the library to check out books. Especially in the summer, just for fun. I remember *The Ted Williams Story*, and *The Autobiography of Ben Franklin*, and a book about space exploration and Werner Von Braun—pre-Sputnik.

Jane:

> All the voices of the old books. One voice is a barrel with a little pig rolling down the hill at dawn. . . . Oh, the cat with the twitchy tail! Oh the dampness and the scurrying! Oh, how I became small, small, in a gray-green garden. It is impossible to extricate that earliest reading from the word-ocean in which it swam. My grownups all sang, and so I sang— "the Rose of Tralee" and "Onward Christian Soldiers" and "Swing Low Sweet Chariot" and "Believe Me, If All Those Endearing Young Charms" were as much a part of reading as the stories my grandmother told me about when she was little, and all are mixed with squares of sunlight in the morning falling on the linoleum nursery-rhyme people on my bedroom floor. . . . At the end of the day when my mother would come home from her work at Macy's, she would get out the black notebook and I would tell her things to write . . . how much children learn from reading without knowing they're learning. I inhaled from *Jo's Boys* and *Eight Cousins* and *Little Men* and *Little Women*, an entire culture.

Jean-Paul Sartre, the philosopher of Existentialism, wrote about the sensuality, sociality, and worldliness of learning to read in his autobiography, *The Words*,

I did not yet know how to read, but I was pretentious enough to demand to have my books . . . I wanted to start the ceremonies of appropriation at once. I took the two little volumes, sniffed at them, felt them, and opened them casually "to the right page" making them creak. In vain I did not have the feeling of ownership. I tried with greater success to treat them like dolls, to rock them, to kiss them, to beat them. On the verge of tears, I finally put them on my mother's lap. She raised her eye from her sewing: "what would you like me to read to you darling? The Fairies?" I asked incredulously: "Are the fairies in there?" . . .

It seemed to me that a child was being questioned: What would he have done in the woodcutter's place? Which of the two sisters did he prefer? Why? Did he approve of Babette's punishment? But the child was not quite I, and I was afraid to answer. Nevertheless, I did. My real voice faded, and I felt myself become someone else. (1964, 44–47)

Through these accounts, we can see that reading words is an extension of reading the world and that public reading is dependent on private life. The split between the public and the private is a major theme for feminist theory. One of the most powerful critiques of epistemology to come from feminist theory is that what we might call private life, experiential life, or personal life, is *not* a retreat from public life; rather, it is objectivity that is a retreat from the richness of experiential life. Feminist theorists like Evelyn Fox Keller and Jane Flax refer back to Plato to show that women have been associated with a private sphere that is deemed necessary, but is marginalized from the public spheres of government and education. They suggest that historically objectivity amounts to a retreat from the maternal love through which humans have been born and most frequently nurtured. While society may acknowledge the power of maternal love, and even idealize it, maternal love and maternal epistemology are kept in a place separate from reason, theory, and political action.

EPISTEMOLOGY ESCAPES THE MATERNAL

How did we get the idea that distance and detachment from what seems to sustain us is desirable? Feminists like Kristeva, Keller, Jane Flax, Mary O'Brien, and Jessica Benjamin ask us to look as far back as Plato to see that epistemologists viewed learning not as a matter of coming to form around others and objects, but oddly as a matter of getting clear of them.

As illogical as it seems to get clear of our origins rather than to extend ourselves from them, there is plenty of evidence that this was a predominant view. Philosophy was written by adult men who lived public and academic lives apart from the presence of women who were their original attachments. Their cultural detachment from women provided a kind of gulf so that when they did go back to write about them and their own infancy, the writing made women's bodies and maternity seem exotic, even chaotic. Kristeva cites Plato's version of what preconceptual life might be like before she reinterprets it:

> Space, which is everlasting, not admitting destruction; providing situation for all things that come into being but itself apprehended without the senses by a sort of bastard reasoning, and hardly an object of belief. But because it was filled with powers that were neither alike nor evenly balanced, there was no equipoise in any region of it, but it was everywhere swayed unevenly and shaken by these things and by its motion shook them in turn. And they being thus moved, were perpetually separated and carried in different directions, just as when things are shaken and winnowed by means of winnowing baskets and other instruments of cleaning corn, . . . it separated the most unlike kinds farthest apart from one another, and thrust the most alike closest together: whereby the different kinds came to have different regions, even before the ordered whole consisting of them came to be . . . but were altogether in such a condition as we should expect for anything when deity is absent from it. . . . Indeed we may fittingly compare the Recipient to a mother, the model to a father, and the nature that arises between them to their offspring. (Kristeva 1986, 125–127)

Plato's passage conveys not only a time, but a place (the mother's body) of chaos. There is some "winnowing" or sorting, but only of the kind as you would expect from a place without divine ordering capacities. The passage is remarkable for its last sentence which is a summarizing metaphor comparing chaos and order to maternity and paternity respectively. Plato's schema of divinity versus chaos sets the stage for his advocacy of a literal flight from maternal space in the creation of a polity that separates the public from the private spheres:

Flax writes,

> A crucial element in Plato's philosophy is the distinction between mind and body, knowledge and sense, reason and appetite. . . . The primary basis of social class in the Republic is the ability to reason. . . . The capac-

ity to reason depends upon the control and sublimation of the passions. In turn, it is for control of the passions which threaten to erupt into public life, that society exists. The state itself thus resembles a vast dehydrating plant for "drying up" the passions of men through education and restraint. . . . The imagery of the cave in the *Republic*, the world of shadows, of the unconscious and of the womb, which the light of reason cannot penetrate or dispel, reveals the fear of regression to that preverbal state where feelings, the needs of the body and women (mothers) rule. . . . Thus reason is in part a defense against regression to those "longings" which threaten to ensnare us forever in the body and the material world. (Flax 1983, 256–258)

Thus the exile of the private, of the personal, of emotion, of the body, of passion and subjectivity, is the exile of the maternal.

Keller and Benjamin show how this proclivity to exile the mother turns into a campaign to conquer her. The conquest of the mother as object is cathected onto all objects and leads to an epistemological paradigm of conquering the environment in general. Benjamin writes,

Indeed, Keller proposes that modern scientific detachment from the object derives from the relation to the mother that I have called one-sided differentiation. Because men originally define themselves through separation from and opposition to the mother, Keller argues, they reject experiences of merging and identification that blur the boundary between subject and object. Thus the masculine stance toward difference accords with the cultural dominance of a "science that was premised on a radical dichotomy between subject and object." . . . She argues that the relationship between the subject of knowledge and his object may be represented in terms of the relationship between the subject and his love object. . . . She contends that as the character of male dominion over women has changed, so has the metaphor of scientific knowledge. (1988, 189–190)

Thus Plato's epistemology is characterized by the self authoring itself, not recognizing its debt to woman and relation to other, but rather valorizing what Keller calls, homoerotic union. Modern scientific method masks human dependency on nature and nurturing by creating distance from them with impersonal authorship. Impersonality is a denial of dependency on the object. "This impersonality of modern science, Keller argues, is actually the signature of masculine identity" (Benjamin 1988, 189).

Feminist theorists have argued that detachment, abstraction, and personal-public and mind-body dualisms, on which Western science and epistemologies rely, are based on the ability to radically separate oneself from objects and other people. We have seen a parallel development in literary theory in which the field sought to distance itself from subjectivity in reading and focus its efforts on the objectivity of the text. Western epistemology has enjoyed the clarity, neatness, control, and efficiency which abstraction, standardization and objectivity provide, but feminists point out that what gets left behind, what is separated out, what is repressed, is the specificity, variability and dynamism of everyday experience, and of the domestic support everyday experience requires.

THE EXILE OF THE MATERNAL TO PRIVATE SOCIETY

Feminists like Keller, Benjamin, O'Brien, and Grumet have convinced me that the sustenance of a public society devoted to detachment, independence, objectivity, and competition, relies on a corresponding private life of attachment, dependence, subjectivity, and acceptance, which is thought inadmissible to public life. O'Brien (1981) writes that from the Greeks forward, men have claimed for themselves the creation of culture or the public realm in jealous compensation for their lack of procreative powers. And Madeleine Grumet writes that schooling has traditionally delivered the child from the private world of our mothers to the public world of our fathers. The context for the division of life into the private and the public is ruled by gender and framed by the family. Benjamin asserts,

> I believe that this insistence on the division between public and private is sustained by the fear that anything public or "outside" would merely intensify individual helplessness, that only the person we have not yet recognized as outside (mother and wife) can be trusted to provide us with care, that the only safe dependence is on someone who is not part of the struggle of all against all, and who is herself not independent. Thus we can only protect our autonomy and mask our vulnerability by keeping nurturance confined to its own sphere. (1988, 202)

Jane's autobiography offers an example of the problematic demands we make of mothers as she describes the kind of support she wanted from her mother and the complex feelings she had about her:

> My mother, who had been an Intellectual in college, owned books but was too busy cleaning and talking to read much. I did not read her

books. . . . But it was my mother who began the family tradition of always giving books as presents, two for birthdays and two for Christmas; and, as I told you before, I was read to from very young and was taken to the library once a week long before I was old enough to walk the thirteen blocks to get there alone. (So my mother must have been reading too—surely she didn't walk us there just for children's books. There is a lot about my mother that I have suppressed from those days.) . . .

I remember discovering Shakespeare's sonnets and rhapsodizing about one to my mother who responded, contemptuously, "Everyone knows that. *I* read those too." So much for all that. Accounts for my attempt to be a better mother to my kids by giving value to their responses. I am hugely ambivalent about this but haven't been able to change my style much. It's pretty clear why I didn't read her books— and yet it was my mother who gave books as presents, books that I loved and claimed as my own (*Mary Poppins, Little Women*). They didn't have my mother's smell; reading them wasn't like sleeping in the bed someone just got out of. I didn't want to see my mother as someone who had a childhood or adolescence because I wouldn't have been able to find room for myself by making her an other, my enemy . . . my mother, a former English teacher, was eighty last spring.

Jane remembers that her mother's responses to her reading could be competitive and jealous, and they intimidated her. She also sees that her mother probably made it possible for her to read, even though she admits she is reluctant to give her credit for it. She understands that she represses her mother's influence because she wants her to be a static, somewhat unreal presence. If the mother is not real and does not have full rights, Jane tries to make her into an object from which to launch herself.

The Women's Movement reacted against this tendency to force the mother or wife to disappear into the background. Furthermore feminists did not like being placed in a tranquil and nurturing domesticity traditionally associated with women, when they could see that this feminine domain was supposed to sustain a competitive, macho, uncaring, and irresponsible public life, from which they were excluded. Some have adopted the tactic of repudiating the personal and domestic as soft and antithetical, and as part of the myth of essential femininity. But many feel that the separation itself of domesticity from public life is one of the most insidious and sexist of arrangements. Their project has been to deconstruct the exploitation of the difference between these two worlds, not to pit once against the other, but to reintegrate and strengthen both. Many do believe, as I do, that the quality of private, personal, and domestic life, long associated with the feminine, has been grossly trivialized, distorted, and undertheorized as the powerful and sustaining force that it can be. Grumet has carved out the point:

> All the cognitive operations that we call knowing, all the methods of the disciplines, their collections of concepts, truths, assumptions, hypotheses, express relations between subject and object, knower and known, person and world. The relations of these terms "subject" and "object" in epistemology, consciousness on the one hand and all that is other to consciousness on the other, are preceded by the subject/object relations within which human consciousness comes to form, the relation of the infant to the person or persons who constitute his world. Becoming a subject means becoming a subject for someone. (1989, 185)

The someone Grumet refers to has traditionally been a woman, and though she need not be a woman, the fact that she was, says much about why her contribution to our ways of thinking is unknown, or neglected if known. Grumet insists that the idealist and materialist rationales of masculine epistemologies are compensations for the inferential nature of paternity and reflections of traditional male parenting roles (p. 186).

CHALLENGING MASCULINE THEORY

The ways humans know are embedded in issues of gender right from the beginning, in what are called the primary processes, since it is females and not males, who carry, deliver, and often feed the child. Nancy Chodorow (1978 and 1979) and Dorothy Dinnerstein (1976) show that even when there is an involved male who is acknowledged to be the father, the inexorable first feminine obligations/privileges in gestation and lactation launch an oppositional matrix of roles and actions for male and females parents that are both competing and compensatory. The situation is further complicated by the projects of the child, who identifies with parents whose gender differences are highlighted by the culture. In many cultures, children are asked to exaggerate an identity with the same sex parent in order to appropriate their own gender role. In turn, they must exaggerate their difference from the opposite sex parent and then compensate for the exaggerations. One of the most pervasive results of the exaggeration of sex roles of the parents, is the effort the child must exert to relate to the parents not only on the basis of need for support and individuation, but on the basis of exaggerated gender identity. At a time when the male child could be individuating gradually within an intimate relationship with parents, he is forced to abruptly move away from mother to father in order to be masculine. The female child may find it even more troubling to individuate, since she gets her gender identity from the original love object, the primary caretaking mother, who has the female characteristics she needs, but from whose oppression and lack of power she may want to distinguish herself.[1]

Freud offered the oedipal solution as a way to manage both gender identity and separation. The boy can safely have femininity in his life if he radically leaves mother, assumes the role of the father, and unconsciously transfers maternal feelings to other females as sexualized, eroticized objects. The female's position is even more complicated. She can safely have masculinity in her life, if she assumes the role of the female by unconsciously taking the place of her mother as an object of her father's desire, and then unconsciously transferring to other men the role of subject who experiences her as object.

In the oedipal solution, the male assumes the role of subject and the woman the role of object. Both male and female children must have a negative experience with femininity as embodied by the mother. The boy must psychologically disidentify with the one whom he has loved and with whom he was merged in infantile life. He must be on guard to be not like he once was. The girl must competitively replace the one whom she has loved and with whom she was merged in infantile life. She has to be better than the female she knows. Gendered parenting with an oedipal "solution" thus leaves children terribly vulnerable. Both sexes must prematurely repudiate the maternal realm of care and intimacy that has launched them into life. This is a good basis for patriarchy, which is the belief in masculine rule.[2] To both sexes, the male appears to be the one who offers the child maturity, as he offers distance from infantile dependence on the mother. It is he who seems to offer a chance for the child to be better than what he or she once was, and even to forget his or her once-fragile state. The *difference* the male offers is exaggerated to create an alternative to what the mother gives, rather than a continuation of care. The most negative impact of the reliance on the patriarchal oedipal solution as the achievement of maturity is that children must *force* power away from the mother by replacing her with an alternative authority, and by that authority, conquer her.

Masculinity is also taken for maturity in life cycle theories and in moral philosophy. Carol Gilligan criticizes Erik Erikson's model of identity development, in which the stages of life are seen as a progress in separation from others (Benjamin 1988, 193). Benjamin draws on Gilligan's criticisms of the ways epistemologists and moral theorists have used the split between public ethics and private choice to validate masculine epistemology and morality:

She writes,

> Furthermore, Kohlberg argues that, unlike justice and rights, women's moral concerns are not sufficiently abstract and universal to be considered proper categories of moral reasoning—they are merely aspects of ego development. It is as if these values were fit only for the nursery, not for the public world. (Benjamin 1988, 193)

Benjamin indicts the crystallization of the public and the private as separate spheres:

> The unbreachable line between public and private values rests on the tacit assumption that women will continue to preserve and protect personal life. . . . In this way the political morality can sustain the fiction of the wholly independent individual, whose main concern is a system of rights that protects him from other individuals like himself. (1988, 197)

Benjamin shows that the oedipal solution encourages the fantasy of a self that is autonomous and self-sufficient. But it also produces a self that fantasizes a repression of the other who raised us and in so doing prevents her from being real to us and outside of us. She becomes simply a split-off part of ourselves. What we rely on as the private is that split-off fantasy, who is not part of the ruthless public world "outside." If we do not acknowledge the source of nurturance, but displace her and conquer her, then we do not like to be reminded of any reliance on her. We have made an escape, and the public world is supposed to be the world to which we escaped. "This scheme preserves the split between outside and inside, so that the individual appears self-sufficient in public but can relax and regress in the safe enclave of the wife-mother" (p. 204). Benjamin warns us of the deleterious effects of the social division of gender:

> As long as the father (and men in general) cannot be depended upon in the same reliable way for tenderness and holding, as long as he represents selfish autonomy, mother (and women in general) will remain the only source of goodness. . . . The ideal of autonomous individuality with

its stress on rationality, self-sufficiency, performance, and competition threatens to negate the mother so completely that there may be no one to come home to. . . . But it is not womens' abandonment of the home that stimulates this fear. Rather, the social division of gender—with its idealization of autonomous individuality—is at fault, bringing about the loss of the very maternal nurturance it is meant to protect. (P. 204)

Benjamin makes the important link between deconstructing the oedipal solution and progress in solving political and social problems. If we deny the support we require to function in public life, because it reminds us of a dependency we repudiate, we are threatened by the helplessness of the needy and we fail to provide "socially organized nurturance—a safe holding environment—" in public (Benjamin 1988, 202).

SCHOOL BECOMES MORE PUBLIC

Grumet expands the psychosocial origins of the public-private split from the oedipal family to the history of the American economy and the history of education. She cites Brownlee's (1979) history of economics to show that industrialization exacerbated our already sexist child-care arrangements when men left the roles they shared with women on the farm and in homes to find work in the factory. Thus men became even more the worldly ones. It was they who were "out there" becoming familiar with commercial and political interests, better equipped to initiate their offspring to enter public life. Grumet tells us that an unfortunate consequence of this sexual arrangement was that the control of public schooling fell to men who supervised it from the top, even though the work force was and continues to be filled by a vast majority of women. Today, nine out of ten education administrators are men, while 75 percent of all teachers, and more than 80 percent of elementary teachers are women.[3] The men in power in education have been best able to include the standards and needs of commercialism and public office in schooling, but least able to acknowledge and include the complexities of the valuable work that women were doing with children in the domestic sphere.

Even the women who made up the majority of the teaching force were rewarded by male supervision and confined to the fantastic and sentimentalized sphere Benjamin identifies. Grumet identifies the ideal woman in industrialized, capitalist contemporary society by quoting Ann Douglas in *The Feminization of American Culture*:

> She was to exert moral pressure on a society in whose operations she had little part, and to spend money—or have it spent on her—in an economy she could not comprehend. . . . The lady's function in a capitalist society was to appropriate and preserve both the values and commodities which her competitive husband, father, and son had little time to honor and enjoy. She was to provide an antidote and a purpose to their labor. (Grumet 1989, 43)

Grumet's review of the feminization of the teaching profession during the transformation from an agricultural economy to an industrialized one, shows that this ideal woman was mapped onto the ideal teacher. By becoming a teacher, a woman "was simultaneously displaced from her position as an active, self-reliant participant in a self-sufficient household and employed as a low-salaried, temporary pedagogue" (Grumet 1989, 39). Meanwhile, the men who theorized and administered education were invested in the values of the public world and institutionalized a curriculum divorced from a student's previous experiences, intentions, and affiliations. Disavowing their dependency on domestic life, the male education establishment relied heavily on testing, standardization, and objectivity.

It is easy to see how the personal experiences of students and teachers were split off from the objectivities of content areas and the standards exacted in business and professional life. Men in charge of schooling held allegiance to what public life demanded, and forgot, distorted, or repudiated what children got in private life. This masculine tradition sanctioned the notion that what kids get at home has to be left behind when they come to school. In school policy today, even when home life is not sustaining, we are ambivalent about whether we ought to provide positive nurturing experiences at school.

The substitutions of the father, that is, abstraction, idealism, and objectivity can be recognized today as the preferred content of our curriculum discourse. The political split between the private and the public retraces the Oedipal split in gendered parenting roles. In missing the continuity between infantile life and the development of cognitive achievements dependent on this life, educators often fail to tap the hopes, intentions, and desires of learners that are pedagogical foundations. The mechanisms by which policy makers hope to transform education are mechanisms that rely on external motivations and standards, not on the most powerful of learning motivations, the learner's felt desire to be better connected to the world and to secure more power to function in it. We will see that Julia Kristeva offers a more productive role for maternal and paternal figures as supporters of the desires, intentions, and achievements of the child started in the maternal relations.

CHANGING OUR THEORY OF LANGUAGE LEARNING

In the narratives that teachers write, it is possible to see that if we shrink from dealing with students as lively and situated bodies with personal desires, motives, and intentions as readers, they have nothing important to carry over into public discourse. Traditional views of language development are strikingly parallel to the Oedipal suppression of maternal care and authority. Structural and propositional approaches to language, including grammars, surface and deep structure architectures, sentence analysis, and the New Critical approach to literary forms, depend on a suppression or exile of subjective life, which is feared to be regressive and even infantile. But Julia Kristeva's view is that the prelinguistic body subjectivity we knew in infantile life with a maternal figure serves as a continuing basis for symbolic achievement, and is not merely the precursor, or failure of symbolic achievement. Kristeva refers to the biophysiological aspects of language as "the semiotic" and we will examine her theory of the body-subject in the next chapter.

Kristeva's work in object relations is directly useful to the language curriculum because it critiques the masculinity and objectivity of the theory of symbolic achievement in language. She even challenges Post-Freudian linguistic theory like Jacques Lacan's, which still relies on masculine oedipal solutions.[4] Lacan imagines a child who is in a largely hallucinatory relationship to its mother, confused by the lack of boundary between them and unsure of the source of its power. Therefore, this child must eventually recognize a gap between what it feels, imagines, needs, and wants, and what is real. Language is viewed as an arbitrary system of signs that bridges the gap. Humans enter into a symbolic realm and offer their experience to be taken up by a chain of signification that has a logic of its own. To use language that is part of a system is to repress the self you imagined yourself to be when you were with mother. Lacan sees the entry into the symbolic order as absolutely necessary if the self is to emerge from the confusion and narcissism of pre-oedipal life. The authority of symbols is sought as a rescue from the oceanic, illusory fusion with maternal life. In the oedipal solution, it is the paternal figure who rescues, who signifies the child for itself, who ushers the child into the realm of the symbolic. Once again, the feminine must be escaped and repressed for the achievement of mature identity.

Lacanian theory is dependent on the Oedipus complex in that it holds that the child must move out of what Lacan calls the "Imaginary" life of fusion with mother by entering what he called the "Symbolic" realm. The "Symbolic" is the realm of the Law, of order, of rules, of letters, of symbols that organize our experience so that we can have a coherent identity. This realm has traditionally been associated with the father by Freud and his followers, including Lacan. Lacan would have it that the child emerges from the dark, viscous underworld of a shared undifferentiated, life with a maternal body, and out of misidentification between mother and child, into the light of reason, of language, of logic, through the influence of the father figure. But Lacan's work is centered on the child who experiences himself through the threatening eyes of oedipal parents. Kristeva believes that we can rewrite the oedipal scenario by retheorizing the value of prelinguistic experience, through remedial transferences in therapy and by representing parental roles differently.

Kristeva attributes much of Lacan's view of symbolic achievement to masculine fantasy. She claims that Lacan projects the male's exile from the female in the oedipal solution onto language development in the form of the gap and repression of desire. Kristeva rejects that view and argues that language develops in continuation with maternal care, not as a refusal of it. Kristeva's theory of language development rests on the notion that the child experiences the beginning of symbolic life in the regulation of body impulses and desires already within his or her relationship with the mother.

Kristeva's important contribution to linguistic theory is to reread Lacan's notion that the psyche is structured like a language. Kristeva contends that psyche and language are structured like a body in a relationship (Oliver 1993, 19). For Kristeva, language is a joint, not a gap—it is both what you mean and what others mean, and it is both not what you mean and not what others mean. Furthermore it is a joint between self and other already experienced in pre-oedipal, physical life with the mother.

For Lacan, the mythology of "the mirror stage" outlines the child's development and serves as metaphor of how the child enters language. The child, on seeing him- or herself in a mirror (a symbol of being seen by others), stands erect and first recognizes its self as a coherent, unified figure. Lacan's story proposes that whereas the child previously felt its self as a fragmented, incoherent mass of drives, spasms, and forces, it can now see its self as a whole creature. Lacan claims that the child is also startled by the gap between how it felt its self to be and what it sees it is supposed to be in others' eyes. The child senses that the Other knows him better than he, and possesses power over him. According to Lacanian theory, the child never knows if the mirror (who represents the Other), ever really reflects or sees him, since the child did not recognize him- or herself. This view of ego development is dependent on a relationship between mother and child that is based on what feminists see as a number of masculine biases. One is that the relationship between mother and child is primarily character- ized by "the look" between them, rather than the physical relationship between them. Another is that the "look" between mother and child is one of alienation rather than recognition. Third, the physical relation- ship with mother allows no space for separation at all, but is simply fusion and merging. As Grumet has pointed out, Lacan's mistake is ascribing to the mother, the inferential relationship to the child the father has (1989, 125). The mother's look and touch are "active and communicating," as are the child's. Grumet cites the recent research of child psychiatrist Daniel Stern, "who reports an emergent sense of self in the early days, related to organized and organizing perceptions of his own body and of those with whom he interacts" (1989, 101).

Grumet challenges "the specular, diadic and patriarchal aspects of this [Lacan's] narrative for excluding the mimetic, maternal, and semiotic identifications" of pre-oedipal experience (p. 125). But she also notes that academia resembles Lacan's scheme. Reading educa- tion has a stake in whether we believe Lacan or Kristeva. If academia operates under the assumption that structure and knowledge can only be achieved in the "Symbolic" realm, we discount the tonal, rhythmic, sensual, fluid, provisional, affiliative realm of the maternal. Mathe- matics, objective science, grammars, and "architectural" literary criti- cism are most securely part of the purely Symbolic realm, and so if we believe Lacan's scheme, the curriculum ought to begin and end with them. Art, poetry, theater, and impressionistic reader response are marginalized as immature and presymbolic. However, if we believe Kristeva's theory, which uncovers the masculine bias and is supported by her empirical research and the research of Stern, Winnicott, and oth- ers, we see the arts as making it possible for the child to carry over his or her intentions, desires, and knowledge from the pre-oedipal semi- otic life into symbolic discourse with more power. Kristeva helps her clients tap into their desires and proclivities by invoking the rich maternal semiotics of body subjectivity, imagination, recognition, and potential space, and by using the paternal figure in a function that sup- ports this kind of maternal love. Furthermore she sees the usefulness of art forms like dance, painting, and poetry to help clients regress in the service of strengthening the semiotic so that they have something to represent in public discourse.

The deconstruction by Kristeva of Lacan's theory of language helps us to critique school's reliance on denuded phonics, grammars, and other propositional structuralisms. Kristeva's critique helps us understand why we have respected these dry, abstract structural forms as not only heuristic and regulatory, but as self-sufficient, and why we have denigrated holistic, impressionistic, culturally dependent language theories and practices as soft, fuzzy, and immature. We have taken Lacan's and other masculinist linguists' word for it that symbolic achievement requires radical separation from infantile subjectivity. The whole language movement in reading education is a good example of an attempt to recover for education the comprehensiveness of language experience that is more representative of education in private life, than a narrow phonics and grammar approach long offered in schools. In our narrowness we are apt to forget that phonics is fundamentally about the body making sounds that correspond to marks on a page, which correspond to sounds others can make, which they have represented as marks on a page. It is, in Kristeva's scheme of things, a reduplication process. The child's body learns to make the sound another body can make, and the child learns to do this through the common focus on an object. The child is tracing with its sounds the pattern the writer has made with marks, which is a trace of sounds the writer's body makes. These sounds as entities, as units, do not directly represent the real word—they are the body's rendition of agreed on abstractions, which are part of an agreed on system of representation of the world, through letters as both sounds and physical marks on a page.

But as Merleau-Ponty has helped us see, words are never only part of an arbitrary system, they are also gestures coming from the body as well. We cannot keep each sound in perfect isolation as a letter unit. Our body develops a history of sounding out letters and words, of visualizing their shape, of imaging where we were other times we heard these words and what was around us or what happened to us. As it reads a string of words, a line of text, the body, which has a cultural history, reacts, anticipates, and predicts its way along the lines of text.

We have to reorient our ideas about reading pedagogy. Those who characterize phonics as "word-attack" skills, to be mastered by each lonely child laboring over a worksheet in isolation, sound all too much like Lacan's child, who must attach himself to symbols as a substitute for human attachment that has completely broken down. Certainly, phonics, or letter-sound correspondence is the basic unit of *a* system of representation by signifiers. But it is not the only symbolic activity in which the child participates and it is a system that is interdependent with other gestural forms of representation related to the body and senses.

The feud between "word attackers" and "whole language" proponents reflects the false dichotomy between the individual and the social. It is true that everyone needs to be in on the game. That means that children do need to know the alphabet and how to sound out words, and to remember vowels and consonant blending patterns. But they take advantage of these phonetic clues, not only as part of a lexical system, but as part of a social nexus of gestures, memories, and anticipations that comprise a life-world.

It makes sense to teach children phonics as part of a choral society, sounding out words together, so that they blend their voices and imitate each others' bodies in efforts to make the right sounds. That they can make the same sounds as others should seem comforting, rather than a threat. That the sounds they make and the words they sound out echo and refer to the real world should not seem threatening to parents, since sounding out words is not different in kind than sounding out the closeness of thunder or the sniffing out the smell of chlorine at the pool. The body knows—it knows letters in the same way as it knows the world.

D. W. Winnicott (1971), the pediatric psychoanalyst, has observed that children who have developed "False Selves" have not been able to play between the maternal semiotic and the symbolic, and are not in touch with their own intentionality. They are susceptible to submission, apathy, and conformity, as well as restlessness and aggressive domination, and cannot make use of the cultural forms. For Winnicott, the maternal role has been the one that could ensure the development of the "True Self," who can manage to adjudicate between "inner" and "outer" reality, and what we call the private and the public so that they can take their place in contributing to society. In the next chapter we will examine more closely the infant's emerging organization of self in its early relationship with the mother. Later in this book, we will see how this insight and research affects the role of the body and relationships in language arts teaching.

THREE

AN OVERVIEW OF MATERNAL LEGACIES: THE BODY-KNOWER, INTERSUBJECTIVITY, AND ATTRACTION TO THE WIDER WORLD

> How much of my scholarly and critical work has been an attempt to learn how to speak in the strong, compelling cadences of my mother's voice.
>
> —Henry Louis Gates, "Whose Canon is it Anyway?"

The fiction of a separate private reality to which we assume anyone can retreat, has the effect of fueling the maintenance and expansion of a dehumanized public life. It is not hard to see that mediocre or failing public institutions and policies seem tolerable to us because we expect another world to make up for it. School can be allowed to be cold and unsupportive, because home is assumed to be warm. And when mothers are associated with a private world that is separated from the public one their own children must confront, their children are likely to experience anxiety as to where they belong, and to deny the importance of the woman and "her world," or cling to it regressively.

We have seen that an oedipal solution forces the child to displace the mother and claim authority over her by appropriating the father's authority. If the child must negate mother to separate from her, maternal contributions to the child are not recognized. And we have seen that we privilege the ideal of rationality as an antithesis to being pulled back into the immature, unauthoritative world of the mother. It seems a good time to look at what we surrender when we trivialize maternal influence in public institutions like schools.

The child suffers in the public realm from not feeling recognized by the loving maternal figure who cared for him. Repressed as the intimate partner who constituted the world for him, the mother of an oedipal child is likely to appear as either immature and a negligible influence, or to be just another demanding authority like the father. In all three teacher autobiographies, there are feelings about maternal influence that suggest embarrassment, nostalgia, neglect, and resentment. In writing that her mother was influential in her reading life, Jane wrote nevertheless, "I didn't want to see my mother as someone who had a childhood or an adolescence because I wouldn't have been able to find room for myself by making her an other, my enemy." Jane assumes she would have to reject her mother if she admitted her mother's independence from her. Philip is more sentimental and nostalgic:

> Usually my mother read to me. As now when I read to my three-year-old Godchild, the communication is mostly nonverbal—and my remembrances, preverbal. I feel anxiety and peace of falling asleep and comfort of voice, and reassurance of presence. I enter that distant place far inside that emerges far away.

Nostalgia emerges when we are afraid something is lost, and we will see how Philip experiences the loss of maternal capacity in his work. And it is April who conjures up the image of a retaliating mother who displaces the sentimentalized one:

> And interestingly too, I remember my mother was the first to steer me away from Buck by first telling me about, then reading me a short story. In this story, again, the strokes are so broadly drawn—the cruel, bitchy, insensitive white woman who hires a poor, starving Chinaman (who is supporting this many children, a dying wife, etc.). At the end of the story she rejects his work, leaving him to certain death.

April's mother doesn't offer up a woman role model, but she does offer up a woman who will not be used or forgotten. She is the antithesis of the angel. We cannot afford to forget or reject her.

Kristeva identifies experiences long associated with maternal care which are the bases of ego development and symbolic achievement. These maternal "legacies" are (1) the creation of the body-subject; (2) the development of intersubjectivity; (3) The provision of a potential space between mother and child, constituting a triadic epistemology that opens up the world to the child, while he or she continues to be anchored in intimate relation. Kristeva's theory serves not just as a critique of traditional epistemology, but as a guide for practice and pedagogy. The three "legacies" I have identified will serve as the instigation for reconceptualizing the practice of English teaching.

THE FIRST MATERNAL LEGACY: THE BODY-KNOWER

The first of what I call "maternal legacies" is the creation of the "body-knower" or "body-subject." Kristeva describes a prelinguistic, pre-oedipal period in which the infant experiences the rhythms and pulsions of its body, and experiences the mother's regulation of its body. Not consciously organized by the baby as symbols yet, vocal and kinesthetic fragments are stored by the body as traces. Kristeva refers to the psychosomatic space for such traces as a "chora," the Greek word for womb or space, and she means it as a receptacle of pre-oedipal experience and a source of impulse. Kristeva conceptualized the chora as a register of body experiences like pulsations, rhythms, drives, and forces that are stored by the creative imagination (Wright 1984, 98). However, what the child feels as a body, is altered by the one who handles him. Elizabeth Wright illustrates Kristeva's concept of chora when she describes how a child's body learns to "expect" it is going to be caught when tossed in the air by a parent. Where once the body registered this frightening and unpredictable experience with tensed muscles, it begins to relax the muscles and laugh when it has knowledge about how it will be saved (Wright 1984, 98). The "chora" is Kristeva's reappropriation of Plato's "chaotic womb" and is a metaphor for the receptacle of knowledge that allows the child to count on and predict its life as a body partially regulated by itself and partially regulated by another.

Kristeva asserts that body experiences prefigure the earliest linguistic expressions of sounds, tone, rhythm, and the order and spatiality of syntax. Laughter, cries, intonations, and gestures extend from the traces of the body knowledge we developed with the mother. Kristeva believes that children do not imitate language initially, but use their bodies to reduplicate the functions of the mother. When the child makes the sounds, "Mum, mum, mum," by pursing the lips, the child is miming the acts of sucking and eating, and thus acting out with his or her own body what he or she has felt to have been gratified by the mother's breast and milk (Kristeva 1986, 244). The child makes a transference from having the breast to being the breast (Oliver 1993b, 74). And in this shifting of positions, as the child takes the place of mother as feeder, along the same trajectory, the child also comes to take the position of speaker. *Just as the child acted out, with its own body, what it has felt to have been gratified by breast milk, the child acts out with its own body what it feels like to have words—to be the speaker as Mommy is speaker to the child.* The child's body itself is the link to the symbolic representation of language introduced by the mother.[1] Knowledge about the body's place in symbolic representation is important, because if language use is, initially, an incorporation, that is, a body making words by the physical experience it has of them in and from the mother, then language use is metaphorical (the exchange of positions) and not merely metonymical (the exchange of names). In other words, if our body makes words in the mouth like it knew breast or food in the mouth, it first takes the *function* of the mother as knowledge, not the specific, discrete, identifiable *objects* of the mother or the names of the objects as knowledge. *Linguistic power and knowledge is first, place, positions, and function, and not the names of things.* My four-year-old draws with his mouth open as if he could control the pen by the shape of his lips. I still do carpentry with my mouth open. The opening and closing mouth is never fully discarded by the body as one of its earliest regulatory mechanisms and means of physical control. It is true that eventually language can take the place of others (the child uses the phonemes, "ooh" and "da" alternately to express "gone" and "there" when the mother comes and goes), but the body itself remains an important, inseparable aspect of representation in speaking and even in writing. As Kelly Oliver has observed, "Kristeva brought the speaking body back into language by putting language into the body" (Oliver 1993a, 13). In chapter 4, we will see how the body figures into thought, speech, reading, and writing, and how language arts curricula can use the body to enhance language and literary skill.

THE SECOND MATERNAL LEGACY: INTERSUBJECTIVITY

The second maternal "legacy" is intersubjectivity. Intersubjectivity involves the complex relations among people as they become subjects who know the world. Kristeva and Winnicott stress that individuation (the formation of the subject) actually requires an involvement with a maternal figure a priori to the individuation project. We are dependent on both our complicity with and separation from our primary caretakers. Being a subject in one's own right, will mean producing lines of difference and yet living close to those lines. There is the difficulty of acknowledging how one can be both part of an other and not a part, or how one was once a part of something and is no longer. Among the complexities of intersubjectivity is the temptation to repudiate what one once was, and the temptation to exaggerate and denigrate differ-ence to secure one's own identity. But Kristeva and Winnicott empha-size that even though the formation of ego-identity is complicated, and includes processes of abjection, parents are often successful at helping their children to secure it reasonably well, and that this early ego for-mation can prefigure successful intersubjective relations all through life. Remember that Kristeva believes that it is a totalistic rejection or abjection of the female body and female love that characterizes Lacan's neglect of the maternal contribution to language and symbolic achievement in his story of the mirror stage. She and Winnicott both tell an alternative story of a mother who reflects the child to the child. She looks at the child and touches the child in a way that shows that she knows how the child feels and who he or she is. She reflects back to the child what she knows about him or her through her touch as well as her look. It is not an uncaring inanimate object that catches the child's interest in him- or herself as a self, but in fact, the mother who functions as a loving addressee for the child. Kristeva argues that the parent-child relationship can be one of intersubjectivity, rather than domination and threat, and that our language development is con-structed by reciprocity, play, and negotiation. We will see in chapter 5 how informal, collegial, and more provisional reading and writing assignments can strengthen literary interpretation.

An important aspect of identity formation and intersubjective pedagogy is the self's ability to reject, or make abject, materials and forces it does not want. Kristeva refers to this divisive, but signifying concept, as the "thetic break" and the "thetic phase" (Kristeva 1986, 98 and Oliver 1993b, 40). The thetic break is a kind of split in experience that divides it and creates borders where there were none before. Dri-ves and articulations in the body rise and crest in thetic breaks. These drives and articulations in the preverbal realm involve our "abjections" or getting rid of what is not wanted through cries, biting, spitting, expulsions. We begin to make and record these breaks as meaningful borders of experience. Kristeva recognizes the link between body expe-rience and thetic signifying practices that constitute symbolic achieve-ment. Indeed, the *Oxford English Dictionary* reminds us that *thesis* orig-inally meant a putting down of the foot to mark the time in music (p. 3288). The thesis, or thetic break, marks experience and affords the child a way to predict and control his or her life better. Remember the child who is thrown playfully in the air by a parent, who at first feels "thrown out," but comes to predict being caught and laughs at the game. Laughter is an articulation of the new meaning of the event.

In signifying practice, we are familiar with thinking of a thesis as an organized, coherent argument with evidence, but it must also be a split from what was said before, a cut the writer makes into reality, an assertion, a marking of difference, a proposition. What the writer chooses to *not* address, is as important as what she chooses to explore. This is how Kristeva writes about the *thetic* break. Thetic breaks involve abjection, that is, the child's getting rid of what he or she does not want. We have said the child incorporates; makes food, air, sounds into aspects of its body and he psychologically takes his mother's body for its own. But he also abjects, that is, he gets rid of fluids, air, sounds, unwanted touching, and psychologically rejects aspects of the mother's body and control. Abjection is as much a prototypical human activity as incorporation, and therefore, negativity, or rejection, is part of the formation of identity and intersubjectivity. The creation of borders within ourselves and among ourselves has roots in the abjective life of infancy. Thetic breaks, which become borders, are forceful and dynamic, and must be tolerated, mediated, and negotiated. Ethical develpment can benefit from the conscious nurturance and extension of these negotiations. Without a tolerance for abjection and negativity, it will always be a temptation to *violently* get rid of elements foreign to our desired position, both as bodies and as subjects. Because Kristeva sees the potential in productive maternal relations extended to other object relations of the individual, her ethical theory steers away from the dynamics of retaliation, her psychological theory steers away from the need for masculine compensation, and her linguistic theory steers away from language as only law.

Kristeva does explore how we can marginalize others in an effort to be ourselves, and how we exaggerate difference from those who threaten our boundaries. In fact, she believes that children attempt to make abject the maternal body from which they came and to which they are bonded. However she also believes, along with D. W. Winnicott, that to a great extent, parents can understand this need to differentiate and allow for it by providing potential space for the child to individuate without fear of retaliation. Jessica Benjamin also believes that in a rapprochement phase, with the parents' guidance, children can come to acknowledge the self's debt to the other and relation to the other without feeling its own identity threatened, Benjamin, like Kristeva, believes in a lesson of intersubjective love which is a maternal legacy. Their view makes it possible to advocate language pedagogies that rely on relationships and that go beyond mastery and rule, which are explored in chapter 5.

THE THIRD MATERNAL LEGACY:
POTENTIAL SPACE FOR ENTERPRISE

The third maternal "legacy" provides for the potential space a child needs for desire and enterprise. Potential space develops within a complex parental love, in which the child learns to imagine his or her powers. Winnicott coined the phrase, "potential space," to describe an area between subjectivity and objectivity in which the child blurs the me and the not-me, the self and the other. Winnicott argues that the ever-expanding appropriation by the child of objects outside itself happens because a "good enough mother" allows the child psychic space for it. By allowing the child to attribute to him- or herself powers that are actually excercised by the mother, the mother frees the child to enter transitional relationships with what is currently out of reach for the child. The child does not have to acknowledge what is inside or outside, or whether he controls his world or mother does.

For example, my two-year-old child thinks he can open doors he cannot really open, because I inconspicuously turn the lock. To his mind, he has opened the door. Because of my protection of his narcissism, my child does not have to acknowledge whether he controls his world or whether his mother does. Another example, more directly related to language development, is that when my son mispronounces words, saying something that sounds like "Sharred Ribs" when he wants to watch a videotape of *Charlotte's Web,* I act as though he has said *Charlotte's Web,* and follow through with the action of turning on the desired tape. He is at first an effective speaker in collusion with me, and he is able to refine his speech using rules only from this powerful position of speaker *as already understood.* The "good enough" mother or parent, provides potential, transitional space, for the child's ego and ascribes her own power to her offspring for the sake of this developing ego. Winnicott believes that if this recognition of separateness with intimate connection is extended, it becomes the basis for reality testing, using objects, creativity, art, and culture. We will see in later chapters how teachers can develop potential spaces in the curriculum for students to take on important projects and explore complex social and scientific problems through their reading and writing.

To describe the function of parents in providing potential space, Kristeva uses the terms "maternal love," "maternal imaginary," and "imaginary father," because she is describing a complex structure that supports the child's bond with the mother, but at the same time, provides the possibility for the child to imagine its separateness from her, often through a third party, like the father, or other representative of the public world. I think that for Kristeva, the terms "maternal" and "paternal" may be cross-functional for males and females and so are somewhat archaic, but not dispensable.

In a memoir about his mother, Henry Louis Gates, the literary theorist, offers an example of how a child may identify with the strength and power of the mother *and* with the public institutions in which she exercises power. Gates writes about a time when he was a young boy and had been practicing all week to recite a Bible class piece at his church's Sunday service. Confident and excited before the event, he found himself in trouble when he rose before the crowd to speak:

> I could not for the life of me remember one word of that piece. . . . After standing there I don't know how long, struck dumb, and captivated by all those glaring eyes, I heard a voice from near the back of the church proclaim, "Jesus was a boy like me/, and like him I want to be."
>
> . . . And my mother, having arisen to find my voice, smoothed her dress and sat down again. The congregation's applause lasted as long as its laughter as I crawled back to my seat. (1990, 45)

Gates remembers his mother's protection of his narcissism in lending her voice to him, and he remembers her also looking beyond him to the attractions and demands of the world outside of the two of them, to the congregation, a public institution. He realizes it is she who sings for him, and knows he must and can raise his voice in public.

Kristeva uses the term, "maternal" to mean a function tradition- ally performed by women, but not a person essentially feminine, and the Oedipal "paternal" function, traditionally filled by males as fathers, is revised by Kristeva, to be one who supports the mother. This "paternal" function can be extended to mean the public world, like the congregation in Gates's story. In contrast to the castrating oedipal father, Kristeva's paternal figure is loving in that he always refers his relationship to the child back through the mother, with whom he has conceived and made the child. Unlike Lacan's detached phallic father who is stern and intimidating in forcing the child to sep- arate from the mother, this father supports the child's bond with the mother, but at the same time, provides the possibility for the child to separate from her. This father can only provide this imaginary func- tion *through* the mother. In the child's unconscious, the paternal func- tion is that which draws the mother's attention away from the child, so that the child knows he or she is separate from her, and even tem- porarily not in her sight, but is always part of her field of recognition. The healthful, egocentric child feels the mother's desire for the father as a desire to make the child. The child learns of the mother's capacity for love this way. Kristeva rewrites Freud so that the child's unconscious imagines his or her own conception occurring out of love, not out of merging or threat.

From an object relations point of view, the third term or "other" for the child is an object of desire for the mother, who was the object of *her* mother's love, which sets up the possibility for a similar link to the child through desire or love. This maternal imaginary or third term function can operate not only through a real father, but through different objects of desire and gratification for the mother, including work, friends, and community, which exist for the child as possibilities because the mother loves them.

This triadic structure unveils an ethic of love, but it also directs us, as educators, away from the dyadic logic of the knower giving to the one who does not know, or objects being apprehended unproblematically by the student. Students need a third space that provides a place for their own new position. Reading and writing education take on new meaning when three positions are acknowledged: student, addressee, and the world beyond, the third calling to the first two to be named and transformed.

SUMMARY

In traditional psychoanalytic theory, both Freudian and Lacanian, the need to leave the mother's body makes it difficult to appropriate what had been nourishing about the maternal bond, including the body and the "chora," intersubjective borders, and the complex maternal love and provision of potential space. In a patriarchal culture, which has abjected women in general in the process of abjecting the maternal body, we struggle with the cost of our loss. Women who abject all that is womanly in abjecting the maternal body, mourn the loss of their own identity. Men who reject the early primary affiliative relationship they had with mother as they abject her body, also reject the imaginative capacity of the chora and the strength of maternal love. And by ignoring the power of maternal desire to shape the child's ego, those who would usher the child into symbolic life are missing a vital source of his or her voice.

Feminist theory has told us why it is unusual for authors to recognize their mothers in their style. Cultural influences mitigate against our recognition of the transformation of the maternal legacies into artistic and scientific forms. Hélène Cixous writes about how important it is to gain strength through the unconscious, associated with the maternal imaginary register, a "limitless country where the repressed manages to survive" (Cixous, "The Laugh of the Medusa," in Marks 1981, 879–890). We pay a high price for the splitting of response into two worlds, one that counts and one that does not, one that is poetic, sensual, experiential, and private, and one that is structured, coded, abstract, and public. Kristeva warns us not to regress to a solipsistic, solitary subjectivity, lost in our own worlds, but to bring our sensibilities to the symbolic order. She asks that we not become hysterics who suffer from reminiscences, as Freud put it, or "move immediately to the other side—the side of symbolic power" (Marks 1981, 166). As teachers who find ourselves in a "woman's profession," we struggle to legitimize publicly, that which moves us and our students, most deeply in private.

PART TWO

EXPLORING MATERNAL LEGACIES
AND PEDAGOGIES

FOUR

RESTORING GESTURE AND THE BODY-KNOWER TO LANGUAGE ARTS

Whole bodies will become ears for the right tumble of words.

—Robert MacNeil, *Wordstruck*

BRINGING THE BODY BACK TO LANGUAGE

An important pedagogical feature of the infant-maternal relation is that the child first learns by incorporation and not imitation. Kristeva emphasizes that the child incorporates the mother; that is, the child goes over to the place of the mother and performs the functions she performs. Kristeva calls this reduplication. The child reduplicates what the mother can do. For example, the child incorporates her speech even before he or she understands, intones like her, makes her noises. The child's mouth readies itself to be fed by her and he fills it himself with "Mum, mum, mum." The child makes himself like her feeding him. His body becomes like her functions and her words. He performs her patterns. It is not an imitation in which one being imitates another. Kelly Oliver writes,

> It does not presuppose an already constructed ego in relation with an already constructed object. It is not one being imitating another, the child imitating its object. Rather, it is a reduplication of a pattern. (1993b, 72)

When Kristeva stresses that the breast is not an object for the infant, but a "model," a "pattern" (Kristeva 1983, 25), we can see that the child does not know the breast as a thing in itself, but knows its function in his or her life and can take a position in the operation of the function not only by sucking, but in reversal by providing what is sucked. The child uttering, "Mum, mum, mum," is putting sounds in the mouth like the mother puts food in the mouth. Psychologically, the child has become the breast by *doing* something with his or her own body. The child has incorporated the mother, the breast. Because of the incorporation, the body taking her position, this achievement is not symbolic in the sense that a word stands for another. It is body being an Other.

This may seem to us as a lot of time to spend on the breast, but Kristeva argues something that is crucially important to language teachers, and that is that speech is taken up by infants in the same way as feeding, not by imitation, but by incorporation. Kelly Oliver (1993b, 72) explains,

> Kristeva compares the infant's incorporation of the breast to the subsequent incorporation of "the speech of the other." She explains that through incorporation of the speech of the other the infant incorporates the patterns of language and thereby identifies with the other. In fact, it is the incorporation of the patterns of language through the speech of the other that enables the infant to communicate and thus commune with others. And through the ability to assimilate, repeat, and reproduce words, the infant becomes like the other: a subject.

This notion of incorporation of the other fills out theories of language learning in social settings, by insisting that there needs to be a chance for incorporation of others, rather than simply chances for imitation. Kristeva writes that the metaphorical shifting of the infant's position from self to m(other), which begins as an exchange of body drives and functions, sets up its ability to shift metonymically, that is to move from being a thing to naming a thing. Just as the infant body's passions were put into the place of the mother who has control over drives, so that the child takes over her powers, so the infant body's passions are put into the place of language. The child learns to take a position in language, much as it learned to take a position as a body. Meredith Skura (1981) gives us a concrete picture of how children use language before they recognize the objects to which individual words refer:

> The child's first relationships take place in a total sharing situation which involves symbolic exchanges. . . . The child who sees his mother offer him a cookie and calls out "ma" (his word for good things-to-eat)

at first does not separate the giver, the cookie, his word for it, his feelings about it, and his identification of it. . . . This is a cookie experience;
there is no clear distinction between self and object; between self and
symbol. (1981, 185–186)

Feminist theory helps us understand why vocal and kinesthetic
experience is likely to be exiled to the realm of illegitimate knowledge.
Associated with the infantile, private, immature, and female realm,
conventional wisdom has voice and body superseded by rational
thought and language. In this chapter we will see that since the body
makes thought, speech, reading, and writing possible, the use of gesture and theater ought to be an integral and central dimension of classroom literary practice.

WE THINK AS BODIES

We start with Merleau-Ponty's line that "the world is the answer to
the body's question."[1] By that he means that the world can only lend
itself to our perception as a function of our bodies. The world is a
temperature, a depth, a height, a brightness, a wetness, and so on,
because we have skin, blood, appendages, eyes, and so forth. It is
easy enough to understand that if humans had the anatomy for
flight, the world would be sensed as a very different place. Experiences of motion, and temperature, and perspective would all be different. But Merleau-Ponty stresses that we not only sense as bodies,
we think as bodies. He asks us to remember that it is not only sensory
apperception, but thought, which functions through our bodies. In
"Throwing Like a Girl" (1990), Iris Young points out that we experience our bodies as capacities and things, and that this experience of
our bodies as capacities and things is gendered. Feminine motility,
Young contends, exhibits "ambiguous transcendence, an inhibited
intentionality, and a discontinuous unity with its surroundings" (p.
147). Of course if females experience their bodies as more "thing"
than males do, they experience the world differently too. Merleau-
Ponty writes that for amputees he has studied, "phantom limbs" are
the effects of continuing to think through one kind of body, even
though that body has been suddenly altered. For the amputee,
thought is still bound to the former body. In order to adjust and function fully, the amputee must gradually learn to redeploy him- or herself in a new world and will think this new world through his or her
new body.

WE READ AS BODIES

Thought is inextricably bound to the body and the body inextricably bound to thought. For the teacher, then, the question is to employ body-knowers rather than knowers for whom the body is irrelevant or in the way. The first-grade body-knower who understands gravity by its ability to stand and by its difference from a falling leaf, uses itself as scaffolding for holding the complex conceptualizations of physics. The body is also what takes up attitudes for us, and so is pivotal in memory and in reading.

Merleau-Ponty reminds us that in the act of memory we project our bodies into time as well as space. He writes,

> The part played by the body in memory is comprehensible only if memory is, not only the constituting consciousness of the past, but an effort to reopen time on the basis of the implications contained in the present, and if the body, as our permanent means of "taking up attitudes" and thus constructing pseudo-presents, is the medium of our communication with time as well as space. (1962, 181)

To illustrate the body's role in interpretation through time as well as space, Merleau-Ponty quotes Proust's *Swann's Way*:

> When I awoke like this, and my mind struggled in an unsuccessful attempt to discover where I was, everything would be moving around me through the darkness, things, places, years. My body, still too heavy with sleep to move, would make an effort to construe the form which its tiredness took as an orientation of its various members, so as to induce from that where the wall lay and the furniture stood, to piece together and to give a name to the house in which it must be living. Its memory, the composite memory of ribs, knees and shoulder-blades offered it a whole series of rooms in which it had at one time or another slept; while the unseen walls kept changing, adapting themselves to the shape of each successive room that it remembered, whirling madly through the darkness. (1962, 181)

Used to projecting his or her body-thought in time as well as space, a reader conjures up countless past experiences of living. A character in a story he or she reads congeals for the reader as a kaleidoscopic composite of his or her own experiences as a body-knower from the past, these experiences presenting themselves as new possibilities for the body-knower in the present. Past impressions are changed, but not replaced, by features from the present reading. The images from past and present cannot be reduced one to the other. They are like metaphor, which compares two things that cannot be reduced, one to the other, but together suggest a new meaning. In her autobiography of reading, Jane notices the metaphorical aspect of reading:

> I still make images so specific that I could (laboriously) draw them after I read, but I don't enter the places myself the same way I did as a child. I think we must construct them from a mixture of cues. The words themselves of course; but they give only a general indication. The rest I think must come from the style—the sounds and sequences of the words and sentences, as well as some visual equivalences, surely metaphorical, we infer from and give to characters. I think I even do that in fleeting snatches with every stranger who, however briefly, catches my attention—I have a mental setting for the barber and the lady at the dry cleaner too. How amazing that the mind is always painting from raw materials!

Jane's reflections on reading are filled with information for us about teaching. Her "raw materials" are striking for their similarity to the past impressions from which Proust's Swann is constructing the room in which he finds himself. We understand Merleau-Ponty's description of hearing and reading (likewise speaking and writing) from his portrait of Swann waking. Swann's body lying on its side remembers itself in many rooms, and rather than starting from nothing, he improves or improvises on these images as his senses sketch out a room using his body's reach and stretching beyond it. Jane's descriptions corroborate this view.

A wonderful writer, as well as a painter, Jane uses these two modes of expression to describe reading. The arts of writing and of painting, together, give us the image. It is this focus on reading as a picture we paint that indicates a pedagogy. The way a picture comes into focus for us will help us conceive of what it is like for words to come into focus and for texts to come into focus.

Proust's man waking in the bedroom illustrates something important about reading that we tend to forget, namely that interpretation is not mental or visual only. Proust's waking body helps him see what is before him, by striking a position that is ready for their shapes and sounds. Merleau-Ponty unites sound, structure and visuals with the body when he describes a word's effect on us. I quote a long passage from the *Phenomenology of Perception*:

What is particularly brought out by the word's behavior here is its indissoluble identity with something said, heard and seen. "The word as read is not a geometrical structure in a segment of visual space, it is the presentation of a form of behavior and of a linguistic act in its dynamic fullness." Whether it is a question of perceiving words or more generally objects, "there is a certain bodily attitude, a specific kind of dynamic tension which is necessary to give structure to the image; man as a dynamic and living totality has to 'pattern' himself in order to trace out a figure in his visual field as part of the psychosomatic organism."[2] In short my body is not only an object among all other objects, a nexus of sensible qualities among others, but an object which is sensitive to all the rest, which reverberates to all sounds, vibrates to all colors, and provides words with their primordial significance through the way in which it receives them. It is not a matter of reducing the significance of the word "warm" to sensations of warmth by empiricist standards. For the warmth which I feel when I read the word "warm" is not an actual warmth. It is simply my body which prepares itself for heat and which so to speak, roughs out its outline . . . we are saying that the body, in so far as it has "behavior patterns," is that strange object which uses its own parts as a general system of symbols for the world, and through which we can consequently "be at home" in that world, "understand" it and find significance in it. (1962, 236–237)

The body outlines an experience for us and stores it. Word and speech cease to *designate* thought and become the presence of that thought in the phenomenal world (1962, 182).

Jane wrote that she does not "enter" the places in texts the same way as she did as a child. She refers to her "mental" settings for texts and how her mind paints pictures of what she reads. But we should pause before we surrender to the proposition of a Cartesian adult mind that subsumes an infantile body-life.

Of course, as we mature, we become more able to remember, imagine, and invoke our world mentally, but it does not follow that these images are abstracted and completely separated from our memory of the world's sensual, acoustic, tactile effects on our bodies. As a child, Jane felt that she entered texts without being self-conscious, or body-conscious about it. As a young reader, she found herself immersed in text as a body in the same way we are immersed in the world as bodies when we are young. But Jane writes that she loses this quality of immersion in texts as she matures. I would submit, however, that the reason for gradual detachment is not simply a shift from affect to cognition, or sensori-motor life to abstract life. Instead, it is likely that we do not enter texts as adults the same way we did as children because we gradually come to realize our bodies are not the world, but that our bodies take up space and are perspectival. As children we are not aware of the mediating quality of our own bodies.

Today, Jane is conscious of constructing places for characters in texts, just as she constructs places for real people in her life—the barber and dry cleaner. She must construct those places just as Swann constructed the room in which he woke—by entering rooms from the past, and feeling them changed by the demands of our own bodies, and then by what we imagine are the demands of the barber or the launderer, or a character in a novel.

As an adult she has become conscious of, and responsible for, this process. Jane compares the construction of her reading response to the construction of everyday consciousness:

> Unlike real places, the places in books had no peripheries. They were like the places I see on a rehearsal stage, before the set is in place— sharply detailed just where the actors are, and though potentially present everywhere else, fading out towards the edges. This kind of imaginative construction of vision must go on all the time. My classroom *looks* different from every class that enters. There is always a time at the beginning of the year, before the kids have come, when I stand in my empty room and remember last year's classes and see the kaleidoscope rapidly rearranging itself in the proportions and colors. But I haven't answered for myself the question of where the ingredients come from with which I paint the settings of the books I read.

We know that in real life places have peripheries, but the painter Jane and the dramatist, Jane, and the body-knower, Jane, know that you cannot see them because of the limitations of our bodies. Thus the lack of peripheries Jane notices in books, may be more similar to our experience of reality than we thought. Jane proceeds to describe from where her reading "ingredients" come:

> For instance, *Little Women*. I haven't read it since childhood, but I can still see its places. The parlor at the March's house is small and dark and brown; the one at Mr. Laurence's is cooler, full of gray and dark green. Both face me—[how interesting!] let us call it north-south orientation. The March's parlor has no windows, but the one at Laurie's has tall floor-to-ceiling windows with a green view and green draperies. Aunt March's parlor, where Jo didn't get to go to Europe (how I hated Aunt March for that!) faced east-west and was closely stuffed with dark fur-

niture over which towered a brass bird-cage for the parrot. The scene of Meg's humiliation at the party (belladonna, pinch your cheeks to make them red, a pale-blue-gray silvery dress) had a tall white wall with a gilded mirror. I understand the place where Jo got her hair cut, because that looked like the barber shop down next to the subway where Daddy went; I don't understand the other places. They were similar in quality to places I was familiar with from our summer visits to the farm (my paternal grandparents' dairy farm in upstate New York) and to "Down South" (my great-aunts' and uncles' homes in Durham, N.C.). All those houses were liberations from the suffocation of our apartment. In the summer I had the freedom of great rambling structures with shadowy stairs (two sets, on the farm) and porches, smell of straw matting and creak of wicker, scratchy feel of sun-warmed wood with peeling paint, stiff slippery horsehair sofas, oilclothed kitchen tables (little patches peeling, showing the fabric underneath), pantries, home-canned tomatoes and home-bottled root beer, singed chicken and bluing in laundry rinse water, warm dapple of sunlight or dank dark smell of piano practicing on wet afternoons. But none of the places in Alcott's books were places I knew. None of the furniture was the same, none of the rooms. Unlike real places, the places in books had no peripheries.

Jane knows that she is not just superimposing rooms she knows about onto novels. Because of the contention between Jane and Louisa May Alcott, the author, a third meaning will arise for those rooms, imagined from real physical sources, but not wholly commensurate with them. There are traces of how both women lived as bodies in rooms, but even more important, there are imaginative projections of how Jane or others *could* live.

A literature text speaks of a possible world and of a possible way of orienting oneself within it, the philosopher, Paul Ricoeur explains. "The dimensions of this world are properly opened up by and disclosed by the text. . . . It goes beyond the mere function of pointing out and showing what already exists. . . . Here showing is at the same time creating a new way of being" (1976, 88). What is made one's own is not something mental in reading (not the intention of another subject, [the author] hidden behind the text, but the project of a world—the proposition of a mode of being in the world) (p. 94).

To move away from the notion of the mental reader to the body reader helps us understand Ricoeur's insistence that interpretation is always perspectival. The reader who knows that he or she is always somewhere in the world, and not everywhere and not nowhere, knows how unlikely it is that he or she can conceptualize a story from all perspectives at once. If the reader must "get into" stories the way he or she gets into the world with the same body/subjectivity, the reader knows that he or she feels the place and situation of first this character and then that. Or that in a dialogue when both characters are "on," he or she may get one character and miss the other. A reader may realize that taking the place of the daughter preoccupies her and so she has not inhabited the mother in the story. She may then choose to inhabit the mother with maternal experiences or to continue to feel her at a bit of a distance as a daughter. We are not thrown back here to a crude identity correspondence reader response, because we can reflect and change our whereabouts in the story. We can acknowledge, however, that we are perspectival thinkers. Our bodies take up space and time, and so do our thoughts, and if you are always in space and time, you cannot be outside of space and time, watching the action from a transcendent or universal position. Emphasizing one's position in literature or science is a way for students to identify their responses, sharpen their understanding of their responses, and to change them if desired. We do not experience a movie, or life, or reading from a universal perspective, rather, we place ourselves somewhere in the novel, say, as the daughter, or the mother-in-law or the children. We may take multiple positions, but we cannot take all positions or no position. We project our bodies into the time and space of the novel and we feel it or live it from there. The medium of theater as a pedagogy can help students identify where they are in the text at any given time and what the text means to them from there.

SPEAKING AND LISTENING AS A BODY

With the help of Merleau-Ponty and Jane, we have found the body in the reading process. We focus now on finding the body in the phenomenon of speech. Merleau-Ponty helps us understand that speech is not merely a representation of a meaning encoded phonetically through letters. Rather, words become the very presence of thought being said. This presence of thought as speech is a gesture. Through the act or gesture of speech—rhythm, tone, cadence, and tempo help make it possible for the speaker to *be* some way toward other people. The words one employs from his or her stock of words do not transcend the *way* they are spoken. The words have the speaker's style— her voice and her movement. If the speaker uses a word incorrectly, some meaning will still find its way to her audience as it was bonded in utterance to a tone, movement, or tempo related to the speaker's meaning and her observed situation by others.

Merleau-Ponty makes another subtle, but important, point about speech to show that it is gestural when he compares how we know and pronounce words to how our bodies move. He reminds us that we do not have to know the distinctiveness of words in order to use them. He writes,

> I do not need to visualize external space and my own body in order to move one with the other. It is enough that they exist for me and that they create a certain field of action spread before me. In the same way I do not need to visualize the word in order to know and pronounce it. It is enough that I possess its articulatory and acoustic style as one of the modulations, one of the possible uses of my body.
>
> The spoken word is a genuine gesture, and it contains its meaning in the same way the gesture contains its. This is what makes communication possible. In order that I may understand the words of another person, it is clear that his vocabulary and syntax must be "already known" to me. But that does not mean that words do their work by arousing in me "representations" associated with them, and which in aggregate eventually reproduce in me the original "representation" of the speaker. What I communicate with primarily is not "representation" or thought, but a speaking subject, with a certain style of being and with the "world" at which he directs his aim. (1962, 183)

We are reminded once again of Skura's child who is having a cookie experience in the last chapter. The key here is that the speaking subject (speaker) directs his aim at a whole world with his gesture. His body prepares itself for that world and shows itself to us as such. From the gesture of such a body, we get an indication of that world toward which he is speaking. Humans comprehend speech, like all gesture, only as a possibility for themselves in the world. As Merleau-Ponty reminds us, we do not understand the sexual gestures of the praying mantis. Merleau-Ponty asserts that we understand speech as the reciprocity of my intentions and gestures with others, not a mere cognitive operation. I witness gestures which outline objects of my possible intentions.

Think of a common situation in a student's life as an example. Every student has the experience of attending a lecture by an appealing professor or teacher. While the lecturer is speaking, the student is transported to the world the lecturer is indicating and speaking within. By her enthusiasm, knowledge of the terrain, and sure footing, this teacher enacts expertise, movement, even joy, in that world. For the student observer, the professor's enactment of secure footing in the world of the subject content runs parallel with the propositions and facts which can be written down as notes. While in class, the student may have the sense of sharing that world with the professor by reading with his or her own body the professor's gestures, but may feel a loss once home with only the notes left from the lecture. The responsive teacher, therefore, provides pedagogies that require the student to maintain his or her immersion in the world of the text or the lesson. This student must reenact the world subtended by the professor, the text, or the lecture notes, or write from within the specific context of the studied world, or perhaps interact with CD-Rom versions. This interactive responsibility, in which gestures are made by both teacher and student, marks the difference between the appealing teacher, who asks students to imagine the facts of a world or to imagine how our world might be different, and the charismatic teacher, who asks students to lose their own sense of the world in order to be dependent on and envious of his or her view.

SPEAKING, LISTENING, AND READING
AS A BODY IN THEATER WORK

In theatrical enactment, we can work with the way the body feels or senses objects and others in the world, and also from the way it moves, to how it looks to us moving. Theatrical enactment provides an objectification of meaning in movement. It focuses on gesture, and it is gesture we can study. Madeleine Grumet's concept of theater in education called, "scoring," patterned after a musical score, offers a fine pedagogy for providing a space for students to take up an attitude about their readings with their bodies. Grumet suggests that students make a "cut" into text like a glazier "scores" a plate of glass. They choose a unit of meaning they want to explore from their reading. Then they work to direct their classmates to physicalize this meaning. Because they emphasize what surrounds the words the text uses and the words they might try to use to interpret, they do not use words in the theatrical enactment, but the gestures that are normally like halos around words. They develop the physical gestures and spatial and temporal rules by which the gestures can be made. The actors/classmates whom they direct try to follow these rules and use their bodies to make the gestures. The creator of the score watches its physical enactment to see the meaning he or she is trying to convey. This creator changes the rules and gestures of the score until he or she believes they convey some meaning of his or her interpretation. The score can then be discussed among the creator and his or her classmates for intention and reception. The text gets the enactment it requires and the reader's response is taken seriously because it is projected onto space and time, so that it can be seen, felt, experienced, and revised. The activity is creative, assertive, sociable, and critical. A score or cut can be made not only from written texts—poems, stories, essays, and so on, but from experience as well, as when Grumet has students score memories from childhood. Just as in life, the body takes up attitudes, but unlike real life, the aesthetic dimensions of theatrical expression delimit an experience for our scrutiny and increased understanding. In the filling out of the text the enactment provides, students acknowledge the surplus meaning mere words exude for them. The surplus is what they have to write about or talk about beyond the text in their assignments.

To express a word through gesture, students can shape their bodies into tableaux, or join with other students to create ensembles. I have seen them show us "warm" in the context of a world with arms wrapped around bodies, or by fanning themselves. I have them seen them show what it was like to run as a child, in the score of repeatedly falling and scraping their knees. I have seen a group arrange themselves as a cage, with one person repeatedly breaking out and being recaptured to illustrate the tiresome burden of responsibility as part of the concept of the word, "freedom." I have see their bodies line up to prepare for a trial by fire as one interpretation of a scene from Arthur Miller's *The Crucible*, and I have seen their bodies line up to be tried by their weight on scales of tradition, gender, and political beliefs in "scores" of the same scene.

The cut of the score echoes the ideas of "cuts" in the theories of Freud, Derrida, Ricoeur, and Kristeva. Carolyn Hill[3] has written that

> Derrida's model [of writing] is Freud's idea of memory as a physical movement inscribing in an organism a trace of temporal experience. From this point of view, all writing is a physical gesture of making a dividing mark, inscribing a boundary, cutting a line through a space (an act therefore of defining, or deciding where the cut goes, creating one category split off from another). The system of traces and relations between "the psyche, society, the world" is an "interruption and restoration of contact between the various depths of psychical levels; the remarkably heterogeneous temporal fabric of psychical work itself." (Hill 1990, 137)

Freud felt that memory was patterned after the way we move physically in time, so temporal experience (the past) was represented by physical-like etchings, traces, or inscriptions that are patterned after movement. The "cut" of memory is like the inscription of a boundary of experience. Likewise, the cut of the theatrical score in the classroom (and the physical movement chosen to play within it like the tune of a musical score), interrupts the seeming cohesiveness of the well-made text and the chain of significance attributed to it by all the others, in order to insert the new subject, an individual classroom reader. Once the "cut" has been made to allow a classroom reader in, the society of the classroom restores contact between himself and all the others by discussing or writing about his insertion into the discourse. A text has been deconstructed, but a meaning has been constructed by a reader in a sociable community.

Grumet's appropriation of the musical score as a model for theatrical enactment in the classroom is a rich one. She notes that Suzanne Langer has characterized a piece of music as a virtual rendition of the passage of time, and we remember that the *Oxford English Dictionary* commemorates a history of the meaning of thesis as marking time in music with the foot. Merleau-Ponty has remarked that like musical notes, words carry us off to a world. The notes themselves, if not played, have no effect. In Merleau-Ponty's words, "The meanings swallow up the signs. . . . The process of expression makes the meaning effective, and does not merely translate it" (1962, 183). "Aesthetic expression confers on what it expresses an existence in itself, installs it in nature as a thing perceived and perceivable to all . . . a reconstitution, not a designation" (p. 182). Because the action of theater requires real space and real time with real bodies, it makes experience more perceivable for students. We will see how theater can work in the literature classroom in ensuing chapters.

FIVE

READING AND WRITING
INTERSUBJECTIVELY:
BEYOND MASTERY AND RULES

There is an impassable gulf between me and my students. I didn't really learn anything about reading in school, so I don't really know how to teach others what no one taught me. Perhaps I was too different for my own experiences to be useful in teaching; or perhaps we have passed a cultural divide too wide to cross.

—Jane, a teacher

Another legacy of the productive object relations between primary caretakers and children, is intersubjectivity. Intersubjectivity involves the ability to negotiate one's stance, positions, and perspectives with others, and to entertain theirs. What maternal object relations theory can offer is a map for alterity—the ability to exchange meanings and differences with others so as to benefit from their strangeness or foreignness, while not letting one's ego boundaries collapse under the weight of the exchange. Specifically, a primary caretaker's interaction with the child can provide a model for the following relations that constitute alterity and intersubjectivity:

1. Assertion and Holding. Drives, impulses, desires, and responses are allowed and held as important in a safe structure. Theatrical improvisation and ensemble work, as well as journal reading and peer writing groups, are pedagogies which provide and require assertion and holding.

2. Projection. The individual places what he or she is not sure of, or does not want, away from herself with impunity. He or she may thus either study it more safely from afar or abject it completely. In the theater classroom, Paula Salvio wrote about children asking classmates to play out their visions of animals at the zoo (see below), so that they could study them from a distance. Writers then go back to their desks, free to take or leave fragments from the improvisations.

   Paired readers and writers provide another opportunity for students to *use* other students to explore their own feelings and thoughts. Reader A may write a note to a friend, Reader B, which contains not only what her own response is, but how she thinks the friend might respond to the work of literature both are reading. Reader A gets a chance to pay attention to clues in the text she thinks an "other" may want. Reader A gets to wonder both why she paid attention to a certain textual issue and why she wants to give that response away. In an unpublished paper on this kind of "double reading," Madeleine Grumet and Bill Pinar use the terms "alter ego" to label this kind of projection, and "persona" to label the process of introjection below.[1]

3. Introjection. This process is to take in some of the "Other's" strangeness or foreignness (Reader B), and to keep it for your own (Kristeva 1991). In theater classrooms, the actor's incorporation of the "character" of the other is the taking on of a new or altered persona. In reading and writing classes, the experience of introjection may be provided in writing workshops in which students discuss their writings with classmates or a teacher, and hear what others make of what they are trying to convey. They may take in some of the foreignness of the other's ideas, or they may see a reflection of their own ideas coming back at them in new forms.

4. Interpretation. This last step is when the reader or writer makes decisions about what he or she believes, after having had chances for holding, projection, and introjection. In this phase of asserting autonomy, the student may choose a topic, or take a position or write a final draft. The student decides how he or she feels about a character in a drama. In Salvio's theater lab, we will see that it may be when writers decide which improvisations they choose to write about in their papers.

   Intersubjectivity is the basis for constructive pedagogies like workshops, labs, and studios in which readers and writers create new knowledge and products by presenting and discussing each others' work. In contrast, "mastery styles" of knowing rely on law and regulation, rather than the effort of real people to come to grips with and balance their needs and ideas.

We can step back from the pedagogical relationships outlined above to the infant-mother dyad again to emphasize the processes that undergird knowledge that is constructed in relation to others.

To locate the seeds of intersubjectivity in maternal life and to learn to extend it in our classrooms, we need to first look at *intrasubjectivity*, since a strong and constructive social relation between a mother and child can nourish a double subjectivity in the child and an alterity in the psychic economy that is a prototype for the development of *intersubjectivity* (see Iris Young, Kristeva, Kelly Oliver, Patricia Elliott, Jane Flax, and D. W Winnicott). Divided subjectivity within the self is related to how we can negotiate with others. In English classes, student readers and writers can learn to nurture, tolerate, and enjoy their own divided opinions and responses and the diverse perceptions of others.

These admittedly ideal relations must be constructed consciously and with purpose. Jane's remark at the opening of this chapter that there is an impassable gulf between her and her students has resonance with many teachers and with many parents. We feel the difficulty of balancing relations between self and other, and we never transcend the difficulty of balancing the heterogeneous demands within our own psyches.

INTRASUBJECTIVITY: BEING OF TWO MINDS

April, Philip, and Jane see in their own reading and teaching the problems of a self "divided." Jane writes about "two realities" she experienced as a child reader:

> *Tom Sawyer, Huck Finn, Little Women,* were home country to me. The puritanism, the conscious do-good, self-sacrificing abnegation of women, the moral rectitude, the large meals, the everyday familiarity of death—those were all as familiar as the smell of my grandmother's ironed aprons. None of those fitted very well with the externals of my life, with air-raid drills in the corridors at school, with the subway, with the crowds of girls my own age whom I didn't understand and who had nothing to say to me. What seems strange to me now is that I didn't think about how those things didn't fit together. In a kind of inversion

of what I suppose is most children's experience of their lives, I lived in two worlds of which the outer, daily one was the unreal one, and the inner, imaginative one was the reality.

Jane may be surprised to know how common an experience her sense of a secret life was. April wrote about her own divided reading life in high school:

> At the same time I was in that tenth grade English class . . . , I read vora-
> ciously at the public school library everything I could find on Indochina
> and America's "involvement." Depressing stuff—accounts by POW's
> mostly—I would pour over these books, as though reading pornogra-
> phy—with titillation, horror, and absolute secrecy. The memory of these
> books, this period, had completely escaped me until recently, when I
> watched *Hanoi Hilton* and I found I knew all about the POW camps—
> and remembered why. My parents were amazed—and somewhat mys-
> tified, dismayed—to hear of this secret obsession.

Both April and Jane tell these stories of their "split" adolescence as though they were transgressions and aberrations. They sense a divi-sion within themselves that seems somehow wrong. But Kristeva argues that it is the recognition and use of the differences within one-self that can form the basis for understanding and using our differ-ences of others (see Oliver 1993a, 1993b, and Kristeva 1982). However, she insists as well that we need to reflect on the difficulties of hetero-geneity.

Although Jane and April's stories sound transgressive, as though hiding and secrecy is warranted, the very memory and invocation of these transgressive experiences are signs that consciousness lives with difference within itself. *Kristeva argues that living with difference within the self, and even enjoying this heterogeneity, is the prototype for living with difference between self and other.* In her development of an ethic of inter-subjectivity, she looks to the mother-child unit. She calls our attention to a mother's divided subjectivity during pregnancy and to the child's divided subjectivity during infancy. Within the mother's body is the development of another body and so within herself, she experiences self and other. She is confronted with the paradox of encouraging a separate subjectivity from her own *within* her own subjectivity, an intersubjectivity and an intrasubjectivity. The child in this dyad expe-riences intrasubjectivity too, and experiences a necessary disjunction from his own experience. Theoretical accounts of this intrapsychic dis-junction offer enlightening theories of object formation, but often neglect the role of the mother or primary parent in mediating the process. For example, David Bleich cites Ernst Cassirer's formulation of the beginning of the symbolic process:

> "The sensory drive, instead of proceeding directly towards its object, instead of satisfying itself and losing itself in the object, encounters a kind of inhibition and reversal, in which a new consciousness is born." . . . Cassirer further links the act of objectification to the development of the inhibitory tendency: he says that the human infant's "clutching at the distance" "is one of the first steps by which the perceiving and desiring "I" removes a perceived and desired content from himself and so forms it into an 'object,' and 'objective' content." The object-concept, in this account, is a compensatory event, permitted by neurophysiological capacity and frustration. Thus both self-consciousness and the capacity for objectification (the combination of which is the symbol-making capacity) originate from accumulated feelings of disjunction from one's own experience. This development is species specific for human beings. (Bleich 1978, 42)

Kristeva's story of object relations within a maternal relation fills out this scenario of disjunction to show how teaching and other human cultural activities form an enabling or disabling context for human symbolic activity as an intrapsychic and intersubjective experience.

Kristeva contends that we are both excited and squeamish about the conflicts within ourselves and with others. She writes about how the self strives to create order from chaos and that we are always in conflict with the lines and rules we draw for ourselves.

In the scenario we have been studying of the self living as a body, the self has a relation with the body's pulses, drives, and fluids. It creates borders which spit and expel excesses. Excesses are defined as other, what is not needed; getting rid of them ensures order from chaos. As part of the effort to expel excess and individuate, Kristeva believes we have a desire to rid ourselves and make "abject" aspects of experience associated with it:

> The abject is that which, although ultimately a part of early experience, must be rejected so that the self can establish the borders of a unified subjectivity. . . . This rejection (abjection) of certain aspects of physical immediacy, whether of the personal body or the body politic, is the act which establishes subjective identity, but this act also establishes that identity as a prohibition, and as lacking an earlier bodily continuity. The subjective self, therefore, is always haunted by the possible return of the abject that was part of presubjective experience. (Oliver 1993a, 144)

Unfortunately as Norma Claire Moruzzi points out, "The self abjects that which is most necessarily inescapable and rejected: the bodily reminders of physical dependence and necessity" (in Oliver 1993a, 145). Moruzzi follows Kristeva's theory of abjection into the arena of the ethical and political:

> Although her analysis is directed at the development and consolidation of personal, individual identity, it can be applied as well to the development and consolidation of national, political identity. The abject is precisely that which constitutes and opposes the self, whether of the individual or of the nation state. It is that which most confounds the self's boundaries. (1993a, 144)

Iris Young uses Kristeva's notion of border anxiety to study phobias about difference as applied to race relations and homophobia (Young 1989). Her thesis, following Kristeva's logic, is that when unsure of our own boundaries, we are tempted to make borderline differences horrible, instead of tolerable. For example, one cannot detect sexual preference by appearance, and so cultural stereotypes are produced in an effort to make borders between straights and gays uncrossable. Another example tells us that differences in skin color lie along a continuum, of course, but race too, is created as a thick uncrossable border in a misguided effort to preserve slight difference. Kristeva reflects on xenophobia, in which we fear getting too close to the foreigner to secure our own borders. Or we identify with the foreigner so much that we unconsciously introject the foreigner's difficulties as our own, and feel that we are in danger of becoming strangers in our own land (see Kristeva 1991, 24).

Because of the strong impulses in the body and the psyche, Kristeva sees that it will always be a temptation to *violently* get rid of elements foreign to our desired position, both as bodies and as subjects. But human caretakers, often mothers, intervene even as the infant's sensations as a body are intense and chaotic. The body's sensations are interrupted and regulated, as Freud remarked (Kristeva 1986, 128), not only by the body itself in its hunger, temperature, and so on, but by the mother/body/caregiver. In experiencing this "Other" in coincidence with experiencing the pleasure and violence of his or her own body, the infant is able to project some of his or her experience onto her, and to introject some of her powers into him- or herself—thus creating two locations of psychic experience, a double subjectivity. There is thus an alterity in the psychic economy of the subject that is divided, but sanctioned and protected by the maternal relationship. We are used to difference *within* ourselves.

MOTHER/CHILD INTERSUBJECTIVITY
AS A PROTOTYPE FOR ETHICS AND EPISTEMOLOGY

As we think of difference as contrary forces, both within the self and between self and other, Kristeva calls for the balance of those forces, not in restraint, but in enjoyment, or in the French word Kristeva uses, "jouissance." "Jouissance" refers to body pleasure and also to the psychic desire that is produced with and through the body, but that travels beyond the body out toward the world through symbolic functions. Kristeva argues that some experience of balancing the forces of pleasure and violence in relation with other people often takes place in a *loving* relationship, of give and take, with a maternal figure. Thus, she argues, love, mutuality and reciprocity likely provide a strong basis for ethics.

Kristeva acknowledges that humans marginalize others in an effort to be ourselves, and that we exaggerate difference from those who threaten our boundaries. However, she also believes, along with Winnicott, that to a great extent, mothers can understand this need to differentiate and allow for difference by providing potential space for the child to individuate without fear of engulfment or retaliation. *Physically and psychologically, the mother walks a line or plays on a border. On one side of the border is detachment from the child, which allows separation and the formation of the child's own identity. But too great an emphasis on separation or difference can result in alienation and abandonment. On the other side of the border is merging with the child, a blurring of bodies and powers. An insistence on too much fusion can result in the lack of opportunity for the child to individuate.*

Mothers know divided subjectivity in pregnancy and they often extend this consciousness of double identity into their relationships with infants. When the mother extends love to the infant in maternal care, she can allow the child to appropriate her power and "confuse" their identities, all the while allowing differentiation. The child gets to try out who he or she is and who he or she is not, with impunity. Because the child is allowed to "confuse" self with mother, what from an external observer would be seen as intersubjectivity, may as easily to the child be experienced as intrasubjectivity. This experience of an internal alterity has resonance in the research of Vygotsky (1962) who found that what we think of as internal thought actually has the structure of internalized dialogue between a self and another.[2]

Kristeva has argued that theorists like Lacan and Freud have explored the question of development from the perspective of the oedipal male child, who is going through a phase of denying the close connections to mother and is obsessed with the "law" of the father as a compensation. Patriarchal law requires mastery, and mastery learning is the style of closed educational systems. (We will see a less oppositional role for the paternal figure in chapter 6.) The perspective of the mother and the child not in "oedipal crisis" is less studied. That is why Kristeva calls this area of ethics (and it can be applied to pedagogy), "outlaw ethics," or "herethics." "Herethics" or "outlaw ethics" questions the submission to prescribed "law" as the pinnacle of psychological or ethical development. "Herethics" reinserts maternal care experiences as providing the space for the nascent ego to confront and integrate social demands. In the view of "herethics," mature autonomy and creativity are achieved through intersubjectivity, not merely submission. The demands of the world, as apprehended and interpreted by people, are the controlling forces to which interacting subjects must respond together. Laws and limits are acknowledged as the results of human effort in the face of material realities. Kristeva claims that an embrace of the differences within ourselves presupposes our understanding of others and the world around us. She writes,

> No restrictive, prohibitive, or punitive legislation can possibly restrain my desire for objects, values, life, or death. Only the meaning that my desire may have for an other and hence for me can control its expansion, hence serve as the unique, if tenuous basis of a morality. (Cited in Oliver 1993b, 184)

As Winnicott and Kristeva have shown, the maternal relationship is one in which desires are expanded and controlled through object relations in a matrix of loving ethics, and we shall see that curriculum can take advantage of the dynamic of the intrasubjectivity-intersubjectivity one knew within the maternal relationship. Kristeva insists that "we are never merely individuals regulated by law; our individuality presupposes a social relation" (Oliver 1993b, 183).

For Kristeva, desire is as important as discipline in ethics and achievement. She asks,

> How is it possible to balance the contrary forces between which we are suspended in such a way as to maximize *jouissance* (enjoyment), to allow the creative production of art, literature and meaning? (1988, 63)

Balance, creativity, and justice are as much about enjoyment as about control and constraint. Subjects come together to draw and redraw the borders that join or separate them, not only when threatened, but based on desire. Difference does not just give itself over to a preexisting law which dominates and controls. Rather, contrary forces can come together to play as it were, around borders, so as to decide where they want to position themselves.

INTERSUBJECTIVITY IN THE CLASSROOM

Paula Salvio (1987) has written about how students help each other bring their visions and desires first to the classroom and then to the page. In a class comprised of students for whom English is a second language, she and another teacher set up a theater lab. When students are trying to write essays, the theater lab is assembled as a support for an individual's writing effort. They begin by asking who is having a problem with their story. After a reading to the class by such a writer, the classmates discuss the story publicly.

In theater lab, classmates are asked to come to the floor to improvise the movements of various animals they had seen at the zoo, especially the polar bears, about which one student, Juan, was writing, identifying them as most memorable. Other students watched the polar bears with the gestures and sounds of an audience at the zoo. From the improvisations of the bear and from the audience's reaction to the bears, Juan regains his footing in his own story. The students go back to their tables and write a few sentences about the zoo experiences they mediated with their bodies through theater work:

> As we began to read the sentences we all wrote, Juan received more and more language to bring himself back to his story. . . . It is the ludic, playful nature of our performance space which extends the one-perspective arrangement of the classroom into a multi-perspectival area which both encourages and receives a broad range of moments from which to render a story. The thinking, speaking, and performing areas are specifically constructed to prepare the students to bracket the ineffable, pre-linguistic knowledge they hold within their bodies, and it is the scoring [choreographing] of a specific bracketed image and subsequent performance of that experience which gives the students the language they need to write, for meaningfulness is something deeper than the logical system of language; it is founded on something prior to language and embedded in the world (Palmer, 1969, p. 34). It is through performative action that we can begin to understand the *onto*logical [emphasis mine] possibilities of words and language, possibilities which reach beyond the congealed referents which are fastened to the law. (1987, 19)

In literature and writing classes, the reader or writer's interaction with others is as important as confronting the rules of grammar, syntax and literary structure. As Salvio showed, other pupils can map out a detailed world with their own bodies and gestures and the writer can go there again with them, remembering his impressions and choosing his words from the milieu. Even after writing, the writer needs others, as Sartre wrote (in Kaplan 1986, 488), because in the process of writing, he or she must appeal to the freedom of readers to collaborate. Writers are asking their readers, as Juan and Kadir in Salvio's class might ask their classmates, "You go out into the world, don't you? Is it not like I have written?" The act of writing is a thetic break from the writer's taken-for-granted immersion in the everyday world because he stops to remember, to make a cut, to ask for confirmation or to differ. Kristeva's work offers us further insight into what roles participants in an English class may take in collaborating with a reader or writer.

THE FUNCTIONS OF THE CARING MATERNAL AS A TEACHING MODEL

By studying the nourishing role of the maternal function, we can find clues to the role of the nourishing classmate and teacher. First, there is the space the mother creates for a nascent ego. By not asking the child to identify the difference between him- or herself and other or to identify what is inside or what is outside, she allows him to appropriate stimulation for his or her own needs, views, and abilities. He or she can enlarge his sphere of power in fantasy. The analogous pedagogy is the indulgence of the egoistic reading response, the improvisation, or the first draft of writing that is an outpouring of inclination. The teacher allows the student to experience his desires and concerns as important to the creative process. She ameliorates the fears young readers and writers have that they will lose connections with others by being themselves.

Second, the teacher allows for negation of what the student feels is not part of his vision. Our drive toward creativity, power, and enlightenment entails trying to get rid of what is in our way. Just as in infancy, we take in food, and we spit some out, in learning, we both accept and repudiate. While thriving within maternal physical and psychological protection, we try to separate from the mother or to abject her so that we can emerge as individuals. Kristeva asks us to notice that mothers can and often do, enjoy, understand, and structure the process of rejection in relationships with children, and for us to presume this process as a model of ethical and pedagogical behavior toward others.

In infancy, the child creates not only by making a mark or by expressing drives, but by getting rid of what he or she does not want. Mother is useful here as the one on whom the child may project what he or she does not want. Winnicott claims that the good enough mother can tolerate this projection. She allows the child to "play" along their borders, mixing his or her identity with her identity so that the child can get rid of material, and reincorporate it with impunity. The child gets to play with who he or she is and is not, and what is and what is not, within the unconditional protection of mother love. The child even gets to project onto her his inadequacies and weaknesses, or whatever the child denies for himself. Remember that the toddler may decide that it is he or she who is able to open the car door and Mother is suddenly "unable." We will see that the teacher, Philip, projects onto maternal life, and women, the personal, sensual, poetic kind of reading he denies himself in the curriculum he teaches. The usefulness of this projection is that it has preserved the poetic for him as an ideal— but the down side is that he has yet to reintegrate the poetry into his teaching.

Whereas Philip may both idealize and exile the maternal register, one of the other English teachers, Jane, writes about her abjection of her own mother. Jane acknowledges that she denies her mother status as a reader and responder, so that she can make room for herself (see Appendix B, Jane's Autobiography #2).

Jane sees that she "made" her mother into a nonreader to preserve her own identity as a reader, but she also sees that she reduplicates this differentiating process with her students, thus creating the "impassable gulf" she refers to in the opening quote of this chapter. After writing about her mother, she muses, "So my teaching is a dangerous act—approach and run away."

By identifying and accounting for merging and differentiation experiences related to language and reading in maternal relations, we have a better chance of using this knowledge to inform our teaching, especially in how we provide for interaction among readers and writers. In the classroom, we can set up opportunities for readers to write to each other about their reading, negotiating what they like and dislike, using each other to define their own individual views. In reading texts together, students can begin to wonder about their individuality—why does another reader have a different response? Are the differences entirely attributable to different past experiences, or do we deny ourselves access to various interpretations? On reflection, how do we want to change?

AN INTERSUBJECTIVE CURRICULUM

Nancie Atwell's ideas for a writing workshop encompass the spirit and ethic of intersubjective negotiation (Atwell 1987). When conferring with a writing student, she asks either teacher or peer, whichever is the conference partner, to refrain from taking responsibility away from the writer. Instead, Atwell asks that the conferee make space for the student writer's desires to expand. Atwell writes,

> Students, for example, need to try out the content of their writing on others and on themselves as readers, hearing what they've said and considering what they might say next. . . . I invite the writer to talk, in this case by waiting and making a space for her to talk, then listen hard, tell back, and ask a clarifying question. . . . Again the purpose of the content conference is to help writers discover the meanings they don't yet know, to name problems and attempt solutions. . . . It's important to remember that you're not asking to hear every word every student writes; if you do, you're taking control and making each of those pieces of writing your responsibility. Instead, ask kids to tell you about the piece. Ask them to read or talk to you about the lead or conclusion, a part that's working well, or a part where they need help. . . . Make eye contact with the writer. This means kneeling or sitting alongside their desks as you talk and listen. Because the student and the student's reaction are the focus of the conference, don't look at or read the paper or allow the writer to give it to you. Don't tell writers what should be in their writing or, worse, write on their pieces. Remember the centrality of ownership in student's growth as writers. The piece of writing belongs to the writer. Build on what writers know and have done, rather than bemoaning what's not on the page or what's wrong with what is there. . . . In questioning students, ask about something you're curious about as an inquisitive human being. Forget you're an English teacher and focus on the meaning. What would you like to know more about? What didn't you understand? (1987, 88, 94, and 95)

In this pedagogical model, the construction of knowledge is structured the way identity is structured by the mother through alterity. To start, the focus is not on prohibition or submission to rules, but on the communication of the student's desire. In the mother-child relationship, the child egotistically identifies with the mother's power and alternately projects onto her his or her weaknesses or inadequacies. In the writing conference, the student takes on the egotistical role of serious writer if the teacher or conferee does not assert his or her own ego in place of the student's. The student writer does not have to defend weaknesses in his work, but can use the teacher or conferee to hold what he or she might want or might not want. The writer knows his or her conference partner is acting as a screen for the writer's own projected ideas because he or she expects some form of them to come back in a "telling back" or clarifying question. A child sees new possibilities for him- or herself in the way the child's mother regards him or her, but the child alternately refuses to be bound by what the mother imagines him or her to be. The child constructs his or her independence out of this alternating rhythm of me/not me, of assertion and negativity. Likewise, the writer sees new possibilities for his writing in the way the teacher-conference partner regards his writing, but is free to choose what he will accept or reject in the conference as the writer continues on with his work. Atwell sees this choice as crucial in the ultimate goal of nurturing autonomous writers. She writes, "Resist making judgments about the writing. If you tell a writer her first draft is good, why should she bother doing anything more with the piece? And how can she be expected to develop her own criteria for good writing if she's dependent on her teacher's judgments to tell her what's good?" (p. 95).

In one of April's autobiographies, we get a glimpse of the alterity that is possible in reading and writing with others in a passage about how April and her sister dramatize Nancy Drew stories (see Appendix C, April's Autobiography #1).

In a portrait of intersubjectivity, April and her sister indulge their individual preoccupations by choosing what to focus on in the stories, even creating their own. Theirs is not a curriculum of assignments, but of what coincides with their own desires. They create alter egos by projecting possibilities onto dolls and to each other. They playfully assume some of the personality traits of the characters by including them in their scripts, and they omit other traits as they choose. Finally they express their autonomy by typing and binding the stories they have created.

A CHILLY CLIMATE FOR NEGOTIATING
READING AND WRITING

Because academic traditions owe more to patriarchal structures of submission to law, rather than to intersubjectivity, we see many examples of the failure of intersubjectivity or the failure to legitimize intrasubjectivity in stories about school. Philip reads the books assigned to his brother in college, rather than read the ones he is assigned in his own classes. By doing this, he chooses to read based on his own desires, but the effort is not extended into an intersubjective relationship between himself and his brother. He writes,

> When I was in high school, my older brother was in college taking English literature survey courses. I remember reading all the books. Robert Penn Warren—*The Cave*. William Faulkner—*Absolom, Absolom*. Ernest Hemingway—*The Sun Also Rises, For Whom the Bell Tolls*. George Orwell—*1984*. I would read for hours, feeling myself important reading college books. I would stay up half the night reading. I don't recall such enthusiasm about my required high school books.

Philip's response remains introspective and not negotiated in a community, as April was able to do with her sister. His brother does not respond as an alter ego, neither are there dolls or scripts to hold experimental possibilities.

Jane, too, writes about reading incidents that fall short of being intersubjective:

> Mostly I realized what a secret, clandestine, ego-centered act it [reading] was (and still is). It is as proprietary as eating, as setting out on solitary trips of exploration, as writing. Sometimes it used to be a knowing gesture—because I was lonely and scared, I was a snob, so I belonged to a select circle of other gawky snobs who dealt in books as partly password and partly conversation-fodder—in other words, books were my substitute for a social life for a long time. They were also a good way of shutting out things you didn't want to see or hear, like calls to dishes. I am still fairly good at walking while reading, but I no longer try to dry dishes while reading. Beth died with the dish towel in my hand, and I was all hot-faced and throat-hurting because I wasn't about to let my mother see me cry. . . .

Obviously there is no reason to expect that any particular mother at any particular time intuitively or essentially provides an intersubjective response, even though the child wishes one. This is especially true when mothers' own experiences as women or girls were ignored, compartmentalized, or trivialized, as they have been in our culture. At any rate, when intersubjectivity is preempted, readers are more likely to regress. Jane feeds her own ego with her reading, but when she attempts to interact with her friends or her mother, they are not willing to take on her readings since they have such an insecure grip on their own. In the absence of a pedagogy of intersubjectivity that guarantees the ego of each reader and time to continue the dialogue with a respondent, each reader scurries back to his original position, holding on protectively. With few successful intersubjective experiences of adequate duration, it is no wonder that teachers simply try to protect each student's right to read on his or her own. Leaving everybody to read alone leaves a lot of class time, however, and many teachers feel pressured to fill it up with structural analysis. For example, Jane values personal response, but states that lessons in structural analysis are most fruitful for her students:

> I still have a big doubtful area about what the literature teacher should be doing in secondary school. . . . Should I be providing texts they might not think to choose themselves, and encouraging them to imaginatively ingest those texts? . . . So my teaching is a dangerous act—approach and run away. Find the emotional meaning, find yourself, retreat into analysis (write a topic sentence, learn to write transitions, all that).

We could go back to a number of passages in which Jane reports having to read alone and feeling that she had to protect her sense of her reading from others. She tries to do the same for her students by suggesting that English teachers ought to let students' "unconscious activities go on in decent privacy." While these "unconscious" activities go on in privacy, the class focuses on analytical structures of the text. Allowing students' responses, but then not feeling supported by the system to respond to them in any depth, Jane skips right to the laws of analysis, coopting intersubjective steps. She explains her choice: "I suppose here I am recapitulating my own reading history, a long period of unsupervised encounters at the level of emotion and fantasy, overlaid with the kind of analytical thinking I am doing now in graduate school."

In *Subjective Criticism*, David Bleich shows that readers always have responses and biases, but in the absence of an opportunity for negotiating them, they may be more likely to couch them in structural terms which are not negotiable, thus hiding their feelings and questions. And so Jane feels, as do many teachers, that her eleventh grade students "read unquestioningly." Not expecting any response, they *have* to read and write unquestioningly and fail to see that their feelings and ideas come from themselves, and not from reality.

Jane writes,

> Since many of my kids don't seem to know how to engage with their reading at a personal level, I try to make them do it (or pretend to do it) in their early journals and in many of their ongoing assignments: write

a diary entry or a letter, etc. . . . This journal will not be so much a dialogue with me as it will be, I hope, a dialogue with themselves about the meaning of the work.

But perhaps our students do not question those of us who seem to not have questions of the text ourselves. Object relations teaches us that children question most within a secure relationship of give and take with someone. Jane also notices that student readers may not have anyone else besides her with whom to have a dialogue. She wrote, "They [books] can provide children with other selves, other eyes to help them see how they fit in the world. I suppose that would be useful to adolescents. Perhaps I should say that to them, and not just assume that it's happening." Jane's reluctance to be both the Other to her students and to have students be "others" for each other, recapitulates the lack of response she has experienced as a reader in school.

Philip tries to be the someone with whom his students can read, but is uncomfortable setting himself up as the one authoritative reader to whom they turn. Remember he wrote,

> I am not as clear about how to respond when students go beyond the text to support their hypotheses with evidence from the text. When I understand how their personal experiences support inferences based on evidence in the text, I see connections. When students' personal experiences seem related to an idiosyncratic interpretation (not clearly based on the text), I feel ambivalence about affirming students' experiences while interpreting the text. Are the "facts" of the text negotiable? Does an individual have the right to an interpretation? Who controls the interpretation(s)? The teacher (authority)? Is the teacher (text) open to interpretation(s)?

Philip is genuinely concerned with his students' responses, but he is unsure about their right to an interpretation. He senses that he is not willing to be a respondant because he does not want to disrupt the authority of the text and perhaps the critical community. In later chapters we will look at how to negotiate individual interpretations, and at the obstacles of domination, submission, and mastery in reading and writing, and at intersubjective alternatives to mastery learning.

SIX

THE TEACHER:
AN AGENT OF LOVE AND ENTERPRISE

> While she spoke, we were alone and clandestine, far from
> men, gods, and priests, two does in a wood, with those other
> does, the Fairies. I simply could not believe that someone
> had composed a whole book about that episode of our pro-
> fane life, which smelled of soap and eau de cologne.
>
> . . . My mother had gone off, not a smile, not a sign of com-
> plicity, I was in exile and besides, I didn't recognize her
> speech. Where had she got that assurance? A month later, I
> realize: it was the book that was speaking. . . . Singing, nasal,
> broken by pauses and sighs, rich in unknown words, they
> were enchanted with themselves and their meanderings
> without bothering about me.
>
> —Jean-Paul Sartre, *The Words*

Sartre's autobiographical account of reading can help us focus on a
third legacy from maternal care which is a culmination and extension
of the two already discussed. The maternal body is the first term in
Kristeva's triad, and we have seen how by sharing physicality with a
mother, the child's bodily experiences are regulated by her and that the
child registers meaning in its body. The second term we have explored
is intersubjectivity, that is, how the child projects, introjects, and
abjects others, like he has done with the mother. The third term will be
the building and utilization of the space between mother and child to
help the child construct a new reality in which he or she can act.

We saw in chapter 4 that an important pedagogical feature of the
infant-maternal relation is that the child first learns by incorporation and

not imitation. Kristeva emphasized that the child incorporates the mother or primary parent; that is, the child goes over to the place of the mother and performs the functions she performs. We can see this dynamic at work in Sartre's taking the parental position vis-à-vis books without knowing what they are: "I took the two little volumes, sniffed at them, felt them, and opened them casually 'to the right page' making them creak."

A HEALTHY NARCISSISM

Remember Kristeva's comparison of the infant's incorporation of the breast to the subsequent incorporation of "the speech of the other" (1987, 26). She explained that through incorporation of the speech of the other the infant incorporates the patterns of language and thereby identifies with the other. In fact, it is the incorporation of the patterns of language through the speech of the other that enables the infant to communicate and thus commune with others. And through the ability to assimilate, repeat, and reproduce words, the infant becomes like the other: a subject and an agent (1987, 26).

Kristeva calls this incorporation of the other "narcissism" because it involves becoming a speaking subject without learning to do so in the sense that one must acknowledge what one knows or does not have. A deficit or lack is not presented. One assumes the position of speaker without knowing the objects of speaking, that is, without knowledge of specific words. In the next, crucial step, the child puts him- or herself in the place of language or signs, just in the same way the child has put him- or herself in the mother's position, as coregulator of fluids, drives, and feeding. At the point of speaking, the child is already positioned within language as a being with drive and intention.

The incorporation and reduplication theory challenges our views about teaching students language arts by confronting them with standards, laws, and grammars. The theory suggests that children do not primarily take up language because they are threatened with something they lack, as Lacan argued.[1] Rather, they take up language as a physical fulfillment of their own desire.

PRODUCTIVE NARCISSISM AS A PSYCHOLOGICAL SPACE FOR KNOWLEDGE AND ACTION

Kristeva maintains that the alterity which is part of mother-infant, body-language, and self-other relations opens up a metaphysical space in which imagination comes to life (Oliver 1993b, 73). Because the child will be allowed to assume the position of the other/mother, without threat, he or she experiences both a stable love and difference at the same time. The child assumes he or she can reduplicate what mother can do even though what the mother can do in reality is receding always out of reach, sparking his or her imagination. A productive narcissism provided for the child by this loving parent protects the child from what he or she does not know and what he or she lacks, so that the difference between himself and the other does not need to be closed by the child; rather the child uses that space to imagine what he or she wants. Narcissism is a structure that teachers will want to preserve and protect. For example, Denny Taylor writes that as teachers we ought to write literacy biographies of students that record how each enlarges his or her linguistic world day by day, rather than testing students' literacy against standards that emphasize deficits.[2] The narcissistic stage is not merely a developmental stage, but an *ongoing* structure of the ego that helps the child negotiate between the maternal body and the symbolic world. Kristeva calls this process a healthy kind of narcissism that "prefigures and sets in motion the logic of object identification in all object relations including both discourse and love" (Oliver 1993b, 72).

D. W. Winnicott's work reinforces the child's reliance on this productive narcissism. He writes about how the material world first begins to get objectified by the child as an extension of the reduplication process going on with the mother. He describes the interplay "in the child's mind of that which is subjective (near-hallucination) and that which is objectively perceived (actual or shared reality)" (1971, 52). Winnicott asserts,

> This intermediate area of experience, unchallenged in respect of its belonging to inner or external (shared) reality, constitutes the greater part of the infant's experience, and throughout life is retained in the intense experiencing that belongs to the arts and to religion and to imaginative living and to creative scientific work. (1971, 14)

Winnicott's conception of how we come to know the world, challenges the notion of splitting reality between what is "inside" and what is "outside," and challenges the notion of keeping what is private, separate from what is shared. He showed that the knower and the known cannot be separated and he sought to understand how the self uses culture to expand his or her world. Winnicott's understanding of human creativity developed from clinical observations in his pediatric psychoanalytic practice, from the descriptions parents gave him of their experiences with their children, and from children's own references to their own experiences (1971, xiii). The modus operandi of the child relating to the outside world in Winnicott's theoretical perspective is transitional objects, the pre-objects which begin to symbolize for the child the maternal reduplication processes to which Kristeva referred.

TRANSITIONAL OBJECTS

Winnicott cites the well-known phenomena of infants using their fists, fingers, and thumbs, in stimulation of the oral erotogenic zone, in satisfaction of the instincts of that zone, and in quiet union (1971, 1). He stresses that after a few months infants of both sexes often become fond of dolls or other special objects which their mothers let them have and to which they may become addicted. Transitional phenomena are the primary "other-than-me" pre-objects that the infant starts to weave into its experience. Transitional objects are thought by Winnicott to be extensions of nursing from the breast and autoerotic experiences such as thumb-sucking. He explains that the baby's fingers may caress the upper lip during thumb-sucking, and that with the other hand the baby may take an external object, like a part of a blanket, into the mouth with the fingers. Sometimes a bit of cloth or napkin is held or sucked, or a piece of wool is plucked along with the caressing activity. Mouthing may occur, accompanied by sounds of "Mum, mum, mum," babbling, anal noises, the first musical noises, and so on. At some point, the piece of wool, blanket, word, tune, or mannerism becomes vitally important for use in going to sleep or as a defense against anxiety.

Winnicott describes an example of a typical, healthy use of such a transitional object by a child he studied in the clinic:

> Soon after weaning at five to six months he adopted the end of the blanket where the stitching finished. He was pleased if a little bit of wool stuck out at the corner and with this he would tickle his nose. This very early became his "Baa"; he invented this word for it himself as soon as he could use organized sounds. From the time when he was about a year old he was able to substitute for the end of the blanket a soft green jersey with a red tie. . . . It was a sedative which always worked. . . . When Y was a little boy it was always certain that if anyone gave him his "Ba" he would immediately suck it and lose anxiety. (1971, 7)

Within this passage, we can recognize that early language is con-
tinuous with what is put in the mouth. Located in the mouth, "Baa" is
body, object (blanket), and also, at the same time, not body (what can be
separated from the mouth). In a symbolic sense, "Baa" can also be read
as mother, substitute for mother, and not mother, all at the same time.
Winnicott focuses on what happens to objects like blankets or teddy
bears because they are artifacts of maturational experience, the use of
which, we can observe as part of a complex maturational journey. I
would suggest, that as we use Kristeva's narrative to reimagine taking
up language, we use Winnicott's narrative about transitional objects to
reimagine students' uses of linguistic objects, like words and texts.

Winnicott explains that the infant assumes rights over the object,
and the object is affectionately cuddled as well as excitedly loved and
mutilated (abjected). This object never changes, except by the infant's
will, and it must survive loving, hating, and abjection. While the infant
feels he controls it, "It must seem to the infant to give warmth, or to
move, or to have texture, or to do something that seems to show it has
vitality or reality of its own" (1971, 5).

To the baby the transitional object does not seem as though it
comes from without as it does from the observer's perspective, nor
does it come from within like an hallucination. There is an overlap of
experience. This overlap of experience was made possible by the
mother who anticipates needs, responds to needs, and allows separation, all the while allowing the illusion that the infant controls these
capacities. Narcissism in maternal relations makes the use of transitional objects possible. When the mother adapts to the infant's needs,
there is the illusion that there is an external reality that corresponds to
the infant's own capacity to create. Progress is made by the expansion
of the rich cultural world the child confidently creates in this transac-
tional process. The use of a piece of blanket or whatever transitional
object "is what the observer can see of this journey of progress" (1971,
6). For the baby the question of who conceived or presented an experience is never formulated—there is a neutral area of experience that
is never challenged. Winnicott sees this neutral experience as that
which always provides relief from the strain of relating inner and
outer reality.

Winnicott believes that the psychic processes that evolved in the
use of transitional objects influence psychic reality for individuals
throughout life as they create and use culture. The impact of Winnicott's
theory is that cultural material (literature, music, arts, sciences) can only
take shape as meaningful reality for an individual by the individual's
capacity for identification and differentiation with objects, which follows

pre-objectal narcissism. In his research and clinical experiences, Winnicott saw that these infantile experiences start in a relationship with the mother or primary caretaker, who creates an arena for safe play with objects. It is there that the infant is first able or not able to move back and forth between subjectivity and objectivity, between self and otherness.

TEACHING AS PROVIDING POTENTIAL SPACE

In *Transitional Objects and the Facilitating Environment*, 1965), Winnicott discusses how the potential psychic space for the use of transitional phenomena is created by what he calls "the good-enough mother." Winnicott's phrasing is patronizing, but the concept can unveil the important function of a caring provider who "meets the omnipotence of the infant and to some extent makes sense of it repeatedly" (1965, 145). In contrast, he describes the mother who is "not good enough" in the following passage:

> The mother who is not good enough is not able to implement the infant's omnipotence, and so she repeatedly fails to meet the infant's gesture; instead she substitutes her own gesture which is to be given sense by the compliance of the infant. This compliance on the part of the infant is the earliest stage of the False Self, and belongs to the mother's inability to sense her infant's needs. (1965, 145)

Winnicott contends that the "True Self" cannot become a reality unless the mother repeatedly meets the infant's spontaneous gesture, and I have suggested earlier that the teacher meet students' gestures through providing space in the curriculum for the individual's response as theater, journal, essay topic, and so forth.

Winnicott sums up the development of True or False Selves and the ability to participate in culture thus:

> In the healthy individual who has a compliant aspect of the self but who exists and who is a creative and spontaneous being, there is at the same time a capacity for the use of symbols. In other words, health here, is closely bound up with the capacity of the individual to live in an area that is intermediate between the dream and the reality, that which is called the cultural life. . . . By contrast, where there is a high degree of split between the True Self and the False Self which hides the True Self, there is found a poor capacity for using symbols, and a poverty of cultural living. Instead of cultural pursuits one observes in such persons

extreme restlessness, an inability to concentrate, and a need to collect impingements from external reality so that the living-time of the individual can be filled by reactions to these impingements. (1965, 150)

So we see Winnicott's research as commensurate with Kristeva's theory that the mother's body contact, holding, feeding, looking at and talking to the child is a process of recognition for the child and reflects back to him or her who the child is and what the child wants. Note that in two pedagogies mentioned in previous chapters, theatrical improvisation and conferences in reading and writing classes, the teacher or other students reflect back to the student what they apprehend of his or her own expression.

A THIRD INFLUENCE

But more is needed beyond mirroring in parenting and teaching for the child or student to mature. Mythologically, as a culture, we have always relied on a third influence to break open the mother-child dyad, and to release the child to become autonomous. Freud's references to ancient patriarchs like Moses and Oedipus, remind us of the omnipresence of the paternal lawgiver and lawbreaker throughout history, and serves as a marker for where we are as a culture. Freudian analysis suggests that a paternal figure must enter into a child's life to disrupt the dyadic fusion with mother, by confronting the child with a third image. Lacan used the "mirror stage" as the symbol of this third intrusion into the child's life, but the theory has roots in a story told by Freud and deemed significant. In Freudian theory, the story of a child's viewing of a specular image of him- or herself in a mirror, focuses our attention on the child's radical and painful move out of maternal relations.[3] This true story from Freud's life tells of how during a separation from its mother, a child acquaintance of Freud notices that he can make himself disappear and reappear in a mirror hung some inches off the floor so that the child can duck below it. The child accompanies his disappearance with baby language Freud recognizes as meaning for the child "baby gone." Freud notices how this activity represents for the child mother coming and going. The child makes himself disappear, like her. He gets control over the lack of or loss of the mother by making himself disappear when he wants to. Thus the image in the mirror makes it possible to reexperience lack, and also to make loss happen and to make up for it.

For Freud, the story of separation, loss, and lack for the child, is overlaid with anatomical sexual difference. For example, to Freud, the lack of appearance of the penis stands for a sense of inadequacy for the girls. For boys, the father's penis presents competition and challenge. For both boys and girls, Freud understood castration as motivation to leave the regressive world of the mother.

Now Kristeva does not dispute that experiences of loss or lack of mother are inevitable, and that in order for the child to mature, he or she must overcome the lack by symbolizing the self as real without mother. She does not dispute that language helps the child accomplish this sublimation. But Kristeva does not believe lack is the only motivation for symbolic and linguistic achievement.

As we have seen, Lacan has reread Freud to powerfully influence linguistic theory. He used the mirror stage as a metaphor for the symbolic order of language. He saw the metaphorical impact of the mirror as a threatening image that lures the child away from earlier maternal relations, by reflecting an image back to the child different from his or her previous diffused experience of him- or herself—more whole and cohesive, but not familiar either. Lacan associates the mirror with the phallic figure who captures the child's attention and diverts it from the earlier maternal connections, by threatening the child with a look that goes beyond him or her.[4] The theory goes that the cohesive image in the mirror makes the child feel that he or she has not been whole without the solidifying image offered by the phallic figure to replace who the child is. The child sees that it has been lacking and wants to make up for what is missing in him or her. In Lacanian theory, the child suffers the threat of deficiency or lack. The child tries to find something to stand in for what he or she lacks. If we follow Lacan's line that the mirror is a metaphor of the symbolic order for the child, then symbolic activity, such as language, is something that the child needs, but lacks, or is always in threat of losing. Lacan believed that the child identifies with language as a "stand-in" for the gap between what he or she means and what others can know of what he or she means. He stresses that it is necessarily like the castration that Freud narrated. For Lacan, the alien, arbitrary, and standard quality of language, suits the child's necessary alienation from what it thought it was (maternal earlier experience) and from what it wants to be (whole, complete, phallic).

KRISTEVA OR LACAN?

Language teachers have a stake in whether they appreciate Kristeva's distinctiveness from Lacan. Lacan's emphasis is that language is necessarily threatening and Kristeva's emphasis is that it must be attractive. Linguistic practice, modeled on Lacan's theory, stresses submission to structure, self-alienation, objectivity, and abstraction. However, Kristeva is not convinced that the child would be willing to leave the mother's body and intersubjective shelter because of a threat. She suggests that there must be an attraction, rather than a threat. Something is needed to attract the child to go beyond the dyadic relationship with mother (and as we shall see, a teacher), and to leave the fusion with her in order to become an individual.

From her theoretical perspective and her psychoanalyic practice, Kristeva sees the importance of a third psychosocial influence extending from and beyond the dyadic maternal relationship. As mentioned earlier, traditionally, the father plays the role of interlocutor in this relationship. Kristeva asserts a different function of the third term in a child's early and primary affiliations, which implies something different for language theory and teaching.[5] I find her story more convincing because of her more careful consideration and theory of maternal relations, her experience and research with clients, and because of my reflection on my own language use and on the development of language in students and my own children.

Agreeing that to individuate, the child must abject the mother's body, but not maternity, from which he or she is inseparable, Kristeva suggests that the child finds a positive and energizing motive for language use and agency, not in a completely new relationship, but in the deepening complexity of the former maternal one. The third or traditionally paternal term, in Kristeva's view, plays an important part in support of maternal function, not in opposition to it.

Kristeva suggests that the third term, represented as the desired father in Freud, need not appear to the child as a new desire in opposition to mother, but as the fulfillment of her desire. The child need not imagine paternity as overtaking the mother to rule or obliterate her. It is more logical from the child's egocentric point of view, that the paternal factor exists to help create the child. Logically the father is there to fulfill the mother's desire to conceive the child, literally and figuratively. The child identifies on two levels with what has attracted and satisfied his mother. On one level his or her own conception attracted and fulfilled the mother, and on another level, a third term—something foreign and other—attracted and fulfilled her. In this kind of productive fantasizing for the child, we see that the child can imagine him- or herself as both identifying with her and transcending her, and as Winnicott's theory would have it, to be both her and not her.

From the mother's point of view, the object of the desiring and caring mother's gaze is a new place in the world made for her and her loved one, a conception. For the child, the object of the mother's desires—other loved ones, work, community, places and objects, does continually recede as a horizon for the child, who cannot in reality have all that she has. But this ever-receding horizon must be in the domain of a world the two can inhabit; the way the mother handles the world includes the needs of the child, of the other, of others. Again, we can see this love as a foundation for ethics and epistemology.

The child's ego is strengthened by the mother's desire for a third party, because the child can only recognize him- or herself as "Other" from mother, if the child sees that Mother has "an Other" besides the child. Kelly Oliver says we cannot take what Kristeva calls a "paternal" Other too literally (1993b, 70). Other primary desires besides fathers can serve as that to which the child sees mother attracted. Other people, community, work, can divert mother's eyes away from the child and fulfill her, in order to make the child realize that he or she is not the only object for her. (These others, or third terms are sometimes called imaginary fathers or maternal imaginaries in Kristeva's work. Again, I think these references seem to Kristeva to reflect biocultural and historical conditions of parentage.) For the child, being the only one for the mother, threatens to be an identification with her—being the same as the mother, with no individuation. However, being one of "others" is a function of love, of a desire, and of choice, and is liberating for the child. The child identifies with the object of mother's desire—perhaps a father or some other love, who fulfills desire—not solely with the mother to whom he or she must individuate. The child becomes not merged with the mother, but loved by her, and by being fulfilling for her, the child can afford to individuate. However, if the desire of the mother is unrequited, ignored, or repudiated, it is hard for the child to imagine that he or she was conceived out of love, power, and choice and is cared for out of love, power, and choice. Instead the child either has trouble separating from the mother to individuate (he or she has to continue to *be* her to have her), or the child repudiates the mother's nourishment as too weak and unacknowledged to sustain the child. The child must then bank on the paternal, symbolic, stern, masculine figures in society to identify with and save him or her from being engulfed by the mother. He or she may either mourn the long lost mother in a kind of depressive nostalgia, pretend she never existed, or spend his or her life making her abject. He or she may develop the False Self of which Winnicott warns, and become compliant to paternalistic authority. From this angle, Freud and Lacan's stern paternal third figure can be read as a failure of support for maternal relations. *The unmasking of society's failure at home and in public to acknowledge and support the power of the mother so that the child can use her power, is an important feminist breakthrough and a breakthrough for understanding our students' teachers.*

ANOTHER POSITION FOR THE TEACHER: AGENT OF LOVE AND ENTERPRISE

The child needs to know that he or she is loved by the mother, but is not the same as her. This knowledge sets up the possibility that the child is a subject who has desires of his or her own. This relationship of love helps us see an alternative for the child to severing the ties to what Kristeva refers to as "semiotic" (body-knowing) life with its drives and passions, as he or she tries to enter symbolic life. If we acknowledge that traditionally the paternal represents symbolic achievement to the child, and that the maternal represents pleasure, Kristeva's triangle suggests that language can carry us back to the source of our pleasures and needs, not in regression, but as subjects doubling back with new tools. This is an alternative to being taken up by the look and law of the stern father in a chain of significations whereby the child does not feel him- or herself as a subject but only as an object of the father's wishes. The referral back to the mother's desires allows the child to keep his or her link to maternity, even through differentiation. If we take another look at the opening scene of this chapter from Sartre's autobiography, *The Words*, Sartre is at first threatened by the difference in his mother when her voice changes as she reads and "goes off" with the fairies. But eventually he identifies with what satisfies her—the charm and excitement of the characters, and he puts himself in their place:

> It seemed to me that a child was being questioned: What would he have done in the wood cutter's place? Which of the two sisters did he prefer? Why? Did he approve of Babette's punishment? But the child was not quite I, and I was afraid to answer. Nevertheless I did. My weak voice faded, and I felt myself become someone else. (1964, 47)

In school teaching, traditionally a woman's profession, we must also be suspicious of customs that cut off the teachers' ability to connect their students with the worldly authority traditionally associated with men. We must likewise be wary of the logic of linguistics that is founded on the detachment of subject from object, word from referent, structure from drive and language user from community. If the mother is most efficacious for the child when she both meets his or her gesture, and when she is attracted by someone or something else, *then the model for a powerful teacher is one who accepts the child's ego and reflects his or her interests back to the child, and who has strong interests and ties to the outside world that are visible to the child.* Before looking at how this revised logic might inform the teaching of April, Jane, and Philip, it may be useful to review the implications of the maternal theory cited for language teaching:

1. The public and administrators, as well as teachers themselves, would reenvision teachers as having the responsiblity and autonomy to provide the opportunity for the student to bring drives, passion, and intention to language arts in schools. Examples of pedagogies that use and shape these intentions are theatrical scores, journals, writing poetry, strong individual responses to reading, allowing students to choose his or her own writing topics, and tapping students' concerns and hopes for the outside world in the development of curriculum.
2. A teacher would provide settings in which attraction to language takes place, rather than slavish conformity to threatening standards or formulas. He or she would protect linguistic narcissism by refraining from emphasizing ignorance or deficits in language. Accumulative accounts of language progress would be more productive, like literacy biographies, drafts, and portfolios.
3. Teachers would encourage negation as part of any intersubjective and constructive process. Classes would provide plenty of opportunity for dialogue in which the reader or writer can project ideas elsewhere, introject ideas from elsewhere, and reject ideas in an effort to construct his or her own position.
4. A teacher would see the value of making visible to students his or her own worldly and literary interests and desires that reach beyond the class and his or her relationship to students. Students would see this "third term" for the teacher as a model for their own license and responsibility to go further than what is known between the student and teacher in school, and to be engaged in the real problems of the world.

At the start of this chapter, we saw a vision of Sartre entering reading within the cozy dyad he shared with his mother. He also suggests the threat of abandonment by her as she turns to read the world beyond him. Her voice becomes infused with the sounds of difference, and as Freudian myth suggests he will, Sartre becomes frightened. By

Sartre's account, he rather magically becomes brave enough to respond to the questions of a threatening world. What Kristeva's narrative can fill in for us, and for Sartre, is that because his mother does not abandon him for the world, but shows him her attraction to it, Sartre is eventually excited by the world and language as something that gratifies him, as well. The challenge for us as teachers is to both show our students our involvement in and excitement for the world beyond the classroom, and to still remain close and responsive to students' needs.

PART THREE

REGENERATING THE CURRICULUM

What happens to a dream deferred?
Does it dry up
like a raisin in the sun?
Or fester like a sore—
And then run?
Does it stink like rotten meat?
Or crust and sugar over—
like a syrupy sweet?
Maybe it just sags
like a heavy load.
Or does it explode?

Langston Hughes,
"Dream Deferred"

SEVEN

PHILIP:
A THINKING READER
IS A FEELING READER[1]

Philip writes that when his all-male class expressed boredom with the novel, *Of Mice and Men*, he asked them to try to separate their own feelings about the text from the feelings of characters in the text:

> In discussion I ask, [about Steinbeck's *Of Mice and Men*], "What feelings do you get at the beginning so far?"
>
> *Dermaine:* "The story has no meaning."
>
> *Erik:* "Lenny and Curley might get into a fight."
>
> I ask students to define "feeling." What are feeling words, emotions? Responses: boring, sorrow, dislike, hate, dull. I say: There are two different feelings going on here. There's the feeling that you're having, which might be boredom or dull; and then there's the feeling that's going on in the story, which might be a different feeling. What feelings do you see going on among the characters in the story?
>
> *Responses:* George, Lennie, and Curley—intense; Candy—sad; Lenny—afraid; Curley—jealous.
>
> *I summarize:* "All these feelings that are going on in the story contribute to the mood of the story."

Philip's lesson plans showed the ways in which he prepares students to group their experiences of reading fiction or poetry into literary categories such as setting, characterization, conflict, mood, rising and falling action, denoument, and climax. In using this classification system to organize reading, Philip is following the New Critics' advice to treat the work of literature as a kind of house that stands on its own. For example, he helps students channel what they may feel in response to a novel into a literary device within the novel, commonly referred to as mood. The category of mood helps him and his students manage and control fairly efficiently, a range of complex reactions readers might undergo in response to *Of Mice and Men*, such as hope, dread, compassion, suspicion, confusion, and revulsion, since they are going to find violence, cruelty, intense love, and competition in Steinbeck's novel. However, Philip finds himself uneasy about his teaching strategy:

> I missed significant opportunities. Was students' boredom real or feigned, jaded? I know from their responses throughout that they were involved and responsive. What about students who hadn't read any meaning into the story? Most important, how could I relate student's feelings to characters' feelings? After all, this relationship is one of my (stated) primary objectives. So why didn't I explore the feelings? Pressure to cover the required curriculum and personal discomfort with contrary and unreconciled feelings.

Kind, thoughtful, and holding multiple graduate degrees, Philip is a dedicated teacher who works in an urban, all-male college preparatory magnet school. In his narrative, Philip reflects on a problematic duality between knowledge and feeling as a student reader and as a teacher. He is beginning to wonder whether his students' interests and knowledge about characters and events in literature can be divorced from their interests and feelings about their own possibilities for self-actualization.

NOSTALGIA AND DEFERRAL

Our culture promotes and relies on blatent gender divisions to organize reality. Traditionally, male influence, linked to public power, can eclipse female influence on children, linked to the nursery and private life. This dynamic can lead to marginalization of maternal influence in cultural institutions, and an exaggerated deference for paternal power. Maternal power and influence are "at risk" in patriarchies. And because maternal power is at risk, we find both a nostalgia for it and an exagerated attachment to paternal power that compensates for it. One senses in Philip's writing about reading and his teaching, a nostalgia when he writes about the body, the desire, and the poetry in language, as though they belonged to another wonderful time and place, lost and irrelevant to present demands. One can also read a magnified investment in external authority in his deferral of student responses. Following the line of Philip's narrative from the first autobiography to the last, and looking at his lesson plans for students, one gets a sense of a movement first toward the playful and imaginative and then away from them toward the prescriptive and convergent. One can discern in Philip's writing about reading, and his teaching, a nostalgia for a "lost" maternal semiotic (body-knowing) register on the one hand, and a deference to the paternal symbolic register on the other.

The style of Philip's first reminiscences of reading could be described in Kristeva's terms as semiotic: bodily drives and rhythms make their way into signification and his language carries the logic of the material body in rhythms, alternations, repetition, space, onomatopoeia, alliteration, and so on. When used to recall his childhood, Philip's prose is informal, impressionistic, almost pulsating:

> There was something about that puppy tunneling under that fence. Something about tunneling underground. Inside self . . . I had the feeling in my teeth, in my jaw—still do. . . . Babaar, the hefalumps—I suppose I identified with them—their size, their strength, their intelligence, their gentleness. I recall a ship voyage from France to America. Waving goodbye separations—catching in the throat, in the heart. Future adventures and past ties. Ocean swell and salt sea breeze. Opportunities and longings. Looking at pictures, listening to voice. The story is alive in those pages. Open them up; let it out. Every day the same stories— familiar friends. . . . Tiny people, miniature villages, vast horizons. There and here together. See yourself floating up there into nothing. See your house sitting down there shrinking away. Voice brings you back. Wake and sleep.

Even the vivid colors of primary books are remembered physically. "Mostly the pictures of the taxi—intense colors: yellow, red, black. Again that feeling in the jaw—." This semiotic style of playful rhythms, repetition, broken syntax, and figurative language, is used not just for reading in early childhood. Philip also writes lyrical, stream of consciousness memories juxtaposed with excerpts from a novel he is currently reading, *A Farewell to Arms*:

"The forest of oak trees on the mountain beyond the town was gone. The forest had been green in the summer when we had come into the town but now there were the stumps and the broken trunks and the ground torn up (p. 6) . . ."

A fantasy: A sunniful beauty day. I'm driving on a country road. My car flips. I am unhurt. My face rests on the soft grass. I smell the earth. Mozart's Exultate Ubilate plays on the radio. Flowers are buzzing. Bees are blooming. A shower passes. The earth dampens and warms. The sky blues. A rainbow sprouts. Water trickles along a furrow where lies my face. My arms are pinned to my sides. I drown.

Walking through the Koinonia meadow. Midnight sky, clear and crisp. Stars, dancing brightly, feeling as close as home and as far as forever. Trees rustling in the wind. Trees never say, "I am cold." The cold passes through me; I do not feel it. Touching the tree, feeling its consciousness. Trees have wisdom which passeth human understanding. Trees communicate. Looking through star-filled branches. Insignificant/Magnificant. One with the universe; absolutely isolated. Unity. Birth/Separation. Death/Unity. Some nows I am in that then space.

Philip uses the forms of personification, onomatopoeia, alliteration, rhyming, and syntactical irregularities to shape and express his reading response to Hemingway's texts. Yet the poetic style and sentimentality of his reading response is in marked contrast to the language he uses in his curriculum assignments, which could be characterized as objective, general, analytical, discrete, and distant. The following excerpts from his lesson plans are typical of the twenty or so he showed me:

Tell students that by the end of chapter 2 Steinbeck has created suspense through exposition and the introduction of conflict and complication. Tell students that they have discovered incidents of cause and that now students must read further to determine the effects and to determine if the effects themselves become causes.

[Langston] Hughes uses five similes when he compares a dream deferred to: _____

Seven unpleasant verbs that refer to a dream deferred are: _____

_____

Hughes uses a metaphor when he compares a dream deferred to:

_____

Introduce FALLING ACTION by asking what makes a reader read beyond the turning point (climax)—need to satisfy lingering doubts about the outcome; concern for the ways specific characters react to the climax. Define FALLING ACTION.

There is a wide gap between Philip's language about personal reading and the language he uses in teaching. Like many of us in teaching, he finds it difficult to carry the emotion and imagery he generates in personal reminiscences or personal reading to the more social and public events of teaching. His narratives about reading and teaching seem to reflect the assessment that mature competence requires overcoming and leaving behind the pleasure, desire, and specificity associated with feminine or maternal life. In declining to integrate the way he read as a child with the way he asks his students to read, Philip seems to identify with the patriarchal educational culture which believes that standard symbolic competence replaces the prelinguistic, fluid, body-knowing register of maternal legacies. Furthermore, in failing to integrate his "private" response to the novels he reads today, with the more structural schematics for literary criticism he offers in his classes, Philip, may, like many English teachers, reinforce the gap between private and public reading, and increase the inclination to marginalize the private and intimate.

Philip's wistfulness and nostalgia reveals that he senses the loss of the semiotic maternal register in scholastic literary practice. A review of his memory of his own reading experiences indicates a yearning for the happy sensuality and comraderie of being read to as a toddler and a parallel contentedness in his reading to toddlers (see his Autobiography #1).

Philip's first autobiographical piece links his emerging consciousness of himself and his identification with the bodies and exploits of the animal protagonists in children's literature. He extends the infantile mimetic experience he has with literary characters into adolescence when he identifies with protagonists who excited his imagination, like baseball players, physicists, and historical figures. In the summer, walking to the library or reading in bed, he experienced the range and freedom he needed to relate to his books as transitional objects, in a way that the confined spaces and protocols of school restricted.

In the next autobiographical piece, Philip describes how he became disconnected emotionally to books as he got older. He suggests that children lose something of their ability to relate to books as they grow older and that school is somewhat to blame. He describes reading before first grade as "a mystical adventure of discovery, joy." "Getting a story, people, feelings, ideas, from page to mind." The "reading method" of sitting on mother's lap as she voices the story, or using his body to mime the conducts of the characters worked well for him. There was the affiliative satisfaction of his aunt reading from *Anderson's Fairy Tales*, as he had lunch with her, the dreaminess of reading for hours in bed, which provided the physical comfort that nourished intellectual courage, and there was the warmth, freedom, and closeness to nature of summer reading. Philip contrasts these sensuous reading experiences with school methodology (see his Autobiography #1).

Although Philip does not object to phonics per se as a methodology, its extraction from the context of illustrations, friendly voices, physical contact, movement, and leisure for imagination, leaves him dissociated from his feelings about stories. He experiences the performance anxiety that comes from trying to meet standards without the imagination and social support on which he used to rely.

It is interesting that as Philip begins to describe his reading for school assignments, his writing style changes. He is less playful with rhythm and syntax. The semiotic elements in language Kristeva described are less pronounced in his style as well as his content:

> If I had been looking forward to going to college to read more college books, I was in for a big disappointment. When I was required to read, reading became tedious. In college and even in grad school—the first time—I remember mostly not reading the books.

Nonetheless, in Philip's second autobiographical piece about his adolescent years, he makes an effort to maintain some of the desire in reading he experienced as a child, and to recover a social aspect to reading as well. At the same time, he sees motivation and sociability slipping away from school reading. He writes that he enjoyed reading some high school books, especially ones he could choose. He happily joins the kids in his neighborhood where it is "required" to read the sports section of the newspapers. In both high school and college he experiences assignments as boring and "only free reading was free." He felt the books he chose to read were good ones by good authors, and one of those, he has recently assigned his own students. Like April and Jane, Philip remembers being touched by literature he chose to read as an adolescent, and he hopes that this literature might touch his students as well. He hopes to transfer his desire to his students.

When his own hopes and intentions for reading were ignored or disallowed in high school and college, he read the books assigned to his brother, in an effort to have some companionship. The books he chose for himself, by Hesse, Doyle, Vonnegut, Fleming, Barth, and Brautigan, like the ones he read with his brother, by Warren, Faulkner, Hemingway, and Orwell, are books he could identify with—about men like himself coming of age in contemporary society.

In his third autobiography Philip celebrates reading cultures which retain the poetic, the intimate, the communal, the feminine. He remembers his most enjoyable reading experiences as those at a Christian missionary center for teaching reading. He describes reading poetry to Girl Scouts and elderly women, Saturday night coffee house readings, marrying one of the other readers, and reading to his stepchildren. But even in this celebratory essay, loss seeps into the text:

> I used to read poetry all the time. It made me feel alive we're alive. Today, I picked up some books of poetry and leafed through them. I realize with many intense and conflicting feelings that I haven't read poetry in years—years and years. I feel sad that I haven't and relieved that I am.

Philip wove a good deal of poetry into the text of his autobiographies. They include parts of T. S. Eliot's "Burnt Norton," Wallace Steven's "Snow Man," William Carlos Williams's "Young Sycamore," and "This Is Just to Say." The poems are used in his narratives as expressions of his deep feelings for nature, loved ones, his fears and regrets, and in the case of a number of works by a favorite poet, e. e. cummings, as a connection of life to words. A thematic refrain for cummings, is that words may refer to life, but they are as not as good as life. One of the lines Philip quotes from cummings, is "And birds sing sweeter than books tell how." For himself, Philip uses the refrain, "I am learning not to let the words get in the way." Poetic citations provide the presentation of a persona for Philip that is more vivid and more emotive. Whereas the poems themselves are asked to carry Philip's feelings *in toto*, neither prose, nor analysis, nor teaching, can be so trusted.

In a fourth autobiographical essay, Philip juxtaposes the texts of Hemingway's *A Farewell to Arms* with his own experiences of birth, separations, violence, and grief. Hemingway'a words stand in for Philip's experiences of loss. Then in his fifth and final reflective essay, it is as though he resurfaces again to compose a rationale for his curriculum. Vulnerable from his sentimental remembrance of childhood reading, and from his melancholy reflections on death and loss, he seems almost relieved at the distance and structure his school lesson plans offer his students. He not only asks students to separate their own feeling from the feelings of characters, but since the assignments do not get back to students' feelings, they are asked to suppress feeling. In a position remarkably like the one Lacan described as the language user experiencing loss, lack, and deferral, Philips worries, "Are the facts" of the text negotiable? Does an individual have the right to an interpretation? Who controls the interpretation(s)?"

OPENING THE TEXT TO OUR READERS

Philip's experience represents how we ask students to suppress their feelings and attachments when they turn their attention to the business of school. However, in shutting down his own feelings, and shutting down his students' feelings, Philip cannot help but shut down their engagement with texts. When their responses are neglected, they are likely to retreat, lose interest in the text, or defer to the teacher or secondary sources.

Philip's assignments, like many English teachers' assignments, vacillate between the poles of nostalgia and deference. His students write about childhood memories, but these are unconnected to what they are reading today or the issues they encounter in the world today. His students write answers to objective questions about the text, but these are unconnected to their own reading responses, or to their hopes and concerns for the world in which they live. Desire is lost, or as Philip puts it, "opportunities missed."

On the one hand, desire for the past is nostalgia. Nostalgia is an inability to integrate the past with the present. On the other hand, waiting for the meaning to be revealed from an elusive someone else or an ever-receding somewhere else is an endless deferral. When a reader believes that meaning is buried in the past or must be deferred to the future, the potential and responsibility for making sense of the text here and now is displaced.

Traditional literary theories like New Criticism espouse literature as catharsis; they welcome the unconscious displacement of the reader's issues onto characters. The child psychoanalyst, Bruno Bettelheim, made a good case for this kind of projection onto characters in fairy tales by children in *The Uses of Enchantment* (1977). Child readers work out many psychosocial challenges as they identify unconsciously with animals and characters. But literature teachers who work with preadolescents and older students see the necessity to demand more of maturing readers. If readers continue beyond early childhood to unconsciously project their fears and losses onto others, they are not learning to actually confront them and transform them. By early adolescence, the child's embeddedness in the magical holding environment of fantasy is threatened and in need of revision. As Robert Kegan, a Harvard educator and clinical psychologist, has articulated in *The Evolving Self, Problem and Process in Human Development,* the preadolescent project is for the children who formerly experienced themselves *as* their needs in an unconscious, egocentric way, to start to become conscious of their needs *as* needs, to objectify them and recognize the needs of others as well. Kegan articulates this process as movement from an imperial position to an interpersonal one, requiring that the preadolescent begin to be able to make reports of interior states, and to be involved with peers in starting to bear the responsibility for creating and maintaining a culture for others and self, rather than asking to be provided for (Kegan 1982, 259). For the preadolescents, the former self-embeddedness in their own needs, interests, and wishes needs to be superseded as they begin to contribute to a community (1982, 109). What helps propel a youth into growth and mutuality is the hope of becoming, with peers, part of a "culturing" community.

CLASSROOM THEATER

For Philip and his students, then, the question is, How can readers be encouraged to express their responses in literature class and negotiate them toward communal, cultural participation? First, students' responses must be elicited, and then they must be negotiated with others. The gestural, personal, and social qualities of theater as a pedagogy seem ideal. In a recent study of theater work with children labeled "at risk," Shelby Wolf outlines how students benefit from a dramatic curriculum in a process that echoes the maternal legacies of not only the body, but of intersubjectivity, and a connection to the wider world that calls the student to action. She writes,

> Much of what we now understand about the interrelationship between reader and text suggests that a creative understanding of text comes when the reader travels through a character or situation as deeply as possible, while keeping sight of personal experience (Bakhtin, 1986). While understanding is uniquely situated in the individual, reading also implies an ability to shift roles and voices and take on the perspective of others. Similar understandings of the interpretation of text occur in theoretical writings on drama that emphasize the actor's ability to take on

the roles of others *through* the role of the self (Stanislavski, 1949).

A second key to classroom theater is the emphasis on the collaborative construction of interpretation through careful guidance. . . . As the classroom opens the door to multiple perspectives, ways with working with text must be explicitly modeled (Delpit, 1988), unpacking and illuminating the discourse processes and conceptual analyses that communicate interpretation. Teachers thus guide children to demonstrate their thinking to others and to see problem solving in and through the text . . .

A third key to classroom theater is the emphasis on nonverbal communication. Vygotsky (1978) also credited other symbolic systems, particularly gesture. . . . Stanislavksi (1961) stressed the importance of communicating the subtext of the meaning underneath the lines of the text, through movement. He believed that the actor's interpretation depended not only on an analysis of the inner life of the play, but on the external physical action that accompanied the words and demonstrated meaning to the audience. (Wolf 1995, 125)

Wolf's study of students' rehearsal processes and performances shows how in a theater classroom, a body/self can use the incorporative and metaphorical qualities we have cited as maternal legacies, to fill the role of an actor who moves and reads texts.

As part of the rehearsal proceedings of the class production of a children's story about an opportunistic fox, Wolf describes the student as actor (Bart) who incorporates a character's qualities and takes the character's place as he moves and gestures so that both self and character are transformed:

> Through cocky endearments slurred carelessly over the tongue, Bart copped an attitude with his character—a fox who was sly and sinister but humorous as well. He also communicated his character through his chosen costume and the way he wore it. . . . Bart's fox was totally played for laughs, and he exaggerated every move. At one point he clenched his teeth so tight and swung his head in such discomfort that he almost fell off the stool. (1995, 126)

We see the development of self through merging with an "Other," in actions both incorporative and metaphorical, meaning both that Bart changes in physical demeanor and that he performs the actions, roles, and behaviors of a sly fox.

Wolf comments on how making the readers' feelings explicit through acting allows them to interact with the text and each other:

Interpretation was heavily dependent on negotiated character analysis. Individual readings, in other words, had to meet group expectations (p. 128). . . . All the children could agree on the character of the fox—he was sly, macho, cool. But the character of the mouse dentist was not so easily discerned—either he was a fool or he was duty bound. Only through discussion did the children begin to see that both points of view played a part in the dentist's character. (1995, 129–30)

Although one of the students hypothesizes a situation contrary to what occurred in the story, as Wolf describes the negotiations, he decided with the others that it would not be fair to put "hypothetical words of negation in the mouths of characters," since these would be "an inappropriate contrast to their roles as professionals" (p. 130). Although only one student actually plays the dentist, he is happy to negotiate his interpretation with others before performing his role. This activity is a lovely portrait of the kind of community that can be set up in a reading and writing classroom in which peers help students with literary analysis and writing.

Finally, Wolf discusses how the students connect their interpretations to wider circles of community and reality. First, in analyzing their roles and plans for action, the students "built worlds for their characters which were only hinted at in the text, or were not at all apparent" (p. 130). Second, the students thought about audiences beyond those in their classrooms and invited peers, parents, and children from lower grades. As Wolf remarks, "They [the student actors] place themselves in three worlds—the actual world of their present decision making and the possible worlds of both the characters in the textual situation and the audience members expecting to enter the text" (p. 132).

Recently I saw the same dynamics of the self merging with "an other" from a text in the actor's role in a college classroom. Undergraduates were preparing scenes from *King Lear*. Student actors had to open their interpretations to the scrutiny of other group members, and having settled on how a scene would be played, they performed for the rest of the class. In rehearsals, one could see the same processes of character analysis, discussion of subtext, and the exchange and merger of visions.

USING THEATER TO NURTURE STUDENT RESPONSE

A primary focus for Philip's class should be to help the boys get in touch more deeply with their responses about the scenes in literature.

Theater work would be particularly appropriate. When the boys use physicality and gesture to "go into" a poem or novel, their memory and feeling and drive are activated, and the space and time of the theater work opens up the texts' possibilities. Their bodies and gestures indicate to them contexts in the world that are possible for the texts' topics.

When students and teachers have not had experience using their bodies to express interpretations in the classroom, they can benefit from the same kind of actors' training and warm-ups that improvisational theater professionals use. Viola Spolin's *Improvisation for the Theater* is a particularly good tool. This text is not only used to train actors for the stage, it has been used in schools, settlement houses, and community centers to teach young people and citizens to communicate through movement and gesture. In any class that I am preparing to work with using theater, I start with Spolin's relaxation exercises, which help students become less self-conscious as objects being watched as they move and gesture. These relaxation exercises are tantamount to reminding students that they are subjects of learning, not objects. When they find and use a point of concentration, they lose their shyness, and learn to think as they move and gesture. Further exercises require them to concentrate and focus on objects, events and actions, sometimes under conditions of great distraction, as they think and move on stage or in the classroom in front of others. Many of the exercises are set up as games, and students find them easy and fun, and are generally surprised to find how quickly they become comfortable using movement and gesture in the classroom. One senses that they enjoy a kind of reactivation of the spontaneous play they used in childhood to explore reality. Spolin goes on to suggest specific kinds of ensemble work, like transformation exercises in which participants exchange voices and gestures, and then change them into something new, or functioning as parts of machines or tableaux. These theater tools provide a basis for students to create renditions of scenes from literature.

In Philip's class, students might start with a theatrical rendition of *Of Mice and Men*, to precede the poem "A Dream Deferred," since its structure as a novel provides more explicit context for a reader than the poem. The novel has place—topography, geography, landscape, climate. It has particular characters with names, dialects, occupations, families, friends, enemies. It has action—these characters do things in this place to and with each other. Student readers will need to construct the historical past that sets the stage of the action. They will need to understand what the characters are trying to do in the present of the novel—how they make a living, relate to each other, and to the ranching culture in the Depression in the American West. Finally, they will need to study what this story points to in the future of the real world in which we live.

As Merleau-Ponty has suggested, the students' bodies will already have "outlines" for many of the experiences they want to theatricalize. A pivotal scene in Steinbeck's novel shows a character fondling a puppy, foreshadowing a tragedy. Many student readers will have held puppies in their own hands (or mice, or guinea pigs, or birds or kittens, or any of millions of other tiny fragile objects). Their bodies will know the tension of holding on tight enough, but not too tight, and the pleasures and dangers of slippery skin or fur. Their bodies will know about the pain of the old man "Crooks's" physical malformations and disabilities—they have had injuries, some fleeting and some chronic. The experiences will not be stereotypical. In a class of twenty or so students, the injuries and suffering will vary tremendously. But all of their bodies will know pain. Students will all know both invigoration from physical labor and debilitation. Theater is both physical compassion and physical difference. When they work to make a showing of the novel together, the variations in their lifeworlds and experiences will provide enrichment for the community and for insight and sensitivity to the text. Their efforts to make the gestures of characters in action in the novel will "show" their own pasts, but they will also provoke them to contextualize more vividly and sensually, where Lenny and George and Crooks are and what their days are like on the ranch, and what they face and fear.

The student's interpretation of the past, present, and future of Steinbeck's *Of Mice and Men* could be juxtaposed with the much more abstract, "A Dream Deferred." Students could map the poem onto the characters and plot. Which characters' dreams dry up slowly like a raisin in the sun? George's? Whose dreams deferred fester like a sore, then run—Crooks's? Whose dream deferred stinks like rotten meat—Curley's? Whose crusts and sugars over? Slim's? Whose sags, like a heavy load, but then explodes? Lenny's? Have they read about other characters who were in similar circumstances or who had similar relations or characteristics? Which members of our communities might be so vulnerable?

"A Dream Deferred," requires students to imagine metaphors for what happens to a dream deferred. Classroom theater can offer them the space and time to recreate these metaphors. Students can physically construct scenes of dreams deferred. Each of a number of small groups of students could be asked to make a theatrical score of each of the possibilities Hughes suggests in his poem. One group physicalizes deferment as a kind of painless drying in the sun. What is that like? Is it okay if the dream turns into something else—like a grape turns into a raisin? How likely is this possibility? Are deferred dreams in danger of slow degeneration? Who else's dreams in fact and fiction dry up like that?

Another dream deferment process is more like a festering running sore. This option turns out to be more incapacitating and offensive to others. It "stinks like rotten meat." Decay and infection may prevent action and repel community. Do they know people and charcters who lost dreams like that? Could Crooks or the villain Curley in the novel be "cleaned up"? Who could do it? Who could have done it?

The group who performs deferred dreams as sugary syrup crusted over may offer the opposite possibility: that repressing dreams is considerate of and pleasing to others. What examples in fiction and real life from individual or group experience suggest internalized oppression?

Those in the next group with the heavy load, improvise the qualities of chronic fatigue, even boredom. What comes to mind about Lenny and George's relationship of "brother" carrying "brother?" Finally, the improvisation of an explosion by the last group brings the students closer to the possibility of how the deferred dream may hurt everyone. Where in our society, especially if we consider that this poem is part of a piece called "Harlem" have we seen deferred dreams explode like this?

Students return to the register of the maternal semiotic to become body readers and body writers. What they feel about characters and events may surface physically before they can verbalize them. They shape them into improvisations and revise them theatrically and socially before they must submit them to writing. Eventually, in writing from these scores of scenes, they will have been able to transform their private feelings and improvisations into public interpretations that contextualize their reading.

As theorists like John Vernon and Julia Kristeva contend, poetry is more like the body than prose is, since poetry is an effort to express reality in a form that mimics the rhythm, cadence, sounds, and pulsations of the body. We have seen that theater is also more like the body than text is and more like the spaces and temporality of the real world. Whereas poetry is an expression of a private thought made into the flesh of a text, that can still be read privately, theater is always a public act that can carry instantly what was private, to others.

EIGHT

JANE:
FROM PRIVACY TO COMMUNITY

> How is it possible to balance the contrary forces between
> which we are suspended in such a way as to maximize *jouis-*
> *sance* (enjoyment), to allow the creative production of art, lit-
> erature and meaning?
>
> —Julia Kristeva, *Tales of Love*

Jane's work with eleventh-grade readers provides an opportunity to
explore possibilities for students coming together with each other and
with a teacher in a community in which language is not merely regulated and mastered, but negotiated. In a class in which interaction
among language users is maximized, students are focused not on
meeting standards per se, or minimizing mistakes, but on what meaning they might be able to make of the world that others could understand, and on what meaning they can make of what others say and
write.

Jane's narrative offers us insight about what kind of support
readers need in order to negotiate their interests and desires, in a
school culture that tends to mask or standardize them. As a poet and
painter, Jane's descriptions of her own literary experiences are personal, lyrical, rich in imagery, and moving:

> Oh, how I became small, small in a gray-green garden. It is impossible
> to extricate that earliest reading from the word-ocean in which it swam.
> My grownups all sang, and so I sang—"The Rose of Tralee" and
> "Onward Christian Soldiers" and "Swing Low, Sweet Chariot" and
> "Believe Me, If All Those Endearing Young Charms" were as much a

part of reading as the stories my grandmother told me about when she
was little, and all are mixed with squares of sunlight in the morning
falling on the linoleum nursery-rhyme people on my bedroom floor
(there were letters, too, which must have been their names) and that
thing on my thumb which was wiry and cold and my tongue could go
between the spaces of the coils just a little and by and by the bad taste
would go away.

In these lines, Jane has rendered the early and easy sociability of
language: "My grown-ups all sang and so I sang." Reading, for Jane,
sounds much as it was for Paulo Freire, mixed up with the songs and
words and customs of her family, and of her natural surroundings. For
Freire, remember, it was mango trees; for Jane it is sunlight on a
linoleum floor and grandmother's stories.

Jane does not claim this world as a paradise, however. She
acknowledges that the same adults who brought her songs, constrained
her from tasting her own thumb with a wire coil and a foul ointment.
By writing about both how attractive and constraining her family relations were, Jane allows her reader to meditate on the joy of being
together, and on the desire and necessity to separate from others.

Her narrative reveals the continuation of this pattern of alternately merging with, and separating from others. She wrote about
reading as an escape from the intrusion and demands of others (see
her Autobiography #1). In passages she described reading as secret,
even clandestine, and of hiding her emotional responses to texts, especially from her mother.

CLANDESTINE READING

As a way to define herself apart from others, Jane emphasizes how
"proprietary," reading and writing are. While describing how people
must share the world, she portrays how reading and writing help individuals create and direct their intentions for it. In the next lines, we see
that it is undeniably her family that provides her world for her—the
farmhouse, the landscape, the food, the labor—but she knows she has
a unique consciousness of her world, and her writing about it is a way
of owning it. In a previously cited passage, she wrote:

In the summer I had the freedom of great rambling structures with shadowy stairs (two sets, on the farm) and porches, smell of straw matting
and creak of wicker, scratchy feel of sun-warmed wood with peeling

paint, stiff slippery horsehair sofas, oilclothed kitchen tables (little patches peeling, showing the fabric underneath), pantries, home-canned tomatoes and home-bottled root beer, singed chicken and blueing in laundry rinse water, warm dapple of sunlight or dank dark smell of piano practicing on wet afternoons.

Jane reports the physical surroundings of her childhood, but she is also describing the little girl who knew them. Like many precocious young readers, she is thrilled that the rooms and landscapes she reads about are *not* created and controlled by those who control her real life. She is glad the places in books have no peripheries, because that leaves space for her imagination. She continued in the same passage:

But none of the places in Alcott's books were places I knew. None of the furniture was the same, none of the rooms. Unlike real places, the places in books had no peripheries. They were like the places I see on a rehearsal stage, before the set is in place—sharply detailed just where the actors are, and though potentially present everywhere else, fading out towards the edges. This kind of imaginative construction of vision must go on all the time.

The closest analogy I can think of is that the book-worlds had the vivid being of those worlds we enter when we dream. Unlike my dreams, which I make, the writers made their worlds. Each writer's style-world was different. When I wrote above that books enabled me to try on different worlds, it was not only—maybe even not importantly— the world of the character's existential or interpersonal situations that was most important. It was the totally different, unambiguous but ungraspable world of the rhythms in which he moved. Today as an adult, this quality in a book is the world I enter. Because I have a stronger circumference to my own identity, I no longer re-enact the characters' story. That I watch from over their shoulders, as it were. But I am just as much *in* the world of the book as I ever was. It is a metaworld, an analogical construction that makes a world.

Jane's respect for the metaworld the dreamer or author creates, is an extension of her investment in the individual's unique grounding in nature and the subjectivity that arises from and conveys that uniqueness. She describes how the painter makes the same investment:

People have painted landscapes for a long time, but Cezanne's world is not the world of Monet, and the difference is everything. It wasn't that the rooks cawed over the graveyard—it was that they existed in their own sound. How the writer does that, and how I recognize it, are the tantalizing questions I try to answer again and again, all the while realizing that any answer will be partial and sterile. To give you another analogy: walk out in the fog of some January thaw. The trees are flattened gray shapes and you apprehend vividly as never before the distances between them. Shape and space are made palpable by impalpability.

Jane, as reader and painter, honors the subjectivity of the artist naming his or her world, but for her, the naming must remain within the art or within nature, to be faithful to it. She states that for her, the author's metaworld, has to take precedence over the situational reality of the characters' actions and predicaments. A focus on the real, "existential" circumstances of characters, as she calls them, can distract a reader from the purity of the artist's consciousness. Here, I think Jane sides with the New Critics and romanticists, over historicists. However, her writing suggests that situational realities in her own biography are not unrelated to her artistic preferences in painting, literature, and teaching, and that events in our early autobiographies may predispose us to guard our thinking and feeling from others. Remembering that she refrained from crying over Beth's death in *Little Women* so that her mother would not know how she felt, Jane believes that it is easier and safer to write about reading books than to talk to others about reading books.

But as Jane will point out, this fear of not being able to share our worlds, a fear we all have, to one degree or another, is a liability in teaching. She may be sensing that teaching is an art and that curriculum design could be thought of as art, like painting, but she does not trust that the customs and culture of teaching in today's schools can support artistic training, vision or technique. She continues her meditation:

> When I see that, [the thaw or the summer or the shapes and spaces of the trees] I want to *do* something about it—but nothing I can do (paint a picture, write a poem) will do more than clumsily point to the experience that moved me to create. So my experience of books is a physical awareness of my own being in a universe. By strangeness they [books] isolate some basic principles of being, they skin the eyeballs of the self. Perhaps the object of my experience is simply myself, experiencing, far below the mind's reach. For this reason, a book read aloud is a different thing than a book read to oneself. For this reason, intrusions of interpretation, commentary, are always beside the point. A summer night sets up yearnings

that no embrace will answer. Should one teach literature at all? Perhaps one's teaching should be a kind of Emersonian presentation, a series of disjunctive metaphors with room for the student to supply the transitions, infer the context, and be moved to his own contemplation, to his own more or less beside-the-point, ineluctable, but life-giving action.

Jane tells a story of a rich interior reading life at home which she hid from others, especially her mother, from whom she was trying to separate, and from daughters, for whom she is trying to provide space for separation. She makes the connection between who she is today with who she was to others at home. Jane uses books as transitional objects. They help her develop a sense of self separate from those around her, and they help her feel aligned with new resources for a creative life. But there is a strong element of guilt and fear intermingled with the pleasure:

> My first daughter was named for two Alices—. One was my great-grandmother and the other was the child heroine of Lewis Carroll's books. To all the world, the name testified allegiance to a family past. That was what respectable people did when they had children; they named them for their ancestors and thus demonstrated that tradition, continuity, all that mattered. But no one knew—this is the first time I have told it to another, not even my daughter knows,—that she was named for a person in a book. Telling her wouldn't have been fair, for the secret of her name had to do with me, not with her, and it would have been taking her name away from her, somehow, to tell her. However, it was important to possess her in that way. Because books were more real than life, that fictional Alice could also continue her secret life and, as memorial or embodiment of some child with bony knees and braids, could also become an ancestor with descendants.

Jane voices an uneasiness about her self-indulgence in reading ["books were more real than life"] and in naming her child out of the desires and experiences of her own life, and not her child's. She writes that she did not notice it as a child, but her grandmother's world did not suit the modern world. That the worlds presented to her by others do not blend well, is a strong theme in her autobiographical writing:

> My mother, who was only superficially gregarious, was an only child; my father, who was an introvert, was one of two. None of my aunts and cousins lived near. Both my grandmothers, formidable women who stamped my childhood with their tales, were older than the usual grand-

mother, not only in years, but in culture. My father's mother, born in 1861, remembered the men coming back from the Civil War; my mother's mother, though twenty years younger, was raised on a farm in North Carolina whose customs, transmitted to me in stories of her girlhood, were those of the early nineteenth century. . . .

In a kind of inversion of what I suppose is most children's experience of their lives, I lived in two worlds of which the outer, daily one was the unreal one, and the inner, imaginative one was the reality. The parlor in Marmee's house, or the one from which Alice went through the looking-glass, are more vivid in memory than the five-room Queens apartment in which I grew up.

I think Jane's experiences are more typical than she might at first suspect. As children we all have to live in varied worlds adults provide for us and our developmental project is to integrate them and transform them into a framework for a future that transcends them. This project is not easy.

(Incidentally, my mother just sent me a birthday package; in with the earrings and the padded dress-hangers and the strange cedar blocks from L.L. Bean were some books she said (she always writes directions on her presents) she was clearing out and I might find some use for. Two of them were books I sent her for recent birthday presents. Oh, well, I didn't get to finish Virginia Woolf's essays before I sent them to her last year. But you can see the kind of emotional load attached to all of this.) . . . My teaching sometimes has the flavor of giving presents of books. They are highly personal but safe presents. . . . At the end of the day when my mother would come home from her work at Macy's, she would get out the black notebook and I would tell her things to write, sometimes doings and sometimes, I think, poems. She would write it down and then read it back to me. But I can't remember that; I have only the notebook, archaeology of buried time.

Jane struggles to define herself from a mother who is still struggling to define herself. Jane both identifies with her and wants to shake her off because she appears weak to the outside world. Notice she "forgets" whether her mother read for herself when Jane was a child. Jane assumes she was too busy cleaning and cooking to read or have a life of her own. Her mother returns the favor in dismissing Jane's knowledge as only what she already knows and as only what "everybody knows." The volley continues with Jane's mother, through forgetfulness, returning Woolf's writings to Jane. Is either to have a room of one's own?

Jane has in fact separated from her mother by producing her own children, her own career, her own art, and her own ways of reading. But because these reproductive and creative activities are closest to a maternal realm, they are too closely associated with things that were gotten rid of or trivialized in our society. Jane associates them both with what is most precious and cherished as well as with what is most vulnerable and criticized. Like many women, Jane is most creative within registers associated with the maternal, but she is apprehensive of bringing them to the public, symbolic, and political world. Not only does Jane protect her own creativity and personal space, she projects her worries onto her students and protects what she refers to as their "decent privacy." Although the story of the abject mother (see chapter 5) does not *explain* Jane's choices, Kristeva's theory does help us appreciate how one can be situated in a rich artistic imaginary domain, and yet not believe that one's efforts in that domain could be interesting to or relevant to public life.

My childhood reading was all autobiographical, as I have indicated in many ways in these writings. The marked impression that Dickens' novels made on me is easy to account for in terms of story; I most strongly identified with David Copperfield because I saw myself as an outcast child at the mercy of half-understood and threatening adult events. The Murdstones made all too much sense. I still react strongly to texts with this mythic pattern, no doubt because it answers unconscious needs. I recently read Sylvia Warner's *The Wide, Wide World* (an 1850's evangelical story of an orphan girl who has to make her way despite an unsympathetic aunt, a radical change of surroundings, etc.) almost as I would have read it as a child—very fast, totally immersed in the story, etc. *Uncle Tom's Cabin* likewise; also *Adam Bede* which tore me apart because the episode of Hetty's wandering and infanticide spoke to deepest fears of maternal abandonment, overlaid now by my own experiences of raising four daughters.

So my teaching is a dangerous act—approach and run away. Find the emotional meaning, find yourself, retreat into analysis (write a topic sentence, learn to write transitions, all that). I am being a little hard on myself here. Since school isn't all of life, and since English isn't all of school, I have made some choices. One of them is to acknowledge the realm in which literature can touch one's own personality while concentrating on the more analytical, perhaps more appropriate and fruitful realm of language—how do words work? What choices does a writer make? What can one do with words that can't be done in other media? To do that even a little bit is enough; let unconscious activities go on in decent privacy.

BRINGING PRIVATE READING TO THE SURFACE

The work of Kristeva proposes that it may be a feminist project, to represent in a new way, our maternal relations, and to save them from sentimentality, nostalgia, or exile. Kristeva does affiliate the unconscious, the "chora," and semiotic life with a maternal register, and she does want to reclaim this register as an inspiration for impulse for art and political change. But she cautions us to avoid regression to a solipsistic, solitary subjectivity, lost in our own worlds. She insists that we attempt to bring our sensibilities to the symbolic order. She asks that we not become hysterics who suffer from reminiscences as Freud put it, or "move immediately to the other side—the side of symbolic power" (in Marks 1981, 166). Another French feminist, Hélène Cixous, like Kristeva, writes that we gain strength through the unconscious, a "limitless country where the repressed manages to survive" (Cixous 1981, 245). Toril Moi concludes that Kristeva believes that "art or literature, precisely because it relies on the notion of the subject, is the privileged place of transformation or change" (Kristeva 1986, 17). Kristeva envisions a space to share reality, to make the personal public. But this act requires a passage, a curriculum, not a capitulation to public demands.

The work of the New Zealand educator, Sylvia Ashton-Warner reminds us of what can happen when the "childhood" drives are carried through to adult symbolic and cultural life. Her uses of a "Key Vocabulary" in teaching reading, parallel how Kristeva posits early language use within the dynamic and organic life of a body-thinker. Ashton-Warner insists that we need to teach students the words that mediate their lives since key words "carry" their minds' illustrations." Like Jane, Ashton-Warner knows that students' impressions are beyond the representations we can make for them. But Ashton-Warner (1961) offers an optimism that the words children choose are gestures for experiences:

> And it seems to me that since these words of the key vocabulary are no less than the captions of the dynamic life itself, they course out through the creative channel, making their contribution to the drying up of the destructive vent. First words must mean something to a child. . . . First words must have intense meaning for a child. They must be part of his being (p. 330). . . . Whether it is good or bad stuff, violent or placid stuff, coloured or dun. To effect an unbroken beginning. And in this dynamic material, within the familiarity and security of it, the Maori finds that words have an intense meaning for him, from which cannot help but arise a love of reading. . . . Out press these words, grouping themselves

in their own wild order . . . the fear words, ghost, tiger, skellington, alligator, bulldog, wild piggy, police. The sex words, kiss, love, touch, *haka* [a Maori war dance]. The key words carrying their own illustrations in the mind, vivid and powerful pictures which none of us could possibly draw for them—since in the first place we can't see them and in the second because they are so alive with an organic life that the external pictorial representation of them is beyond the frontier of possibility. We can do no more than supply the captions (p. 39). . . . And it is the most vital and the most sure vocabulary a child can build. It is the key that unlocks the child's mind and releases the tongue. (p. 41)

Jane respects the power of words, but she wants to bind the personality and the unconscious to a private realm, protected from public, analytical work with words. In experiencing herself "far below the mind's reach," Jane begins to invest in two worlds—the pre-oedipal imaginary world of the semiotic Kristeva describes, and the rational world of analytical choices:

I am a creature who mediates life with words. To do that, I have to be working out of a reservoir into which I dip and select in order to make public representations—but everything in me says, it's better not to bring it all to the light of day because the creative part, the pattern-formation, has to go on underground. Analysis is a necessary death.

But she is ambivalent. She wrote that the analytical is for pedagogy "perhaps the more appropriate and fruitful realm of language" and that "reading in school just wasn't reading, that's all. And maybe it shouldn't try to be—maybe it should just be the material from which we teach skills." But remember, her own objection: "The trouble with that [choice] is that it denies everything I believe in about literature, everything I have formed myself around." In her last autobiographical piece, it is the split-off analytical world that Jane chooses as the one the secondary English curriculum can best serve. But not because it is the only world that Jane values. The realm of acute sensibility to one's experience is so special that she claims, . . . "intrusions of interpretation, commentary, are always beside the point. A summer night sets up yearnings that no embrace will answer." When Jane's physical and imaginative sensitivity intensify, she is not convinced that the experience can be shared and developed. She uses the word, "sterile": "How the writer does that, and how I recognize it, are the tantalizing questions I try to answer again and again, all the while realizing that any answer will be partial and sterile."

But remember that in her most radical proposition for curriculum change, Jane asked,

> Should one teach literature at all? Perhaps one's teaching should be a kind of Emersonian presentation, a series of disjunctive metaphors with room for the student to supply the transitions, infer the context, and be moved to his own contemplation, to his own more or less beside-the-point, ineluctable, but life-giving action.

The last phrase in this piece, "life-giving action," is the opposite of "sterile." Jane's fascinating idea for curriculum design which leaves space for interaction between text and student, and which might be developed in theatrical activity, or video or hypertext productions, double reading with friends or research, or computer manipulations of texts, blazes for a moment, but fades out. Jane's narrative shows us that she herself is close to the semiotic and subjective, but that she is not sure how she can legitimate this imaginative, desiring realm for her students or help them share their subjective worlds.

However, her students' journal entries provide possibilities for using the literature classroom as a community of readers.

COMMUNITY IN THE CLASSROOM

In his book, *Subjective Criticism*, David Bleich makes a good case that subjective response statements from readers in which readers talk explicitly about their feelings about texts and recognize them as their own feelings or opinions, are more negotiable for making knowledge than response statements that read as though writers were talking about reality. Bleich redefines objectivity as the ability to make one's subjectivity objective—that is to put one's feelings and perceptions out there to be studied and negotiated. Bleich believes that a "judgment of taste is a proposal of knowledge that can gain public authority through its shareability and its subjective efficacy for other readers and communicators" (1978, 190). These judgments can be negotiated into knowledge in a variety of contexts, "such as for an author, genre, a period . . ." (p. 190). One of Bleich's reader respondents wrote:

> I found that the procedure of response analysis required a high degree of objectivity—i.e.—treating my response as though it belonged to someone else—before I could subjectively evaluate it. The most difficult part of the analysis was avoiding the temptation to rationalize rather

than understand the response. I think I responded to many of the same aspects of the story that I would have chosen to discuss in a traditionally "objective" paper. The essential difference between the two critical methods is that through a subjective approach I accept responsibility for focusing on particular features of the story and attempt to understand why I have done so. (1978, 197)

Bleich claims that however we progress with interpretation, judgment and criticism, the reader's desire is paramount for developing knowledge. He asserts that intellections are useful if "the presentation of her [a reader's] affects and associations were advanced and not inhibited in the process" (p. 210). Bleich's critique of the reader who claims to be writing objectively when he writes about the text, and not himself reading the text, echoes Jessica Benjamin's critique of domination/submission described in chapter 2. We can think of "dominating" reading, on the one hand, as that which takes over the terrain of reality because the reader finds no addressee who might set limits by his or her response or counter his or her ideas. Submissive reading, on the other hand, fears retaliation or being wrong, and the reader masochistically eradicates his or her own feelings or opinions. We can revisit Winnicott's warning of the False Self and the pitfalls of a curriculum that denies personal response:

> In the healthy individual who has a compliant aspect of the self but who exists and who is a creative and spontaneous being, there is at the same time a capacity for the use of symbols. In other words, health here is closely bound up with the capacity of the individual to live in an area that is intermediate between the dream and the reality, that which is called the cultural life. . . . By contrast, where there is a high degree of split between the True Self and the False Self which hides the True Self, there is found a poor capacity for using symbols, and a poverty of cultural living. Instead of cultural pursuits, one observes in such persons extreme restlessness, an inability to concentrate, and a need to collect impingements from external reality so that the living-time of the individual can be filled by reactions to these impingements. (1965, 150)

Perhaps a student who has been treated as a reader who has freedom and responsibility to make something of the text given to her, will be less likely as a *writer* to try to overwhelm, flatter, and dominate her reader, and more likely to have to construct her text carefully as an appeal or proposal. Jane could help her students balance their tastes, desires, and knowledge in a reading and writing studio that encourages both enjoyment of each other (jouissance) and limit setting.

We first looked at Nancie Atwell's work in chapter 5. She abandoned units, tests, lectures, and assignments in her eighth-grade English class to make room for reading and writing workshops that simply provide time for reading and writing and for classmates and herself to respond to writing. By students' own report, by the work accumulated in their portfolios, and by standardized testing measures, her program is a success. Atwell modeled her public school program after the way she and her husband read, write, and talk at the dining room table, earnestly and seriously about what they wanted out of reading and writing and what they were getting out of them. She based her pedagogy on conferences and dialogues between her and her students and between students. She created an environment in which students could ask for what they need as readers and writers. Students read and write what they want to read and write, what they feel attracted to. As we saw, she does not take students' papers during conferences to correct them; she asks them to talk about their intentions—what they are trying to do and why it is important, and they rewrite from their conversation, ultimately meeting the editing demands of their intended readers, often publications, or people in their families or communities. Students choose the genre that suits their need, and semiotic forms like poetry and drama are as valued as prose by readers and writers, for capturing desires that more propositional prose forms cannot capture.

What Atwell accomplished and what has made an impact on writing classes nationwide, is to place desire and intersubjectivity at the center of the language program. She writes, "Right from the first day of kindergarten students should use writing as a way to think about and give shape to their own ideas and concerns" (1987, 17). She takes the role of the "Other" in the process of helping a writer find and express his or her intention very seriously:

> I need to look at writers' faces because I'm an inveterate English teacher. If I look at a draft-in-progress, it's all over. While writers are drafting, their primary and overriding concern is with meaning, and when a writer reads or talks to me about a piece, I can focus on his or her meaning. When I read a draft, my eyes are drawn inexorably to errors. I'll want to focus on errors eventually, but only after the meanings are worked out and the student has submitted to me to edit. So as I move I avoid looking at the writing and, early on, if a student hands me a piece-in-progress and says, "Read this and tell me what you think," I hand it right back saying, "I don't read drafts. I need to listen. Why don't you tell me what you think?" . . . I wait, listen hard, tell what I heard, ask

questions about things I don't understand or would like to know more about, ask what the writer might do next, and offer any options I might know of. (1987, 70)

Atwell sees that the student writer will change the way he or she thinks because of the effect his or her thought has on an "Other"; that there is mutuality in the process. But she recognizes too, that as a writer, a person stakes out the right to speak for the dialogical encounter him- or herself, and that the ultimate boundary drawn around the piece of writing is the writer/artist's to draw. There are echoes here of Winnicott's "good-enough" mother who enjoys merging with the child on the child's terms, but does not challenge the child to declare the difference between what is self and what is other. The fruits of their encounters eventually go toward the child's side of subjective development.

Atwell fights the obsession in English studies with plagiarism, skepticism, and rigid boundaries, by encouraging students to borrow subjects and styles from published authors, from other students, and from her. It is as though she realizes that boundaries congeal naturally around our differences in intentions and experiences, if they are genuine, and that it is good to be attracted to somebody else's words. This curriculum is dependent on desire and students are allowed to drop writing pieces or books they are reading that are not working out and encouraged to understand why.

Starting with her students' journals of reading (see samples copied below) Jane might help her students serve as partners or doubles for each other. Along with Bleich I would argue that those responses in which students objectify what they think and feel are more suitable for developing literary criticism than those that do not.

Using the responses found in the journal entries from Jane's class, those students who have few negotiable items could be paired with those who are more reflective. Student A and Student B have both read Jack London's *The Sea Wolf*. Student A's response below offers more affect than Student B:

> When I first was introduced in the book to Wolf Larsen, I thought he was a heartless and brutal sea captain. However, as I read more of the book, I realized that this was a man who I could hate and yet feel sympathy for at the same time.

Student B confines himself to expectations about the structure and plot. He concludes his response by writing,

Now in the final chapter, Wolf Larsen must die and Humphrey and Maud must either reach civilization on the "Ghost" or be picked up by a larger vessel. Since all the loose ends, other than Humphrey and Maud reaching civilization, have been tied up, I don't think anything major is missing.

What Student B wants to "tie up," could be opened up by Student A's comment that he feels both sympathy and hatred for Wolf Larsen. Even if Student B cannot be convinced of Student A's position, in the process of conversing with him, he would have to find his own position, and realize it is a position. Students can be taught to respond to each others' reading responses and writings, and to look for and enjoy tension between each other. I also think that Jessica Benjamin offers a helpful response to Jane's worries that different generations suffer a gap in cultural experience too wide to bridge:

> One of the most important insights of intersubjective theory is that sameness and difference exist simultaneously in mutual recognition. This insight allows us to counter the argument that human beings fundamentally desire the impossible absolutes of "oneness" and perfection with the more moderate view that things don't have to be perfect, in fact, it is better if they are not. It reminds us that in every experience of similarity and subjective sharing, there must be enough difference to create the feeling of reality, that a degree of imperfection "ratifies" the existence of the world. (1987, 47)

Jane or any teacher may serve as "the Other" for her students as she responds to their reading journals and preserves difference. Consider the following exchange between Jane and Student D:

> Student D: *Ethan Frome's* ending really shocked me. The accident in the snow involving Mattie and Ethan scared me because I didn't know who would live or die. The end was also slightly confusing to read. The next thing I knew, Zeena was caring for an injured Mattie, and Ethan wasn't there anymore. It was really quite sad for Ethan and Zeena, but in the same respect joyous for Mattie, and Zeena really cares about Mattie, got well, and was a changed person.

Jane's response:

> Do you think she *really* cares about Mattie? Ask yourself—if you were Mattie, how would you have felt to be helpless and to have to be dependent on Ethan's wife? And, how do you think Zeena felt, suspecting that Ethan loved Mattie? Do you think her resentment would have gone

away? This book has one of the most excellent endings I've ever read—my own suspicion is that Zeena was happy *because* Mattie was destroyed—and that's horrifying.

This response works well to keep the dialogue going, because the negation Jane provides in the conversation is presented clearly as part of a subjective response, an opinion. ("This book has one of the most excellent endings I have ever read—my own suspicion is . . .") Here Jane and her student are in a relationship of reciprocity. Benjamin helps us appreciate the value of reciprocal relationships between subjects (in this case readers), over the fantasized relationship between a subject and mute objects. Just as a mother's response to an infant is both more attuned to the child and more unpredictable than inanimate objects, resulting in greater pleasure and focus from the baby, so relationships that combine resonance and difference "open the way to a recognition that transcends mastery and mechanical response, to a recognition that is based on mutuality," yielding mutual influence (1987, 26).

A teacher who responds to a student reader or writer, has to be careful to not let the potential space between him- or herself and the student collapse. The teacher's words have to be chosen for their dialectical potential, and not be taken as retaliatory or dominating.

To take a contrasting sample from these journals and replies, Student E has not offered his judgments as reflective or as proposals of knowledge. Instead, he has all-encompassing answers: "After reading the first chapter, I start to understand what Ethan Frome is all about." Although he makes subjective observations, they are not recognized as such or proposed as such. Most of his statements are presented as textual problems, rather than reader interests. Another example: "The final chapter should tell whether or not Ethan and Mattie will part. . . . Lastly, Ethan and Zeena's relationship and various marital problems should be solved." This student could be helped to own his or her interests as interests by doubling up with the someone like Student D who wrote more directly and feelingly, "*Ethan Frome*'s ending really shocked me. The accident in the snow involving Mattie and Ethan scared me because I didn't know who would live or die." At issue is not which student read the book more closely or more ably, but that for knowledge to be developed, interpretation must begin with negotiable matters of concern. It is in social relations that adolescent readers are more likely to find the support they need to sustain multiple perspectives and complexity. Intersubjectivity allows them to repose in the other, to rest there, to test reality and reposition themselves. "All literary work is an appeal," Sartre writes (in Kaplan 1986, 487). As indicated in Jane's sample journal entries (located at the end of this chapter), the students' likes and dislikes are often listed as afterthoughts, and thus marginalized, function as final assertions rather than appeals for response. The reader is free to peruse the journals for further examples of negotiable or nonnegotiable responses.

Finally, Jane could encourage students to use various genres to bring form to students' work. Being a poet and painter herself, and a patron of drama, Jane could teach the structure of the genres by providing the opportunity for students to find a mesh between their intentions and literary forms, from poetry to plays to research papers, fulfilling her "Emersonian idea" to help a student move "to his own contemplation" and to the student's own "life-giving action." What if she and Student C, who share the experience of reading the world through the novel, *Through the Eyes of a Maniac*, both made theatrical scores of what they saw through those eyes? The student begs to know: "Why is it such an odd experience seeing the world through her eyes?" What if they made poems, or at least lyrical, impressionistic studies? The two would probably move from their initial experience of feeling as though they both are having the same experience, to positions with more differences, and enjoy the differences. Jane need not feel threatened that "there is an impassable gulf between me and my students," that they don't remember a time "before there was orange juice or instant coffee." As Jessica Benjamin wrote,

> Experiences of "being with" are predicated on a continually evolving awareness of difference, on a sense of intimacy felt as occurring between "the two of us." The fact that self and other are not merged is precisely what makes experiences of merging have such high emotional impact. The externality of the other makes one feel one is truly being "fed," getting nourishment from the outside, rather than supplying everything for oneself. (1988, 47)

READING JOURNALS FROM JANE'S CLASS

Each sample is comprised of a single student's entries in a reading journal.

STUDENT A'S READING JOURNAL

October 2, 1987
Jack London's characterization of Wolf Larsen in the novel *The Sea Wolf* provides a fascinating look into a man who is fighting against the

world. When I first was introduced in the book to Wolf Larsen, I thought he was a heartless and brutal sea captain. However, as I read more of the book, I realized that this was a man who I could hate and yet feel sympathy for at the same time.

Even his physical features make him look as if he was a wild creature. Five-feet ten-inches high and of massive build, with a deep chest and broad shoulders, it seemed that he was a primitive ancestor of man. His face, from his lips to his mouth, his chin, his jaw, and his beak-like nose bespoke of savagery and power. With his cigar in his venomous mouth, the smoke curled from him like he was a dragon. The sinewy, knotty strength that he owned was ferocious and alive in itself. It was the strength that makes an insect or snake writhe when it is dying or almost dead.

Response:

(Top of page)
        Excellent start—now go on to support your other point (has sympathetic qualities)
        Well written
(Line 6) Good
(Line 7) Good transition, good support
(Line 13) Either bespoke savagery—or spoke of savagery

STUDENT B'S READING JOURNAL

London, Jack. *The Sea Wolf.* New York: Bantam Books, 1981.

1) 9/19/87
        Since the picture on the cover shows that the ship's name is "Ghost," I know that the title cannot refer to the ship itself. Perhaps the title is a nickname for one of the main characters. Surely, one of the characters must act with primitive instincts like a wolf. Possibly, this character is evil and cruel. Usually a wolf is a predatory animal that preys on the weak or sick by using its brute strength. Furthermore, a wolf is heartless and ruthless, for it is a wild animal that must kill to survive. Basically, the "sea wolf" has to be a character who is brutal and merciless. Also, being a "sea wolf," he must make his livelihood upon the "Ghost."
        After seeing the ship on the cover, I hoped the book would be full of adventure on the high seas. Perhaps the characters would perform courageous deeds as they struggle to overcome the perils of a stormy, unpredictable sea. Additionally, I wanted to discover the reason the author refers to one of the characters as the "sea wolf." Since Jack Lon-

don's *Call of the Wild* takes place in Alaska, this book also might take place in a cold climate. I expect this book to also involve a struggle to survive against great odds.

2) 9/19/87

At the end of chapter one, the narrator is about to be rescued after being shipwrecked in the cold January waters off San Francisco Bay. As he was being rescued, the rescuer shouted at him in an annoyed manner, "Why in hell don't you sing out?" Since the rescuer is already irritated by the shipwrecked man's lack of initiative and resourcefulness, he is surely not going to extend any great amount of kindness to this individual facing life and death in the icy waters. Once the narrator is rescued, his life will probably change for the worse as he struggles to deal with the lack of compassion of his rescuer. While he is aboard this other ship, the narrator may have to become more resourceful in order to survive. Probably his calm life as a writer will drastically change after he is taken aboard this strange ship. If this strange ship is the "Ghost" as depicted on the cover of the book, then the narrator will probably be kept on it against his will for a long time. Since Jack London gives the reader a strong sense of foreboding at the end of the first chapter, the narrator will probably be faced with further bad luck once he is on the ship. Furthermore, since the rescuer had the destiny of the shipwrecked man in his hands, he may not want to relinquish this control for quite awhile. If the rescuer is the "sea wolf," then the extremely civilized narrator is about to face a ruthless, primitive man.

3) 9/25/87

Basically, the characters' problems center around dealing with the "sea wolf," Wolf Larsen. As the captain of the "Ghost," Wolf Larsen is merciless and brutal to his crew. The narrator, Humphrey van Weydon, has left behind his gentlemanly life to unwillingly become a cabin boy aboard the "Ghost." As Humphrey performs his menial tasks during his involuntary servitude, he is shown no compassion when he is injured during a storm. In fact, Wolf Larsen says that the injury may cripple Humphrey, but he'll learn to walk and stand on his own two feet for the first time in his life. Actually, the entire crew is callous to suffering. Often Wolf Larsen physically hurts Humphrey with his brute strength in order to emphasize that "might is right" and the "strong eat the weak." Even the cook, Thomas Mugridge, is domineering and bellicose toward Humphrey. Eventually, the crew tries to attack Wolf Larsen, but their lack of organization leads to defeat. Amid all this brutality, a woman is brought aboard after she was shipwrecked. While Humphrey wants to protect her from Wolf Larsen's savagery, Wolf will probably want to ravage her by his brute force.

Since all the problems center around Wolf's brutality, the solutions revolve around getting rid of Wolf Larsen or escaping from the "Ghost." I think the crew should forget all their petty squabbles and organize themselves, to be able to effectively use their collective strength to kill Wolf Larsen. Cooperation is the key to their problem. Being an intelligent man, perhaps Humphrey can plan an escape from the "Ghost."

4) 9/26/87

Most definitely, the problems have been settled, for Wolf is paralyzed, dying, and no longer a threat. In previous chapters, Humphrey and Maud Brewster, the shipwrecked woman, had escaped from the "Ghost." After they escaped and landed on an island, Humphrey learned to use the island's resources for food and shelter. Soon after Humphrey and Maud gained their freedom, the crew of the "Ghost," offered better pay, deserted Wolf Larsen to join the crew of Wolf's brother, Death Larsen, on his ship the "Macedonia." Eventually, the "Ghost," with Larsen alone on it, drifts onto the shore of the island where Humphrey and Maud are struggling to survive. Humphrey then plots to use the "Ghost" to escape from the island to find civilization.

In the next to the last chapter the "Ghost" has been repaired by Humphrey. Furthermore, Wolf is totally incapacitated by his brain and nerve impairment. Now, in the final chapter, Wolf Larsen must die and Humphrey and Maud must either reach civilization on the "Ghost" or be picked up by a larger vessel. Since all the loose ends, other than Humphrey and Maud reaching civilization, have been tied up, I don't think anything major is missing.

5) 9/26/87

Liked

1. London effectively used similes.
2. London utilized vivid descriptions.
3. The book was exciting and full of adventure.
4. The main character, Humphrey, learned to be independent, resourceful, and self-confident. It was a pleasure to see the character learn to fend for himself.
5. It was ironic that in the end Wolf's sickness totally destroyed his brute strength. He became a prisoner of the body he once was so proud of.
6. I was glad that good triumphed over evil and that might really didn't make right.

Disliked

1. When the crew members spoke in dialect, they were sometimes difficult to understand.
2. The overabundance of nautical terms often made passages difficult to understand.
3. Sometimes the author quoted lines of poetry which I did not always understand.

I liked the author's effective use of similes because they added to the vivid descriptions. For example, the author states, "The fog seemed to break away as though split by a wedge, and the bow of a steamboat emerged, trailing fog-wreaths on either side like seaweed on the snout of Leviathan." Another example described the shipwrecked women as "shrieking like a chorus of lost souls."

Whenever the author used an overabundance of nautical terms, I became somewhat confused. For example, he talked about the main boom, the secondary tackle, the windlass, guys, watch-tackle, hoisting tackle, etc. All of these terms slowed down my reading as I tried to find their meanings.

STUDENT C'S READING JOURNAL

"Through the Eyes of a Maniac"

While reading this book, I had one of the most unique and odd experiences that I have ever had reading.

The reason, or rather the person who is responsible for this is the main character, Mary Katherine Blackwood, since this book was written in first person.

Why was it such an odd experience seeing the world through her eyes? In order to answer that question, I think it would be best to give you a little background information on this unique individual.

Mary Katherine a 18 year old girl who, when she was ten, was involved in a family tragedy. Apparently one evening when the Blackwood family ate their dinner, four of the members suddenly collapsed. They were soon reported to be dead from arsenic poisoning which was found in the sugar.

The only remaining members of the Blackwood family were Mary, Constance, (Mary's older sister) and their Uncle Julien. The person who was suspected the most was Constance, who had made dinner that evening and had washed the sugar bowl immediately before the police arrived.

Since this incident happened all of the members of the Blackwood family, were acquitted of the murder charges. That apparently didn't mean anything to the people of their community. As far as they were concerned, one of the members of that family was a crazed murder.

Throughout the years Constance and especially Mary, had been ridiculed and publicly humiliated. Mary soon developed an insane hatred for these people. She constantly thought of evil and wicked thoughts of them. These thoughts were my first indication that she was a psychologically disturbed person.

If you can imagine seeing the world through the eyes of a paranoid, self-conscious, insecure, psychologically disturbed person who often wishes for people to crumple up and die so that she can walk all over their bodies for revenge, it could prove to be quite terrifying and confusing for the reader.

Then finally toward the end that this person who you have begun to know most intimately, turns out to be the killer.

Response:

Good for you. Some students read the entire book and don't realize that Merricat was the killer. You *must* tell me how you felt at the end, and what you learned—because Jackson is engaged in pulling the rug out from her reader's feet. She involves you with Merricat and then makes you rethink the whole thing.

STUDENT D'S READING JOURNAL

Ethan Frome's Impact on Me

The novel *Ethan Frome* provided me with much entertainment and kept me interested throughout the entire book. I had my own ideas about what should happen from chapter to chapter, and virtually none of it occurred. For what I thought was going to be a dull, boring book, I was surprised at how much I liked it.

Response:

(Paragraph 1)
Good for you!

Student:

I'd have to say that the best experience the book provided me with was the ending: "Zeena taking care of Mattie?" I just couldn't believe it!

The entire book was the exact opposite. Zeena was the ill one, and she never got along very well with Mattie. After Mattie's and Ethan's accident, everything changed. Attitudes changed, feelings changed, and so did the actions of Mattie and Zeena. It was really very surprising.

Response:

(Paragraph 2)
An example of life's irony—life has a way of tripping people up—or maybe of giving them what they've set up for themselves?

Student:

Throughout *Ethan Frome*, Mattie and Ethan were becoming closer, and closer, falling in love more each day. With Zeena being Mattie's cousin, and the circumstances of Zeena's illness, nothing much ever resulted between Mattie and Ethan. While reading I was secretly hoping that one of two things would happen. First, that Ethan and Mattie would stay together and eventually get married; or second, that Zeena would get well, and resolve everything with Ethan, her husband.

Reading of the feelings shared between Mattie and Ethan, I really felt sorry for both of them. I could imagine how distraught they both were not being able to get married. I believe that they were two special people who deserved each other and eternal happiness.

Response:

(Paragraph 4)
She made her reader hope so much that they will find a way to get together.

Student:

I also slightly felt sorry for Zeena because she was so ill. I disliked though, the way she let her illness dominate her life and her relationship with Ethan. She was too much like a baby and acted ridiculously helpless! When Mattie broke one of her dishes she was furious, and she eventually wanted Mattie to leave because she "supposedly" needed better care.

Response:

(Paragraph 5)
Me, too.

Student:

Ethan Frome's ending really shocked me. The accident in the snow involving Mattie and Ethan scared me because I didn't know who would live or die. The end was also slightly confusing to read. The next thing I knew, Zeena was caring for an injured Mattie, and Ethan wasn't there anymore. It was really quite sad for Ethan and Zeena, but in the same respect joyous for Mattie and Zeena really cares about Mattie, got well, and was a changed person.

Response:

(Paragraph 6)
Do you think she *really* cares about Mattie? Ask yourself—if you were Mattie, how would you have felt to be helpless and to have to be dependent on Ethan's wife? And, how do you think Zeena felt, suspecting that Ethan loved Mattie? Do you think her resentment would have gone away? This book has one of the most excellent endings I've ever read—my own suspicion is that Zeena was happy *because* Mattie was destroyed—and that's horrifying.

Student:

Overall, I experienced many feelings while reading *Ethan Frome*—some were good and others were bad. If I had to choose a book all over again, I would still definitely choose the one I did. After finishing it, I had warm emotions, and it really left me thinking the way the characters had, and I realized what a fun interesting book it really was!!

Response:

(Paragraph 8, Line 6)
This is unclear, Sherry.
(Paragraph 8, Line 7, Word: *fun*)
Maybe another adjective would be better here.

STUDENT E'S READING JOURNAL

1) Wharton, Edith, *Ethan Frome*. New York: Charles Scribner's Sons, 1911.
When I first read the title of my book, *Ethan Frome*, I was a little hesitant because it doesn't sound very interesting. I guess that the title is just the name of the main character in the novel. For some reason, the name makes me think of a rich family. It also sounds English or

European. The book looks slightly boring, but also a little interesting.

One reason I picked *Ethan Frome* was because of the introduction inside written by the author. Another reason was that it looks fairly easy to read and understand. Next, in class when we learned more about all the authors on our Independent Reading List, Edith Wharton's style of writing appealed to me. My expectations of this book include excitement, and a heart-warming family oriented story. I also hope it keeps me entertained throughout, and is easily understood.

2) After reading the first chapter, I start to understand what Ethan Frome is all about. It's a flashback to his own personal family like I guess one thing that's going to happen is that Zeena, his wife, is going to keep getting sicker each day. She can't even care for herself, and her doctor told her that she needs extra care.

Another thing that I believe will happen is a deeper relationship between Ethan and Mattie. This is because of all their time spent together just walking, talking and learning. It's also because of Ethan seeming jealous at the prospect of Mattie marrying Dennis Eady, and the fact that Ethan shaves everyday for her and helps her clean the house. He shows much kindness and affection towards her.

Lastly, I think that Mattie will eventually marry Denis Eady because Ethan is already taken. I think she might marry him just to make Ethan jealous, and also to show Zeena that she has no feelings for Ethan.

3) The main conflict in the novel at this point is Ethan's struggle with himself to stay away from Mattie and to not pursue her. All he does is dream about her and wish that they were together all of the time. I think Ethan should start concentrating on getting his wife well, and being happy with her. This is logical because Zeena deserves his love and support since they're married, and Mattie should be getting on with her own life. Besides, relatives shouldn't be treating each other the way they have been.

Mattie's problem is her vulnerability and uncertainty concerning her feelings. In my opinion, she should move away, get married, and start his [sic] own life so that Ethan and Zeena can be happy again.

Most of Zeena's problems concern her bad health. Someone needs to be there to take care of her, and help her to be able to be a better wife. If she was, then her and Ethan would be much happier together.

4) In the next to last chapter, the problems haven't been solved yet. Mattie and Ethan have had an accident, and their problems aren't

resolved. The reader doesn't know if they'll be okay or not, and if Ethan will eventually have Zeena for Mattie. Zeena's illness still hasn't been resolved, and she's still upset with Mattie because her dish was broken.

The final chapter should tell whether or not Ethan and Mattie will part. It should also tell the result of their accident and if there were any injuries or not. Also, Zeena's illness should be further explained or cured in some way. Lastly, Ethan and Zeena's relationship and various marital problems should be solved.

The one thing that's missing right now is returning to the man who wrote the chapter before the first. The entire book was a flashback, and now it's time to return to the present, and explain how the past and present tie in together.

5) *Liked*

1. The characteristics and developments of all the characters.
2. The speed at which the story was described and eventually resolved.
3. The idea of the novel being a flashback instead of just a normal book.
4. The length of the book.

Disliked

1. The title of the book—it sounds boring.
2. The ending, especially the last chapter.
3. Some of the names of the characters (Zeena, Ethan).
4. The way the book began.
5. Some of the vocabulary in the work.

The main thing that I liked about *Ethan Frome* was the fact that it was written as a flashback, and not just an ordinary book. Because it was different, it appealed to me more and kept me interested throughout the entire story. I couldn't wait to finally reach the end so I could see how the beginning would tie in with the rest of the book. The entire flashback explained the beginning, and also made the ending interesting. I wasn't expecting the ending to have Mattie returning with Ethan, and Zeena caring for Mattie. It was a very surprising ending, and it was both good and bad. I was hoping for it to be different, but it was still a good book.

One thing that I didn't like about the book were some of the vocabulary words. There were some words that I had never heard of, so I just had to use context clues to determine their meanings. I'd rather have an easier to read book, but I was able to still figure it out and enjoy it. Also, some of the words were spelled the way they sounded instead of their real spelling. I guess this was just the author's style of writing though, and as long as the reader can understand it, it's fine. Even though I didn't like some of the vocabulary and wording, I learned from it!

NINE

APRIL:
TAKING ON THE WORLD FROM SCHOOL

TROUBLED BY CONFLICT

During the reading of two contemporary texts, Pearl Buck's *The Good Earth*, and Maxine Hong-Kingston's *Woman Warrior*, conflicts about the curriculum surface for April and her eighth-grade students. *The Good Earth* was an inherited part of the curriculum. April writes that she understands its popularity among students because she and her sisters loved the book as children, acting out scenes from it, and absorbing its values. It was popular among the faculty at the school because it was so popular among students, and as April points out, because of the sentimental film made of the text in the fifties. However, April is offended by its stereotypes, racism, and sexism. In a move that seeks to modify the sexism and racism of Buck's book, April decides to juxtapose it with another text, Hong-Kingston's *Woman Warrior*. She writes,

> I am still quite new to teaching; in my first two years, I found—as the Red Queen tells Alice—it took all the running I could to just to keep in one place; I'd have to run twice as fast as that to get somewhere else. Maybe I've finally increased my speed, but happily, in this my third year, I at last have some time to examine what I'm doing—how, and why I'm doing it. At the top of that list of consideration is my reading curriculum. I have never felt comfortable with it, and I feel it is important

to make sense of the eighth grade reading program—because all our other study focuses around it, because it is something that is important to me. I suppose I have been fighting toward this all during these three years—and though I feel I am making headway, I'm still frustrated.

. . . The curriculum I inherited seemed to be a confused hodge-podge of readings. When questioned, the members of the department admitted that these books were left over from various eighth grade courses, which had been organized around themes such as Mystery, Adventure, Fantasy. Somehow, these texts remained, but they didn't "hang together" in any way.

The categories that group the books in this eighth-grade bookroom may not be exactly the same as those that group the courses in the undergraduate catalog's English department. But in either location, one is likely to find courses or units named by form: The Novel, Poetry, Short Fiction; or by major canonized authors: Shakespeare, Chaucer, Milton, Blake; or by region: Survey of American Literature II, English Literature I, African Literature; Southern Literature; or by literary school or period: American Realism, The Courtly Tradition in Medieval Literature; or even increasingly by gender or race: Women Authors of Color. It would not be unusual for an undergraduate program in a small liberal arts college or a large research university to offer thirty-five such individual courses, some required and some elected, but sequenced, in one semester. Middle school and high school English teachers would have been prepared by such programs, but are not perhaps prepared to decide how to choose across category lines for the benefit of the middle school and high school age readers. As we have seen, for example, in Jane's teaching autobiography, there is a canon related to Advanced Placement Courses, and other standardized curricula. However, Jane, Philip, and April all worry about their responsibility to choose what their students should read in any given year. Because secondary school students are minors, their teachers have an implied relationship with students' parents and the social mores of the community, which makes curriculum particularly contestable. And because they spend the day in relationships with developing adolescents, these teachers worry about whether the events, texts, and activities they design for their classes will help them mature. April continues:

I particularly objected to *The Good Earth*, which I consider poorly written and racist. When I read this book, additionally, I see Buck perpetrating unhealthy stereotypes about women and to a lesser degree, men: "Good girls" like O-lan make suffering and sacrifice their badge; nobody who has read that book can forget how O-lan delivers her first child with no assistant, then returns to work in the fields two hours later. O-lan is silent, subservient, noble; her one selfish act is to request two pearls from her husband, which of course, he denies her, giving them instead to his mistress. The melodrama is served up fairly thickly in this book. Bad girls show up in the person of that same opium-smoking mistress, and men are shown as having uncontrollable lust (of course, none of the women possess any sexual desires).—The strokes in this book are fairly broad and crude—but that is how the book speaks to me—interpretation right?

It fascinates me how many people in their late fifties extol the virtues of this book—and I have to wonder if their view is not colored by their memory of Louise Rainer in the film. But I have also considered how thirteen-year old girls respond to this book (—especially because I remember reading it when I was an adolescent, and loving it;) for weeks my sister and I imitated the heavy and sorrowful tones of these characters, speaking as they did: "It is meet that we should do it thus." It was at this point that my sister began to argue vehemently for my grandmother to hold onto her farmland (the land! the land!). And, interestingly, too, I remember my mother was the first to steer me away from Buck by first telling me about, then reading me a short story. In this story, again, the strokes are so broadly drawn—the cruel, bitchy, insensitive white woman who hires a poor, starving Chinaman (who is supporting this many children, a dying wife, etc.). At the end of the story she rejects his work, leaving him to certain death.

What of my students? In the first two years, the department implored me to "at least try it," so I gave in, assigning *The Good Earth* as summer reading. Most students responded to it with enthusiasm—they enjoyed the foreign setting, the elemental-ness of the living—life and death, starvation, floods. Only a few were disturbed by the portrayal of the Chinese and the women. When we re-read the book later, we took more time to examine the writing and the attitudes of the author. This was successful/not successful. Though in most cases the students felt triumphant to re-evaluate a book and to go beyond and deeper than their first reading, others felt resistant and even resentful—I was ruining their relationship with this book in asking them to view it in a different, more judgmental way.

April's attempt to steer controversy into formal literary analysis is familiar to us. We saw it in Jane and Philip's classes, and we see it in English classrooms everywhere. Literary analysis, can, of course, unpack what is going on in texts. Students may have missed the causal relationships in the plot of *Of Mice and Men*, without Philip's direction, and thus miss why both the economy and Curley's marital jealousy may threaten the solution to George and Lenny's problems. But students have the right to ask what these particular predicaments have to do with the world, the future and their lives. These secondary school teachers know the danger of dropping students' interests and concerns en route to analysis. Analysis that merely explicates the text can cool off controversy to the extent that students lose interest in reading. Reaching beyond analysis, April tried to help her students develop a perspective on *The Good Earth*, by reading another book about Asians, *Woman Warrior*. She describes her disappointment with that experience:

> Incidentally, as part of that second-read, I had my students compare GE to Maxine Hong-Kingston's *Woman Warrior*. This book, written in 1975 by a Chinese-American woman, explodes some of the stereotypes and attitudes about Asians. It is also fairly bitter in its feminist viewpoint—something which the students felt perplexed and irritated about; something which I had not focused upon until they pointed it out—(we spend some time discussing this—their reactions, my non-reaction, etc. It was exciting for me to have them discover something I had "missed.") Despite my best efforts, this book was not well-received, for a number of reasons. Kingston experiments with her writing style freely, mixing fantasy and reality. Her progression is nonlinear. She will establish a truth in one chapter, only to violate it in the next, and come up with a third solution in the following chapter. A number of my students felt completely lost with this book and (interestingly) very angry at the author for these techniques. Some were also overwhelmed by the graphic images—of a strangled fetus, of monkey brains, and other disturbing passages—a crazy woman who is stoned to death by villagers.
>
> And yet—though at first I thought this [the juxtaposition of *Woman Warrior* with *The Good Earth*] would be an exciting way of showing students how to re-evaluate a book, reconsider it in a different way, after consideration, I have come to think that there are other, less "violating" ways of accomplishing this same task. In my first two years, I hear often, "why do we have to analyze *everything*? It destroys [a book, a poem]; why can't we just enjoy some of these things? And I felt particularly responsive to the complaint, because I used to voice it myself. I haven't heard that complaint recently, perhaps because I've been able to guide the students into interpretation and analysis in a manner which is more acceptable to them. (This December we viewed an RSC video

called "Interpreting a Character" in which two actors discussed their different portrayals of Shylock. The students took notes and then discussed what they agreed and disagreed with—how they pictured Shylock, which choices they accepted or rejected and why.)

April does find an effective way to teach interpretation. By using actors to argue the points of diverse portrayals, it becomes more clear to students that texts do not furnish a reading, but an opportunity for a reading that is potentially contestable. Because students defer to expert actors, they suspend their own judgments to entertain new perspectives on literature. As an end in itself, however, the deferral of response can cool off reading interest. April has mixed feelings about her decision, but she especially wants to prevent her students from feeling lost or abandoned in a text. She writes,

> So *The Good Earth* and *Woman Warrior* left the curriculum after two years. In the case of the first book, I was relieved; it never made sense to me to teach a book I don't value. I dropped *My Antonia* for similar reasons—I felt I knew so little about the American Midwest that I could not find an approach for the book and therefore could not help my students in reading the book. Of course, it's not to say one shouldn't explore a text that is foreign to one's experience—but I do think that as a teacher I have to make sense of a text, find an approach for it—

April's problems trying to find an approach for the troubling *Woman Warrior* echoes her own experience of being troubled by certain texts as a child. It is understandable that she does not want to reproduce for her students the threat that she felt in reading disturbing books. *Woman Warrior* is an autobiographical novel about an Asian-American girl who comes of age in the San Francisco area. The protagonist must deal with the double-bind of being too Chinese for American cultural standards and too American for her family and community's Asian standards. The overlapping space she is forced to occupy is one of crisis, not of smooth transitions. What is particularly difficult is that there are whispered legacies and experiences from the purges in China from which the girl's parents fled. Deeply wounded by these experiences, the girl's parents will not speak about them directly with her, and so they become like ghosts to her, since she lives with their effects.

The triumph that adult readers and critics acknowledge is that the protagonist learns how to appropriate some of the strong cultural legacies of her Chinese ancestry, which her mother embodies, but won't articulate for her. As an adolescent she rejects her mother's choice to repress anger, and then beats up an introverted Chinese-American girl in the lavatory at school. Eventually she learns to confront racism and sexism more directly by assuming a strong persona derived from the Chinese legends that have been imparted to her by her mother in riddles and whispers. Her transformation is not aesthetically pleasing—it is violent, bizarre, threatening. Hong-Kingston chooses a style that shatters chronology, personality, and a coherent voice to mirror the protagonist's struggle to achieve an identity from the disparate elements of her biography.

As April reports, the girls in her class reject the *Woman Warrior*, but find *the Good Earth* much more palatable. O-Lan, the Chinese heroine of Buck's book, achieves wholeness and serenity by hard work, love, and devotion to her man, something that April implies her students can relate to and want to believe. In the face of their rejection of *Woman Warrior* and their endorsement of *The Good Earth*, April decides to drop both books from the curriculum.

SHARING A READING LIFE

April's strategy as an English teacher has been to merge her interests with students, to read the books they like to read in her leisure time, and to guide them carefully as they read more demanding material. Although her curriculum is split between informal social reading and formalized and objective skill development, both kinds of experiences ensure that the girls will have security and company in their reading lives. Like her aunt, Judy, a teacher whom she admires, April feels a duty to guide her students through literary experience with a firm hand through a specific approach. When she cannot find a definite approach, she excises the readings from the curriculum.

However, April finds herself troubled by the fact that the girls seem unprepared to cope with material that unsettles their preconceptions. She teaches in a small, well-known, religious-affiliated girls' intermediate school in a large metropolitan area. She teaches classes of up to twelve or fifteen girls in a comfortably furnished, handsome school in an affluent neighborhood. The long elegant windows of her classroom open onto a lovely old tree-lined street. The desks face each other seminar-style, and a fuchsia velvet lounging sofa, draped with a black silk shawl, adds to the room's coziness and drama. April prints her syllabus and work packets for students on colored paper, presides over informal, intimate reading groups, entices the girls to read new books by hosting "book talks," and offers to read some of her students' favorite books at home on her own time. She shares an almost domestic rapport with her students. She wrote:

> The day before break, I gave each of my classes a "book talk." I lined my blackboards with all sorts of books, but mainly those that would make for entertaining reading—*The Adventures of Sherlock Holmes, Rebecca, The Portrait of Dorian Grey, The Martian Chronicles, Passage to India, The Spoon River Anthology, The Wide Sargasso Sea, Robert Frost's Collected Poems, All Creatures Great and Small,* and a number of others. I began by talking at length about *Rebecca* by Daphne Dumaurier—I read the first chapter, and described the overall feeling of the book—the mystery involved, and the romantic/luxurious/ominous/mysterious exciting feel of the story. This was the book I had come up with about a month ago for two girls to read, because their mothers complained to me that they were reading far below their ability—Nancy Drew mysteries, mainly. I told Barbara and Eugenie about *Rebecca* and I promised them that if they read the book, we'd get together to discuss it, and then watch the movie. A number of other girls heard about our "bargain" and asked if they could get in on the deal. After I spoke about *Rebecca* to the class, I turned to the other books and described each briefly—then I left the last ten minutes of class open, so they could mill about, examine the books, and take home any of those that caught their interests. I in turn was challenged to read *Frost in May* and to come back and discuss it.

April's own love of intimate reading experiences runs deep and back to her early childhood living in Nepal. She recalls,

> When we were even younger, my parents would read to us. There were all sorts of different books, from Chinese and Japanese fairy tales, with delicate water color pictures, to Grimm's Tales, Winnie the Pooh series, and Dr. Seuss books. There are two books that stand out when I think of Mother reading aloud. The first to come to mind, oddly enough, is *Wind in the Willows.* This strikes me as peculiar because at the time we considered the book a failure—Mother kept trying to push it, but the children lost interest, and in the end we never finished the book. But today, I can still clearly envision my favorite character, Mr. Toad. Mr. Toad was one of the few spunky, colorful animals. Something of a cavalier, Toadie was very wealthy and spoiled. He wore a smoking jacket, puffed on cigars, and terrorized the other animals by ripping about in a 1920's roadster. Later Toadie gets thrown in jail and repents all his sins, which I considered grossly unfair.

April gives a running account of her pleasures and worries as she reads:

My other favorite read-aloud was a large book with unusual angular, stylized pictures and tales from the Greek myths. I remember pouring over the book and stories with my mother and siblings, as we discussed the characters and their adventures. We were particularly fascinated by the Trojan war and the gods and goddesses who helped the various mortals; Odysseus' adventures seemed frightening and sad to me, and I kept worrying about inconsequential details—the poor Cyclops with the stake in his eye, the men whom Circe turns into swine, and Odysseus' faithful dog . . .

Her feel for the inconsequential details helps her build a vivid world for the myths, and sensitizes her later to her students' responses. She still savors the times when she can afford to get into bed with a good book, a cup of coffee, popcorn, propped up pillows, and read all night. Reading has been both a private and sociable pleasure for her.

April seems to have the same easy rapport with her student readers and their families as she has had within her own family:

Some of the families still read together, especially when they are on vacation; some of the children read their assigned English books with their parents so they can discuss the stories together. I always ask my classes to see if any of their parents have read/memorized *The Rime of the Ancient Mariner* or Portia's "Quality of Mercy" speech, or other famous bits. They find it very exciting to report that "my father knew all of it! He sat there and recited for us over dinner."

One cannot help but notice that differences in the classrooms of Philip, Jane, and April, are associated with class and gender. I have argued that Philip's male students may well identify with patriarchal features in our culture, such as repression, splitting, and objectivity, in their reading practices and attitudes. These masculine identifications may present special challenges to teachers. Jane, like many English teachers in large, public schools, finds herself having to overcome the deficits of a standardized, abstract, and alienating English program which disregards students' hopes, intentions, and need for community. April's female students may well be both less repressed and less alienated by virtue of their gender, their socioeconomic privilege, and the extraordinary degree of attention they get from adults at home and in a small and prestigious school.

April acknowledges the shelter a private and small school can provide. Having transferred in the 1970s to a large suburban American high school from a very small one for diplomatic families living in Nepal, she wrote about feeling alienated and frightened in her new high school. Remember she blamed her teacher for not taking care of her or the class (see p. 29).

> I do remember *Lord of the Flies*, and the feeling of despair-repulsion—I remember slumped low in the back of the room, watching the boys in front of me rolling a joint, thinking that my worst nightmare would be to be trapped on an island with this English class—wondering who would be killed first (the English teacher and the fat girl with heavy glasses who always had a cold but no handkerchiefs, and then maybe me, unless I could get away). What was that teacher thinking when she chose her book list? What did she title the course—"Alienation and Despair?" The first time I began to think about systems of education was when I came to West High School—how could a school have such extensive modern equip-ment—science laboratories, the newest books, movies, film strips, records, a fabulous arts studio—and yet be such a demoralizing place of study? What I remember of WHS are long underlit halls, bathrooms stinking of cigarettes, and everything bureaucratized, systematized, regulated—being sent to the principal for my habit of sitting on my knees ("who do you think you are, Pocohantas?"), being caught reading instead of going to the pep rally ("what do you think you come to school for?") . . . but here we go again—Fear and Loathing in Suburban USA; enough.

In this memory, April has marked a decision she made about what kind of teacher she wants to be and does not want to be. She does not want to be "a mouse," taken advantage of, frightened, and ineffec-tive, and she does not want to be the kind of teacher who abandons or alienates students as she was abandoned. In her remarks about unruly boys, and a teacher who cries, she struggles to resist the role of the dis-empowered female who cannot command respect and who cannot lead her students with strength and authority.

READING AS TRANSITIONAL EXPERIENCE

Much of April's narrative about her own literary experiences as a child and adolescent are about support and intimacy. She notes disturbing reading as exceptional:

There are only a few unpleasant stories that have stayed with me from that time in my childhood. One—which all we children still remember sadly—is about a Duck named Ping who lives in the Hongkong Bay and who catches fish for a living. The horrible part was that Ping has a metal ring around his throat which chokes him and made it impossible for him to ever swallow the delicious, fat fish which he catches for his employer. Undoubtedly, Ping's life took a turn for the better, but I hated to think of his life in subjugation.

The other story is one that a nun told me in Religious school. About one hundred and fifty years old, Sister Elizabeth was a crotchety, mean-spirited nun who told my class a story about a family that goes on vacation. As they get into their car for the outing, their youngest daughter prays to Jesus that the family will travel safely. But on the highway, a truck swerves into the car, and everyone perishes—except for the youngest daughter, because she remembered to say her prayers. The story panicked me for months after, and I desperately urged my bemused parents to pray before they went on trips.

Although April writes that she had been frightened by reading as a young child, reading also became pivotal in her struggle to individuate:

As a child, it seemed to me that my parents were always going out; the house seemed impossibly empty and lonely. The three of us would usually spend the evening in our playroom playing with our dolls and toys, with the ayah sitting in the corner. The books, stories, and recounting of stories were a solace. At different times, different ayahs took interest in joining in, and we'd read the "American" books to them, while they in turn told us their stories. From ayahs I learned folk tales, ghost tales, tales of village life and superstition. In Bangkok, we learned the stories of the Ramakien (the Thai version of India's Ramayana)—we followed the adventures of the heroic Rama, his kidnapped wife and loyal brother, and the wily lascivious monkey-god, Hanuman. When we felt very bored, on rainy afternoons after school, my sister and I would amuse ourselves by watching Chinese soap-operas on television—we'd make up elaborate stories to match the action and try to put English words to the Chinese songs.

April describes how reading facilitated her becoming her own person as an adolescent. For example, when she felt exiled on moving to the United States, she took the initiative to read about American soldiers "exiled" in Vietnam (see her Autobiography #3).

April's reading about POWs, Indochina, and America's involvement in Vietnam seems an odd refuge from the nightmare of her
school experience that year. Yet having Chinese ancestry and having
lived in a culture exotic to the United States, it may be that April identified with the American POWs in Asia as fellow exiles. Her preoccu-
pation, or "secret obsession" as she calls it, may have provided a kind
of potential space or sanctuary of transition for her to work at recon-
ciling conflicts she experienced among Nepalese, Chinese, and American cultures.

At one point April is critical of her tenth grade teachers' syllabus
of "alienation and despair." Eventually, though, she found writers like
Sartre, Borges, Camus, and Beckett "fascinating." The autobiography
suggests that it was not so much the texts in the curriculum per se that
were unsuitably depressing or alienating, but that a basic environment
of security was required as a backdrop to do this serious reading. April
seems particularly comfortable in an AP class in which the reading
was challenging emotionally and intellectually, but probably more
important, she was in the company of a more companionable group of
students who were cooperative, sensitive, and articulate, and who
respected the teacher. At this point, she begins to venture out to the
city to do research and stake her own intellectual territory:

> In the next two years of high school I settled down, learned to work the
> school's system, discovered some of my best friends in the teachers, and
> began to explore wonderful books. A course called "World Literature"
> introduced me to a whole realm of translated material, and, for the first
> time, fascinating existentialist works—Sartre, Borges, Camus Beckett. In
> that class I first discovered Dante, Milton, Tolstoy; in a creative writing
> class I read Oates, Barth, Gorki, Woolf; in the AP class, Kafka, Conrad,
> Faulkner. I was immersed in a whole world of reading—and a new
> world of university libraries. I used to drive an hour out to Columbia to
> "research" different projects—and find myself instead walking the
> stacks and collecting armfuls of books.

Thematically, April's narrative shows the value of transitional
experiences which help a reader bridge the familiar with the strange or
threatening, and the self and the other. The children read books to
replace absent parents, make dolls, and plays to represent characters
and her father taped stories they could hear when they were gone.
They in turn wrote books that he would bind at the office. The *ayahs*,
or nursemaids provided another bridging experience as they stood in
for the parents and entertained the children with stories from their

own culture, while April and her siblings read American books to them. As she and her sister moved toward more independence from their parents, they read boarding-school stories together and stories about adventurous teenagers solving mysteries, like the Nancy Drew series and the Hardy Boys. As April gets older, she carries with her the desire to make herself at home wherever she is when she reads:

> The libraries. I remember the sad American embassy library in Kathmandu. Tucked away in an attic room of an obscure administration building in the USAID compound—one small room, packed mainly with crumbling paperbacks or hardbacks with that ugly 1950's feel to them—cheap paper already ruined by the acid of the print—with those stiff plastic covers—mylar?—always dirty, always brittle and torn on the top, so that you'd rip your hands up when you'd try to read, and the only solution would be to cautiously tear off the tape and slip the book out of its cover. There was something mysterious and pleasant about that library—half the time it would be locked and I'd get the key from the manager of the commissary—slip up into the cool, dark room, mingle solitarily among the books, load up with an armful. . . . A very sensory reading setting—white plaster walls, cool and dark, with uncomfortable rattan mats, which would leave impressions of their design on my legs if I sat too long. . . . I'd usually sit myself at a particular window that overlooked the compound—overlook the broad thick trees with heavy foliage and armies of Nepalese cows—the irregular red-brick paved courtyard—and the impossibly blue skies and ghosts of Himalayas in the distance. It was a good secret-nook . . .

She reflects further about the large American suburban high school she attended later:

> Ridiculous as it seems, I still have nightmares about that school; nightmares of being lost in vast, anonymous halls with rows of lockers and faceless people—and a particularly panicked nightmare of trying to find my locker and then trying to remember my combination—. So my memories of high school reading are inextricably woven into the experience of being a teenager, of living in that particular suburb. But when I look back, I think a number of negative experiences from that time continue to inform and influence my teaching now.

The books April's students choose and the ones April encourages them to read are often romances or exotic adventures, or classics that are not controversial. In her lessons, students are given the help and approach to the text April claimed so important in her autobiographical writing. She teaches how the figures of speech work and the meanings of archaic vocabulary usage. She shows videos of theatrical productions which illustrate alternate interpretations of dramatic scripts, she draws cultural parallels between the historical context of literature and today's issues, and she provides the opportunity for students to perform scenes from *The Merchant of Venice*.

When April was growing up, literary pieces served as classic transitional objects in that they provided elements of a previous way of life, as well as a link to a new metropolitan way of life she began to live as an adolescent in the United States. But as a literature teacher today, she is torn between wanting students to enjoy the shelter of escape, romance, and the strong guidance of a teacher as they read, and the challenge of reading texts that contest and expand their views.

In her close identification and rapport with her students, April has a solid basis for being the strong teacher she knows her students need. For many nurturing teachers, though, the question of how to allow space for students to challenge the world and themselves through their reading is daunting. April looks for ways that are not "violating." Moreover, to prevent on the one hand, the self-effacement of "the mouse" and on the other hand, the paternalistic effacement of students' responses, a powerful teacher has to choose texts wisely, and present herself to students as a worldly, active, and powerful person with whom students want to identify.

THE NEED FOR A WORLDLY TEACHER

In chapters 5 and 6, we looked at a model for a powerful teacher as one who accepts the child's ego and reflects his or her interests back to the child. We saw, however, that mirroring was not enough, and that children (and students) need a caretaker who has strong interests and ties to the outside world that are visible to the child. The prototype was Kristeva's "third term," embodied in a teacher who could see the value of making visible to students her or his own attraction to and involvement in the world beyond the classroom. Students would see this "third term" for the teacher as a model for their own license and responsibility to go further than what is known between the student and teacher, and to be engaged in the real problems of the world.

Already successful at building rapport and community with her students, April senses from the conflict over *The Good Earth* and *Woman Warrior* that her students need more support for maturation, differentiation, and separate initiative. She can help them individuate and become stronger readers through the roles she embodies as a teacher, and through the curriculum. First, she can help students identify with the excitement and pleasure she gets from her *own* projects in the world. She can assert her own autobiography, her own reading interests, her work in graduate school, and her traveling. While an autobiography is egotistical, it invites others to acknowledge their own specific anchoring and relation to the world. April's life in Nepal may be quite different from the lives of any of her students, but her telling it to them both differentiates her from them and invites them to assert their egos in differentiating from her. Likewise, she may talk about her love of Chinese poetry in a way that does not imply that they need to love it too—but that they may find their own individual reading favorites. She is working on a master's degree and has recently traveled to Brazil. This is the enterprising and satisfying life that she should not hide from them, nor expect them to follow. Her life is an invitation for students to try to find their paths of individuation, their "voyages out," in Virginia Woolf's phrase.

In April's case, it is clear that she has autonomy and interests in the outside world, but that she has difficulty interpolating them into her relationship with her students. Furthermore, the school culture, with its hierarchical supervisory structures, inhibits the revelation of her power to the students by controlling the curriculum. The curriculum should be developed and negotiated with the larger academic and political worlds *through the teacher.* Secondary English teachers need to be acknowledged as readers and writers in their own right, and as communicators and actors with the outside world, and so do students. For the students, being readers and writers only for the teacher, threatens to be an identification with her domestication in school. That is why Nancie Atwell and her colleagues (writing theorists Donald Murray, Donald Graves, Lucy Calkins, Ellen Giacobbe, Tommy Newkirk), are right in insisting that writing and reading never be taught as school exercises, with no purpose for the student. Exercises are products of the domestic, of the confinement of the child to school. Furthermore, tests created by and for outsiders, are the vehicles by which the domesticated teacher is controlled through standardization by the "outside." Both are part of a paternalistic system. The movement toward "authentic learning" since Dewey, has tried to make this point, but has been hampered by not conceptualizing the issues with a critical, sociological, and feminist theory of the teacher's position. If the desires and interests of the teacher are ignored, repudiated, or confined, it is hard for the child to imagine that he or she is thought of as interesting and respected by the system either. And if students cannot imagine their teachers as both inside and outside the school, it is harder for them to imagine themselves as ever being ready for the outside world. If we remember once more, Sartre's introduction to reading in Chapter 6, we remember that even though he felt threatened by his mother consorting with those foreign characters in the text, he began to identify with her fun, with her excitement, and he gradually took the position himself of one who could be fulfilled by reading. Teachers can help students recognize themselves as readers and writers who transform reality only if the students recognize the teachers as such active agents in the world. Teachers need to be seen as separate enough from students and school, to have their own worldly interests, autonomy, and power.

If their teacher is excited and engaged in worldly business, as an individual and as a community member, students can identify with that excitement and satisfaction. They need not love the same objects the teacher loves. If he or she loves literature, is stimulated by worldly issues and committed to meaningful projects, they can identify with this position as an autonomous person who desires and gets fulfilled. They will develop a narcissistic confidence in a powerful *position*.

In order to provide this nourishing narcissism for students, the teacher needs to be seen as an actor in an open system. He or she needs to be seen as the person who designs the curriculum not only of what is known, but about what must be done in the world. The teacher's hopefulness and involvement in making the world a better place is taken by his or her egotistical students to be the construction of a better place for *them*, a healthy presumption. The teacher's leaving the classroom physically and symbolically to go elsewhere is taken not as abandonment, but as his or her meeting her obligation to transform reality for them. Kristeva believes that the object of the desiring and caring mother's gaze beyond her child, is a place made for her and her loved ones, a conception. To repeat the theme of chapter 6, her desire as desire must continually recede as a horizon for the child, but it is not regressively fantastic since it searches for a place in which both she and the child can live. For April this means that her interests and abilities may always outstrip those of her students, but it also means the horizons of readers' education must always recede beyond the text or the class. The focus of the curriculum needs to be on the interpretation of worlds beyond the classroom and the page, worlds that we are actually trying to make habitable.

A CURRICULUM THAT REQUIRES STUDENT INITIATIVE

The literature curriculum could help readers cut a new path toward the complexities of the world and their opportunity and responsibility to transform it. In the development of an "authentic" curriculum in which readers try to use literature to take on the real world, April can look at the works on her syllabus in a new light. The point is not to decide which works are good or correct, but to help students decide how they can be used. In an article entitled, "Why Write?" (in Kaplan 1986), Sartre discusses how the text is a gift and an exigence—a proposal and an appeal to act. He asserts, "However bad and hopeless the humanity which it paints may be, the work must have an air of generosity," and the more disposed one is to change it, the more alive it will be" (1986, 497). Sartre believes that writers must appeal to the freedom of readers to act on the text:

> The novelist's universe would lack thickness if it were not discovered in a moment to transcend it. (P. 496)

The challenge for April is to help students develop their motives and freedom to use the literature on the class reading list such as *The Good Earth, Woman Warrior,* and *The Merchant of Venice* toward an end that is important to them and that connects them to the world beyond the classroom. A prototype for such an enterprising curriculum might be found in a community research project developed by the anthropologist/educator, Shirley Brice Heath, and Amanda Branscombe, a classroom teacher in Auburn, Alabama. Heath and Branscombe worked together to bring to their ninth grade students the opportunity to become researchers of language use in their communities (1987, 214). Branscombe contacted Heath and from California, Heath directed Branscombe's students to serve as research assistants to her. Students had a "felt need" to assist Heath in her writing about patterns of using reading and writing across communities of the United States. The students stepped back to analyze the familiar literacy of the community in which they lived to help their teachers understand it.

Students wrote autobiographies as a way "to begin recording who they were, where they were from, and what they wanted for themselves (as far as goals, a future career, and a family)." The students gathered data and Heath wrote "critical comments on the students' fieldnotes, reports, and letters describing their communities" (1987, 214). Branscombe reported:

> The students continued their personal letters to Heath, but expanded their writings to include fieldnotes, interviews, observation, and timed writings. They taped oral histories of older people in the community and young children learning to talk. . . . In late spring, Heath came to the

class and talked with them about their final tasks as a group and as individuals. She divided the class into smaller groups for those tasks. One group interviewed people about language used in sports. (1987, 215)

Branscombe described how she gave up her classroom and "changed it into a learning lab in which the students and I equally focused on gathering the data that we needed" (1987, 217). Branscombe took on the role of the teacher as an agent of enterprise. She describes this role:

> She [Heath] encouraged the students by broadening their worlds through her letters about her travels, and gave them a real audience who needed their data. She also helped me to make a shift from a teacher who imparted skills and knowledge to a person who was a co-learner. . . . We had become co-producers of knowledge with other researchers in other areas of the country. We became researchers who would take our data and release it through analysis so that other teachers and researchers could use it in the larger body of knowledge about student's learning patterns, teachers, patterns, and classroom activities. . . . The students and I felt that we were in a real work setting, doing something that mattered. (1987, 218)

This model for constructing authentic work could be adapted to April's class. April could help her young readers study issues of gender and culture subtended by the texts they read in class, *The Merchant of Venice, The Good Earth,* and the controversial, *Woman Warrior.*

It could be argued from a Kristevan perspective that in responding to *Woman Warrior,* April's students are identifying too much with the Chinese-American victim turned warrior. Because they identify with her, they see themselves in her place, threatened and misunderstood. Kristeva writes that fear and hatred for immigrants can result from the oppression of foreigners triggering in natives their own feeling of foreignness, of being "other," of being displaced, of not fitting in, as though their problems were even worse than the immigrants' (see *Strangers to Ourselves,* chapter 1). Given this sense of threat that her young eighth grade girls seem to feel, April drops the book in retreat. But she is not happy with the romanticized texts the girls like and she thinks the girls should be concerned about issues of racism and sexism.

Like Branscombe's class, April could send the girls out to do research on the experiences of females in different cultures. They could interview both males and females of different ages so that comparisons could be made between gender experiences in different ethnic groups. They could talk to relatives, friends, neighbors, professionals, owners and patrons of businesses and restaurants, and churchgoers from diverse ethnic groups about their lives. They could ask them about their experiences and expectations in life, their roles, what others expect of them, about their education, their hobbies, sports, and pastimes.

After their field work, the readers would be in a better position to contextualize the various texts on females they read in class. The texts of the female characters, Portia, O-lan, and the Woman Warrior could more purposefully take a measured role as transitional objects in the lives of April's students.

A community research project on the intersections of culture and gender for this class has a number of advantages. First, it is an active empowering way for girls to get out into the world and construct knowledge for themselves and for others. Second, "foreignness"— because it is being sought in the study, becomes attractive, rather than merely threatening, and so more likely to be introjected. In an important sense, allowing foreignness to be introjected is a primary requisite for learning.

To follow up their empirical work, April's students could write essays, articles, scripts, autobiographies.

Students might also formulate their own questions about migrations. If people have always moved and yet always honored borders, who draws these borders and how do they get redrawn? What border problems does the international community wrestle with today? What immigration problems must the United States address today? What do students know about proposition 187 in California?

They can write autobiographies of their own migrations. What is it like to move to a new community or change schools? What do philosophers, sociologists, and psychologists write about the self-other identity issues that the subject of immigration subtends? Students can do interviews with family members or ancestors who had immigration experiences. Have they seen films or read other texts about the topic? What were their impressions?

What is it like for Pearl Buck to write about China as a Caucasian woman? They might write a critical analysis of the film starring Caucasians and made for white audiences. They might read film and television criticism from the 1950s to get a sense of the aesthetic and political preoccupations of the time. What borders does the heroine of Woman Warrior cross? They might do research on the history of Chinese immigration to the United States, especially at the turn of the century, when Chinese came in large numbers to help Americans tame the West with their labor. What is similar and different about the Chinese immigration experience from other migrations to the United States? Ronald Takaki's *From Different Shores* is a good source. How did women tend to fare in these migrations? They might read another narrative about women' roles in Chinese immigration to Canada in the early twentieth century, *The Concubine's Children* by Denise Chong.

Students might look at what accounts for the different artistic visions about the same topic by Amy Tan in *The Joy Luck Club* and by Hong-Kingston. What textual boundaries does Hong-Kingston shatter to make her point? Could this be seen as effective? What gender borders are crossed in these texts? Why does the metaphor of "voice" emerge across so many texts about women? They might consider Mary Belenky's "silent" way of knowing in *Womens' Ways of Knowing*, Michele Fine's *Disruptive Voices*, and Hong-Kingston's secret versus public voices.

Finally, how do the girls in April's class feel about their own ability to speak in various settings, private or public? In what institutions do they have "voice?" or would they like to have "voice?" Whether April were to have students wait to read *Woman Warrior* in later years, or whether another text is preferable, students may be glad for her partnership with them in asking these worldly questions. How do they want to take their place in the world as contributors? How will they learn to take strength from the heroines in literature and life and to confront the ghosts and demons as well?

PARTING WORDS

Language comes from childhood. This truth cuts across our theories, our research, and our teaching. A less obvious truth is that language comes from motherhood and fatherhood. In our eagerness to outgrow our parents, especially our mothers, it is more difficult to admit language's tie to them. Parenthood is not the same for everyone, we do not understand its complexity very well, and it is constantly changing. Nevertheless, motherhood and fatherhood are as much institutions as our schools, legislatures, churches and our courts are. Freud got us thinking of our parents as limitless countries, and Kristeva reimagined the maternal relationship as both wildly joyous and painstakingly structured. The way our parents nourish and regulate our body and our relations will nurture our imaginations as well as our language.

But the realm of the private realm is not the walled-off garden of Rousseau's fantasies and the public realm is not a perfectly ordered one with a predictable set of rules. Our children's language must travel from the private to the public and back to the private and out again. Our job as educators is to construct a curriculum that contains these passages between attachment and individuation: a vibrant literacy that links love, imagination, and action.

APPENDICES

THE TEACHERS' AUTOBIOGRAPHIES

APPENDIX A

PHILIP'S AUTOBIOGRAPHICAL WRITING

AUTOBIOGRAPHY #1

My memories of first being read to are before naps when I may have been about three years old. Although there were probably many books involved, there are only a number of titles I remember. Since I cannot remember the details of the books, there must have been something about them that has made an indelible impression. In some intuitive way, specific images must have resonated within me. For one, *The Pokey Little Puppy*. There was something about the puppy tunneling under that fence. Something about tunneling underground. Inside self. The mystery of deeper consciousness. At the time, I had not the words; but I had the feeling in my teeth, in my jaw—still do. I remember the puppy as being brown and white, and tunneling under that fence. The rest is gone.

Usually my mother read to me. As now when I read to my three-year-old Godchild, the communication is mostly nonverbal—and my remembrances, preverbal. I feel anxiety and peace of falling asleep, and comfort of voice, and reassurance of presence. I enter that distant place far inside that emerges far away.

Babaar, the hefalumps—one named. I suppose I identified with them—their size, their strength, their intelligence, their gentleness. I recall a ship voyage from France to America. Waving good-bye separations—catching in the throat, in the heart. Future adventures and past ties. Ocean swell and salt sea breeze. Opportunities and longings.

Looking at pictures, listening to voice. The story is alive in those pages. Open them up; let it out. Every day the same stories—familiar friends. Memorize and read along.

Babaar—colorful hot air balloons. Hefalumps floating with the breeze. Power and grace and celebration. (A retrospection: How could they have floated with the breeze and not have felt the air on their faces? Not have heard the wind?) Floating free—imagination. Tiny people, miniature villages, vast horizons. There and here together. See yourself floating up there into nothing. See your house sitting down their shrinking away. Voice brings you back. Wake and sleep.

The Taxi That Hurried was my favorite. I remember no details— something about getting some people, a family, to somewhere. Something about a little pull-down seat on the side for children. Fragments of images. Mostly the pictures of the taxi—intense colors: yellow, read, black. Again that feeling in the jaw—palpable feeling, frozen in time. Then and now.

Why do writers of children's books have so many nonhuman agents? Where are the people? Even *The Little Engine That Could.* Any why do I remember *these* stories?

After college, I was surprised to find the series of Little Golden Books in stores. When I picked them up, the memories-feelings were intense. On the back of the book was a list of titles in the collection; I remember having remembered most of them. Now I remember only these. I have saved my collection. I vaguely remember reading them from time to time for confidence of a more simple, comforted, reassured time. I gave my first books to my stepchildren. They were getting a little too old for first books, but the giving seemed important— reconnecting time. Now I'm giving my later childhood books to my Godchildren. They are getting a little too young, but . . .

I must have been reading before first grade. Reading wa a mystical adventure o discovery, joy. Getting a story, people, feelings, ideas from page to mind. A simple miracle—human. In the first grade—Miss Jarvis—I learned phonics; I could do that. I learned to read—one word at a time. Still do. I remember anxiety and stress. I couldn't name the feelings. I could perform. The fun was gone. Reading for school was usually work. Reading for me was always pleasure.

When I was seven or eight, I used to go to my aunt's for lunch. She would read *Andersen's Fairy Tales*; I remember "The Tinderbox." I loved to hear the story, over and over, I remember the soldier finding the tinderbox and calling on the dogs with eyes as big as saucers. Of all the tales, something about that one feels good in my chest.

During my elementary school years, I loved to go to the library to check out books. Especially in the summer, just for fun. I remember *The*

Ted Williams Story, and *The Autobiography of Ben Franklin*, and a book about space exploration and Werner Von Braun—pre-Sputnik. A book about baseball records: Who pitched two consecutive no hit games? Johnny VanDer Meer. Who completed an unassisted triple play? I can't remember. I would read for hours. Time would suspend. I'd read at bedtime—especially at bedtime—long into the next morning. My imagination would reach and gather and grow. School assigned readings were had to's, not want to's—a horrifying thought for a teacher.

AUTOBIOGRAPHY #2

In high school, I enjoyed some required readings: tenth grade, *As You Like It*; eleventh grade, *Macbeth* (I just heard a news report on *All Things Considered* that today is the 947th anniversary of the date Macbeth killed Duncan); twelfth grade, *The Tale of Two Cities*. But mostly, school assignments were tedious; free reading was free.

In high school, for book reports I remember reading books that I could choose. I enjoyed choosing good books by good authors. Sinclair Lewis—*Mainstreet* and *Babbit*. John Steinbeck—*Of Mice and Men*. Hemingway—*The Old Man and the Sea*. Aldous Huxley—*Brave New World*. I enjoyed exploring new worlds. New experiences. New ideas.

When I was in high school, my older brother was in college taking English literature survey courses. I remember reading all the books. Robert Penn Warren—*The Cave*. William Faulkner—*Absolom, Absolom*. Ernest Hemingway—*The Sun Also Rises, For Whom the Bell Tolls*. George Orwell—*1984*. I would read for hours, feeling self important reading college books. I would stay up half the night reading. I don't recall such enthusiasm about my required high school books.

Of course, I always read the sports section of the newspaper. That was required reading in my neighborhood.

There was something mystical about reading all those great books. I seem to have learned more about life from fiction, more about people from characters. There must have been many more novels, but they all merge.

If I had been looking forward to going to college to read more college books, I was in for a big disappointment. When I was required to read, reading became tedious. In college and even in grade school—the first time—I remember mostly not reading the books. Instead of feeling involved and lost in time, I felt distracted and out of time. While reading for myself, I was living in an emerging present. I couldn't tell the dancer from the dance.

While reading for myself, I read every book I could find by Herman Hesse, Conan Doyle, Kurt Vonnegut, Ian Fleming, John Barth, Richard Brautigan. Remembering reading in those gone days I feel energized, enthused. Remembering reading in those school days, I feel not.

After grad school, my teaching at Koinonia was a time for reading and sharing. I read Merleau-Ponty and Edward Albee and Wallace Stevens and Samuel Beckett and e. e. cummings and Henrik Isben and Jean-Paul Sartre. We shared and talked with students and other community members. Time was creative with drama, with art, with philosophy, with music, with poetry.

Then the hiatus: graduate school—the second time around; graduate school—the third time around; and, now, graduate school—the fourth (last? . . . not likely) time around. More about in the next installment.

The most significant reading in my late adolescence was *Winnie the Pooh*, and *Tigger Too*.

AUTOBIOGRAPHY #3

I'm learning not to let the words get in the way.

When I was on the faculty at Koinonia in 1972, I was invited to talk with a troop of Girl Scouts at Goucher College. One bright, crisp, springtime day I was gazing at hundreds of fifteen-year-old shining morning faces wondering, "What do I say?" So, I read to them: [A poem by e. e. cummings about how much more life is than the words we can use to convey them.]

Along with e. e. cummings, I could say, "i thank You God for most this amazing day." Hundreds of fifteen-year-old shining morning faces listening, sharing, living. We talked about organic gardening, quantum physics, mathematics, nature. Afterwards, girls scouting the grounds: seeing the world in a leaf. Girls raiding the college bookstore, buying cummings's poetry, reading together. Sharing favorites, I read: [He quotes lines from cummings's "you shall above all things be glad and young.]

That was fifteen years ago. Those girl scouts are fifteen-year-olds times two. How many are reading to their Brownies? Since half their lives ago I haven't much thought about that day. no

w
i'm
(t)
her
e

I'm learning not to let the words get in the way.

I knew once a woman at Goucher—an English major. Sh(w)e liked to read together. We read *Rosencrantz and Guildenstern Are Dead*: "Words, words. They're all we have to go on." On rainy afternoons she'd read to me Dylan Thomas, *Under Milkwood*. I sometimes wonder if she would have known what an old fool I've become. . . . A few years after college I saw her once when she visited me at Koinonia. I hope Patti has a daughter.

I'm learning not to let the words get in the way.

Koinonia was founded in the early 1950s as a Christian missionary center for teaching reading—the Frank Lauback literacy method: "Each one teach one." When I first started visiting Koinonia in the sixties, it was starting to change; when I joined the faculty in the seventies, it changed. We integrated the intentional community—not commune—with an alternative semester college curriculum for students to receive credit from their colleges and for adults to take a sabbatical from life.

We read with and to each other. One reading group was meditation or vespers. Traditionally, the leader read the Bible. I was somewhat controversial by reading—may God forbid—poetry. I would begin by reading *The Gospel According to John*—thus lulling my unwary audience into a false sense of security: "In the beginning was the Word, and the Word was with God, and the Word was God." Old ladies would smile angelically and begin to nod off. I would continue: "You cannot step twice into the same river, for fresh waters are ever flowing in upon you." A few eyes would start to reopen. "Time present and time past / Are both perhaps present in time future, / And time future contained in time past."

Eyes begin to search out each other as if to ask, "Ecclesiastes?" or "1 Corinthians?"

"No, dearies," I think to myself, "'Burnt Norton.'"

Who's to say that T. S. Eliot isn't as sacred as Saint John?

[Philip quotes lines from "Burnt Norton" about how words cannot fix reality since like music, they move as much as life does.]

I'm learning not to let the words get in the way.

We had other contexts for reading together. One semester I offered a poetry seminar on Wallace Stevens—enrollment, one. Cindy, a recent graduate of St. Timothy's, reciprocated by teaching me operatic singing, giving me horseback riding lessons, and beating me at tennis. I figure I came out ahead. Another semester we read plays— enrollment, all women. I remember a roomful of women of various ages and backgrounds reading *Hedda Gabler* and *A Doll's House*. That semester I offered a poetry writing seminar—enrollment, one. I found myself reading poetry while Mary reciprocated by teaching me how to write poetry, showing me how to cook breakfast for 120 people, and marrying me. I figure I came out ahead, again.

The Koinonia library was small and focused—mostly theological texts. So I opened my literature library to the students. I still go to my bookshelf to get a book I know I had; then I remember that book must have been borrowed. My only consolation lies in the hope that most of my bookseeds were cast on fertile ground. I hope there's another generation out there reading to each other and to their children. Well, each one read to one.

The most enjoyable reading experience was our Saturnight coffee house where I would give readings. I would wear my pink beret and puff on Camel cigarettes-unfiltered, of course. I'd read Emily Dickinson or Robert Frost (or Paul Simon). Then I'd read William Carlos Williams: [Philip cites the lines of Williams' poem, "This Is Just to Say," which concerns an implied domestic relationship. One party writes a formal note to the other asking for forgiveness for eating a plum in the icebox, and describing the temptation.]

Then, I might conclude with Richard Brautigan, "It's Raining in Love."

I'm learning not to let the words get in the way.

I used to read poetry all the time. It made me feel alive we're alive. Today, I picked up some books of poetry and leafed through them. I realize with many intense and conflicting feelings that I haven't read poetry in years—years and years. I feel sad that I haven't and relieved that I am.

The past many years I've been in a How To phase. Practical reading such as *Plumbing for Dummies, Masonry and Concrete Work, Practical Electrical Wiring,* and *Inside the IBM PC* had purpose. Pleasurable reading such as poetry, drama, and fiction had conflict. The only pleasurable reading I did was required for school-teaching or taking and I didn't even read all of that. Reading to write papers was easy. Read the books. Follow the process. Write the paper. Graduate school now and again, and again, and again. Following procedures was easy. I wasn't nurturing myself. I was in reading limbo or Purgatorio on my journey to reading Paradiso, regained.

When my children were young to me, I read to them. Our favorite was *Dr. Seuss.* The narrative didn't seem very important; the sounds did, and the illustrations. We'd read in bed before lights out, among book-strewn petals. (The floor around my chair is book-strewn now.) We'd laugh out the day's tensions and feel relapsation. After lights out, Rachel and Matt would take their books to Whoville and read themselves to sleep with flashlights.

When my Godchildren were young to me, I read to them. Our favorites were dinosaur books. When Zak was four, he knew more about dinosaurs than I'll ever know. We'd look at the illustrations, and Zak would name dinosaurs I'd never heard of. Then he'd explain that this one used to be called "thus" because of some anatomical feature, but not due to recent fossil discoveries it's called "so"—very interesting, Zachariah. Don't ask me the names. When Kaz was two, she'd grab a handful of books and dump herself and them into my lap. Then I'd read. First, she would turn the pages—randomly. The fact of this anomaly didn't seem to matter. Next, she would identify the animals, objects, and colors—randomly. Again, no matter. Finally, Kaz would squirm, laugh, wrap her arms around my neck, rub cheeks, and pull my ear—randomly. These activities mattered, most of all. Often as now, I can feel Kaz in my lap, arms around my neck. I can smell her baby's breath. My shoulders relax, my breathing deepens, my heart rate slows. Then, as now, my eyes tear. I miss my Kaziah.

I'm learning not to let the words get in the way.

What I've come to know:

Reading connects people, not as much with the author as with each other.

How I've come to know it:

I don't remember most of the poems I read to the Girl Scouts then. Now I remember the fifteen-year-old look on the fact of the fifteen-year-old Girl Scout when she returned from the college bookstore holding her own copy of e. e. cummings' poetry.

I don't remember most of Dylan Thomas's *Under Milkwood* then. Now I remember half a life ago a rain gray day and Patti's voice, reading.

I don't remember most of *Hedda Gabler* then. Now I remember the energy and the family of my women-filled study.

I don't remember most of the books I shared with my children then. Now I remember my children who, long away and far ago, feel closer to me than hands and feet.

AUTOBIOGRAPHY #4

In the Resistance: Reading *A Farewell to Arms*

"There were mists over the river and clouds on the mountain and the trucks splashed mud on the road and the troops were muddy and wet in their capes; their rifles were wet and under their capes the two leather cartridge boxes on the front of the belts, gray leather boxes heavy with the packs of clips of thin, long 6.5 millimeter cartridges, bulged forward under the capes so that the men, passing on the road, marched as though they were six months gone with child" (p. 4).

Birth and death. Irreconcilables. The ultimate human paradox.

I have resisted writing this autobiographical essay. Why?

A Farewell to Arms: no more war? Or no more individual power? Arms symbolize power, ability, freedom. Raising arms in anger, joy, or love. Bound or missing arms symbolize impotence, disability, constraint.

A fantasy: A suniful beauty day. I'm driving on country road. My car flips. I am unhurt. My face rests on the soft grass. I smell the earth. Mozart's Exultate Ubilate plays on the radio. Flowers are buzzing. Bees are blooming. A shower passes. The earth dampens and warms. The sky blues. A rainbow sprouts. Water trickles along a furrow where lies my face. My arms are pinned to my sides. I drown.

"The forest of oak trees on the mountain beyond the town was gone. The forest had been green in the summer when we had come into the town but now there were the stumps and the broken trunks and the ground torn up" (p. 6).

A reality: A cold winterful night, 1972. I've been reading Wallace Stevens: [Philip cites Stevens's "The Snow Man." The poem identifies ones' own human body with cold and snowy trees in winter.]

Walking through the Kiononia meadow. Midnight sky, clear and crisp. Stars, dancing brightly, feeling as close as home and as far as forever. Trees rustling in the wind. Trees never say, "I am cold." The cold passes through me; I do not feel it. Touching the tree, feeling its consciousness. Trees have wisdom which passeth human understanding. Trees communicate. Looking through star-filled branches. Insignificant/Magnificent. One with the universe; absolutely isolated. Unity. Birth/Separation. Death/Unity. Some nows I am in that then space.

[Philip includes the text of William Carlos Williams's poem, "Young Sycamore." This poem, too, compares a tree's trunk and its branches to one's human body.]

I know an old sycamore near the willow stream. We have togethered one annual. Its trunk stands straight and strong—earth rooted. It has a mind of winter. A consciousness of its nature transcending conscious nature. Living eternity in the moment present.

"The river ran behind us and the town had been captured very handsomely but the mountains beyond it could not be taken and I was very glad the Austrians seemed to want to come back to the town some time, if the war should end, because they did not bombard it to destroy it but only a little in a military way" (p. 5). What is the military way? Humanity's inhumanity to humanity. "People lived on it and there were hospitals and cafes and artillery up side streets and two bawdy houses, one for troops and one for officers."[5]

And man's dehumanity of wo/man hisself. I've never experienced nor understood how the biological drive can drive over the humanizing drive. Have others never understood how it cannot?

"She was looking at me in the dark. I was angry and yet certain, seeing it all ahead live the moves in a chess game" (p. 26). How can a person manipulate another person? Where is integrity and authenticity?

> "She looked at me, 'and you do love me?'
> 'Yes.'
> 'You did say you loved me, didn't you?'
> 'Yes,' I lied. 'I love you.' I had not said it before."

> . . .

> "I did not love Catherine Barkley nor had I any idea of loving her. This was a game, like bridge, in which you said things instead of playing cards. Like bridge you had to pretend you were playing for money or playing for some stakes. Nobody had mentioned what the stakes were."

> . . .

> "She looked down at the grass.
> 'This is a rotten game we play, isn't it?'
> 'What game?'
> 'Don't be dull.'

> . . .

> 'Do you always know what people think?'
> 'Not always. But I do with you. You don't have to pretend you love me. That's over for the evening.' . . .
> 'But I do love you.'
> 'Please let's not lie when we don't have to.'" (Pp. 30–31)

When I first read this dialogue, I must have been about fifteen years old. The deception bothered me then as much as now. But I'm still not sure if it's self-deception or other-deception or both. How can people live in the world without integrity and authenticity? How can

I understand others whose experiences and perspectives so differ from mine? How can Frederick Henry be such a self-absorbed dunce?

"I went out the door and suddenly I felt lonely and empty. I had treated seeing Catherine very lightly, I had gotten somewhat drunk and had nearly forgotten to come but when I could not see her there I was feeling lonely and hollow" (p. 41). I feel uncomfortable that Henry is not in touch with his feelings. Conflicts are difficulty to reconcile.

"The sun was going down and looking up along the bank as we drove I saw the Austrian observation balloons above the hills on the other side dark against the sunset"(p. 46).

Matt, my auto mechanic son, took me to the Air and Space Museum. Matt showed me the 24-cylinder 2,400 horse power engines and explained how they work. We saw an exhibit of hot air balloons, the first circa 1750. How exhilarating to be the first to fly. What a giant step for humankind. What impressed me the most: within a few years, humans were using balloons to bomb other humans. [Philip quotes e. e. cummings's poem, "pity this busy monster manunkind." The poem laments the world of nature cultured and victimized by humans.]

In the dawn of the twentieth century, the Wright brothers pioneered powered flight. It didn't take long to see the WWI flying aces' planes—bombing people.

With quantum physics, technology exploded in quantum leaps—the power and the glory that were created during WWII. And to what end? To what end? A proud grandpa shows his childgrand the plane he flew in the war, in the good old days. "Bombing houses, kids, women and villages." Lest we forget—the Enola Gay.

Then the rocket age took off. Satellites and space stations.

The creation and the energy that has invested air and space. To what end? To what end?

"Through the other noise I heard a cough, then came the chuh-chuh-chuh-chuh—then there was a flash, as when a blast furnace door is swung open, and the roar that started white and went red and on and on in a rushing wind. I tried to breathe but my breath would not come and I felt myself rush bodily out of myself and out and out and out and all the time bodily in the wind. I went out swiftly, all of myself, and I knew I was dead and that it had all been a mistake to think you just died. Then I floated, and instead of going on I felt myself slide back. I breathed and I was back" (p. 54).

I have been out of my body in the otherwhere. There is a longing to be, misplaced in time.

"I sat up straight and as I did so something inside my head moved like the weights on a doll's eyes and it hit me inside in back of my eyeballs. My legs felt warm and wet and my shoes were wet and warm inside. I knew that I was hit and leaned over and put my hand on my knee. My knee wasn't there. My hand went in and my knee was down on my shin" (p. 55).

When I was in high school, my friend Marty played lacrosse for another school. Marty was a superior athlete. Fast. Strong. Built like an Olympic statute. In a lacrosse game, an opponent body blocked his knee. Surgery. Rehabilitation. Marty was not a superior athlete, dragging one leg behind. Even on one leg, Marty was superior to many.

When I was teaching high school, my friend-spouse Mary fell ice skating and injured her knee. Arthroscopic surgery, a few days rest, and Mary was back to normal. In her hospital room after surgery, Mary's roommate commented how caring and supportive I was. I've never revealed how anxious and frightened I was. I wouldn't abnormally fear breaking a foot, an arm, or even a leg. But I'm petrified about knees. Maybe due to "fight or flight"—I'm a world class distancer.

When I was coaching high school lacrosse, an opponent slipped in the mud and fell into Richard's knee. His leg broke. His knee cap slid around the side of his leg. (This is painful to write.) In the emergency room, the doctor made several vainful attempts to replace Richard's knee. The following fall, Richard sat out the season. The following winter, Richard wrestled. The following spring, Richard played lacrosse; he carried the team. The following fall, Richard played football.

One past summer morning while I was jogging, my legs started to hurt, and I started to bitch. Then I saw an old man returning home from grocery shopping. He pushed himself along in a home-made chair with wheels. He had no legs. And I thought, "What am I bitching about?" Then I thought of Marty, whose high-school aged son I was tutoring in writing that summer. Marty was probably home. When his sons were little boys, Marty contracted multiple sclerosis. While I had been celebrating at the Shakespeare Institute and running around the quad, Marty had been out of his home only five times all summer because he couldn't breathe the outside air. I thanked God that my legs hurt.

We take our immortality for granted. We expect to live forever. Life is fragile. Tenuous.

"I slept heavily except once I woke sweating and scared and then went back to sleep trying to stay outside of my dream. I woke for good long before it was light and heard roosters crowing and stayed on awake until it began to be light. I was tired and once it was really light I went back to sleep again" (p. 88).

When I was a senior in college, I used to stay up all night and go to sleep at dawn; then wake up for supper. Around midnight, I'd take a group to the Top Hat. The straws said, "Eat, drink and chat at the Top Hat." We'd play the pinball machines and listen to "Carroll County Accident" on the jukebox.

We'd go to the hardware store and get metal tubing to make a blow gun. Then we'd bombard the next door fraternity house with wet toilet paper. In the afternoons after classes we'd shoot at cars. Convertibles were in open season. I used to be bad. One cool, sunny, spring afternoon, a car stopped in a row of traffic at the light. The window on the passenger side was cracked open several inches. From the second floor window, all I would see were a pair of attractive legs under a short, flowery spring dress. As she waited for the light to change, her left leg was raised and slightly turned out. Her right leg was down, foot on the brake. The sunlight glistened on the red leather seat between her creamy thighs. The traffic light turned green. She flexed her right leg to step on the gas. I shot my wad. Through the passenger window. Splat. As her car accelerated, I saw, against a background of red, a wad of wet, white toilet paper nestled between her lovely thighs.

"That night a bat flew into the room through the open door that led onto the balcony and through which we watched the night over the roofs of the town" (p. 101).

When I was a senior in college, the night before my final final, a bat invaded my space. Stump and I put on lacrosse helmets and gloves; then we attacked with lacrosse sticks. We trapped the sucker in the guest bedroom and barred the door. I was living on the third floor of my grandfather's house. Since he was a doctor, we searched his office for supplies. I got out the blow gun and made darts with hypodermic needles. Once, we made a glancing hit. Then, in desperation, we soaked cotton swabs in alcohol to make flaming darts. We almost incinerated a poster of Janis Joplin. By daybreak we were all tiring— including the bat. Somehow we trapped the fiend on a board and put a bucket over him. We took the monster into the middle of traffic and snatched off the bucket. He wasn't there! Then, in horror, we remembered: we had left open the guest room door.

"You're pretty wonderful.' (Henry said)

'No I'm not. But life isn't hard to managed when you've nothing left to lose.'

("Freedom's just another word for nothing left to lose.")

'I'm going to have a baby, darling. It's almost three months along. You're not worried, are you? Please please don't. You mustn't worry.' . . .

'People have babies all the time. Everybody has babies. It's a natural thing'" (pp. 137–138).

The last year I coached women's basketball, in 1983, at the beginning of the season my power forward came to practice and said that she wouldn't be able to play that year. "Why not?" I asked.

She explained, "I'm pregnant." But she added that she would like to help out at practices. One morning we were shorthanded to scrimmage, so Alethia (not her real name) volunteered to help. As soon as someone passed her the ball, I blew the whistle and yelled, "Violation!"

"What's the matter?" she complained.

I explained, "Too many players on the court." For weeks, Alethia ran around at practices laughing and telling everybody, "Too many players on the court."

I love irony. I have no biological children. And I never will. When I married Mary, she had borne three children, had adopted one, and had suffered many miscarriages. I have felt anxious and overawed about conceiving child. Now that I feel all's right with the world; I won't.

At our twentieth college reunion, I hosted Heide and Gary, friends I hadn't seen for fifteen years. They have been married for nearly twenty years and had been trying unsuccessfully, to have a baby. Now in their forties, they were despairing. Last summer after the Shakespeare Institute, they invited me to visit. When I gave Heide a hug, I knew she was pregnant. I don't know how I knew, but I knew. Years ago at Kiononia, before supper one night, I snuck up behind Betsy and gave her a hug. I knew Betsy was pregnant. Two weeks later she made the announcement. Heide told me that she was pregnant and that she had previously suffered two miscarriages. I visited for the weekend, and fifteen years' absence felt like fifteen days.' Rachel's emergence is expected near the end of February.

Maybe my many students my many years are not my children. When I was in tenth grade, I knew I wanted to be a high school English teacher. When I was a senior in college, I realized I knew.

I love irony. When I was adolescent, my friends called me Daddy Otts.

"I know the night is not the same as the day: that all things are different, that the things of the night cannot be explained in the day, because they do not then exist, and the night can be a dreadful time for lonely people once their loneliness has started. . . . If people bring so much courage to this world the world has to kill them to break them, so of course it kills them. The world breaks everyone and afterward many are strong at the broken places. But those that will not break it kills. It kills the very good and the very gentle and the very brave impartially. If you are none of these you can be sure it will kill you too but there will be no special hurry" (p. 249).

As I am writing, on the radio is a broadcast *Remembering Anne Frank*:

Wednesday, 3 May 1944

Dear Kitty,
What, oh what, is the use of the war? Why can't people live peacefully together? Why all the destruction? Why should millions be spent daily on the war, and yet there's not a penny available for medical services, artists, or poor people? Why do some people have to starve while there are surpluses rotting in other parts of the world? Oh, why are people so crazy? There is in people simply an urge to kill, to murder and rage, and until all mankind without exception undergoes a great change, wars will be waged. Everything that has been built up, cultivated, and grown will be destroyed and disfigured, after which mankind will have to begin all over again.

Yours,
Anna

A few years after college, I was visiting Mark and Beth in Philadelphia. Mark, another college friend, was a senior medical student. I left to visit Stump, and Beth and Mark went to the park to enjoy the autumn sunshine. That night I got a call: Mark was dead.

It must be a mathematical function of aging that a person experiences more death. But it never gets easier. Especially with children. When Bobby C. was in my ninth-grade class, he was under treatment for a congenital heart defect. Bobby was brilliant and sensitive. When he was in my eleventh-grade class, one spring Sunday he was playing baseball when he died. Charley played on our football team I coached. I remember Charley was always laughing and celebrating life. His freshman year in college, one night Charley developed a fever. At the infirmary, they couldn't bring down his fever. By morning, Charley died. Robert was the senior quarterback on the football team. He wasn't a gifted athlete, but he was dedicated. Robert helped everybody, even the junior quarterback who beat him out at mid-season. During the summer after graduation, Robert was earning college tuition working for an armored car company. One morning in a Columbia Mall parking lot, they found Robert in the back of the armored car—shot in the head.

One night around midnight while I was passing Kaziah's bedroom, she awoke crying she had to go to the bathroom. Her parents were busy elsewhere, so I took sleepyhead to the bathroom. When I put Kaz back into her crib, half-asleep she reached her arms around my neck saying, "I love you." After Kaz fell asleep, I watched her breathing imperceptibly. The miracle of life. And the tenuous cord connecting life.

"I went out into the hall with two babies and closed doors all down the corridor. It smelled of hospital. I sat on the chair and looked at the floor and prayed for Catherine" (p. 314). . . . "And what if she should die? She won't die. People don't die in childbirth nowadays. That was what all husbands thought. Yes, but what if she should die? She won't die. She's just having a bad time." . . . "Why would she die? What reason is there for her to die?" (320)

"'I'm not brave any more, darling. I'm all broken. They've broken me. I know it now'" (p. 323).

"I had no feeling for him. He did not seem to have anything to do with me. I felt no feeling of fatherhood.

'Aren't you proud of your son?' the nurse asked . . .

'No,' I said, 'he nearly killed his mother'" (p. 325).

"'What's the matter with the baby?' I asked (the nurse).

'Didn't you know?'

'No.'

'He wasn't alive.'

'He was dead?'

'The couldn't start him breathing. The cord was caught around his neck or something.'

'So he's dead'" (pp. 326–327).

I know an actual Cathy. After her son Patrick was born, they would visit and Patrick would sleep on my chest: he listening to my heart, I listening to his breath. Patrick's baby's breath is sweet his lifetime later. I can feel him on my heart as a ten year day. Cathy laid her second baby in the crib one night. In the morning her baby was dead.

I cannot imagine a life lost.

"'Mrs. Henry has had a hemorrhage.'

Catherine looked at me and smiled. I bent down over the bed and started to cry.

. . .

It seems she had one hemorrhage after another. They couldn't stop it. I went into the room and stayed with Catherine until she died. She was unconscious all the time, and it did not take her very long to die'" (pp. 330–331).

Before I met Mary, she had birthed a son Andrew, Matt's baby brother. Andrew had a congenital heart weakness and in a month died in Mary's arms. I never held Andrew to my heart. He would have been our child. Mary wrote a poem comparing Andrew to a spring crocus— blooming for a moment, then dying. Last year after the snow melted, I was feeling emptiness in my belly. Then as I saw the blooms I realized that this was the time of year that Andrew died. He would have been sixteen. I wish the life unshared with my never-child.

Philip's Final Reflective Paper on Reading and Teaching

In lesson plan #2, I mention that the plot is a sequence of events based on cause and effect relationships. In whose eyes are these cause and effect relationships? Are they debatable?

In the handout requiring students to rearrange a list of events, the cause-effect relationships are limited. In the home assignment asking students to select events and identify their causes, students are free to apply their own points of view and to support their perspectives.

On study sheet #4, under the category of mood, I ask, "In the first two chapters one might get the feeling that. . . ." Do I mean "one" to be a universal one or you or the student who is answering the question?

In editing the curriculum guide, I overlooked that "one." I mean one to be you, the student who is answering the question. Also, I am interested in the mood among the characters within the text and how this mood relates to the student's mood however, this intention is unclear (to me also).

Most students' written responses state: "boring," "dull," or "uninteresting." One student wrote: "Something is going to happen to change everyone's lives."

In discussion I ask, "What feelings do you get at the beginning so far?"

Dermaine: "The story has no meaning."

Erik: "Lennie and Curley might get into a fight."

I ask students to define "feeling." What are feeling words, emotions? Responses: boring, sorrow, dislike, hate, dull.

I say: "There are two different feelings going on here. There's the feeling that you're having, which might be boredom or dull; and then there's the feeling that's going on in the story, which might be a different feeling. What feelings do you see going on among the characters in the story?"

Responses: George, Lennie, and Curley—intense; Candy—sad; Lenny—afraid; Curley—jealous.

I summarize: "All these feelings that are going on in the story contribute to the mood of the story."

I missed significant opportunities. Was student's boredom real or feigned, jaded? I know from their responses throughout that they were involved and responsive. What about students who hadn't read any meaning into the story? Most important, how could I relate student's feelings to character's feelings? After all, this relationship is one of my (stated) primary objectives. So why didn't I explore the feelings? Pressure to cover the required curriculum and personal discomfort with contrary and unreconciled feelings. Based on my autobiographies, I avoid conflict (and rejection) while encouraging reconciliation, empathy, and other perspectives. I need to acknowledge an empathize with others' feelings. I need to become conscious that I feel discomfort and that it's all right to feel discomfort and that I can reconcile my emotional response with my subsequent actions. I need to reconcile between conscious intention and emotional reality.

On study sheet #5, I ask students to identify desires, conflicts, and complications in the novel. Do I consider these matters of opinion or are there right answers? Can students make a case for their opinion in class or in an essay?

Opinion. Yes.

My responses between student's answers: "That's one reason. Any other reasons? What else? Okay, what kind of a problem? Okay. Anything else that Curley might do to create a problem? Anything else that Curley might do? Those are possible complications."

Worksheets on structural analysis. I cover the literary terminology that is required on the final exam. I prefer to minimize explicit terminology for analysis and to use analysis to encourage interpretation. Metaphor is needed for literary language. Foreshadowing requires inference and interpretation. Structural analysis as an (oversimplified) construct in itself is counter processive to interpretation.

In lesson plan #4, I ask students to write three "what if's" that would change the course of events in the novel.

I ask what would happen if you change one event in a casual chain of events. Central to my curriculum is student's making inferences and predictions. With responses such as, "That's a possibility," I encourage students to speculate; then I require students to support their hypotheses with evidence from the text. I am not as clear about how to respond when students go beyond the text to support their hypotheses with personal experiences. When I understand how their personal experiences support inferences based on evidence in the text, I see connections. When students' personal experiences seem related to an idiosyncratic interpretation (not clearly based on the text), I feel ambivalence about affirming students' experiences while interpreting the text. Are the "facts" of the text negotiable? Does an individual have the right to an interpretation? Who controls the interpretation(s)? The teacher (authority)? Is the teacher (text) open to interpretation(s)?

I encourage students to venture beyond the text (before and after). In a music imagery writing experience, I ask students to speculate about Lennie's childhood. Students express personal childhood experiences. In an essay, I ask students to speculate about events after the novel and to justify their opinions and values.

Is interpretation teacher-centered, student-centered, or text-centered? I appreciate a dialectical process. This process, for one, requires getting the curriculum out of the way. This process privileges students' discovering interpretation. Therefore, the media (curricula) either encourage or discourage discovery.

In lesson plan #7, does the home assignment to compare Hughes' poem to Steinbeck's novel encourage or coopt interpretation? Do I get original interpretations? Does it lead students toward concensus or diversity? How do I feel about that?

Comparison encourages interpretation by opening spaces among texts and among people. Originality is enhanced by students discovering additional experiences from which to vantage perspectives. My intention is to lead students toward concensus *and* diversity. Inter-textuality leads to inter-views. Rather than creating premature closure around the text, comparison opens creative spaces for interpretation. Comparison inter-connects social/cultural experiences and helps students relate experiences. Langston Hughes's "Dream Deferred" is alluded to by Lorraine Hansberry's "A Raisin in the Sun." Hughes' poem relates to the theme of John Steinbeck's "Of Mice and Men." Steinbeck alludes to Robert Burns's poem "To a Mouse" which contains the lines "The best-laid schemes o' mice and men' Gang aft a-gley." Centuries, continents, and cultures inter-relate.

APPENDIX B

JANE'S AUTOBIOGRAPHICAL WRITING

AUTOBIOGRAPHY #1

Childhood Reading

There are secrets hidden in names. They are the vehicles for the private allegories we form in childhood, whose tenors are generation, self, and time. Nathaniel Hawthorne, whose first purchase with his own money was a copy of *The Faerie Queen*, named his oldest child Una. It is a fair name, he wrote a bit defensively to a friend who had remonstrated against giving a child such a symbolic burden to carry. In it was not, I think, so much Spenser's character as the child Hawthorne had been when he first began to read.

My first daughter was named for two Alices—. One was my great-grandmother and the other was the child heroine of Lewis Carroll's books. To all the world, the name testified allegiance to a family past. That was what respectable people did when they had children; they names them for their ancestors and thus demonstrated that tradition, continuity, all that mattered. But no one knew—this is the first time I have told it to another, not even my daughter knows,—that she was named for a person in a book. Telling her wouldn't have been fair, for the secret of her name had to do with me, not with her, and it would have been taking her name away from her, somehow to tell her. However, it was important to possess her in that way. Because books were more real than life, that fictional Alice could also continue her secret life and, as memorial or embodiment or some child with bony

195

knees and braids, could also become an ancestor with descendants.

It all has to do with family and not-family, my early reading. I am told that I learned to read from having my father read to me. What I remember is a knee, just there, down and to my right, and starch smelling shirt, and a picture on the side of a page, long-necked grainy gray black-lined Alice with the little bottle in her hands. And the rabbit ("Oh, my ears and whiskers!"). It was a voice that was not my father's voice (since the voice is also the words, and these were not the words my father owned, but had a different color, texture, smell, sound of words, a voice that made a place entirely my own, not to be shaped, formed, shared in walls of command and interjection—eat this, wear this, say this, don't.) The voice that made the reading was entirely an adventure of self. Not, either, the words of self, or the words of Jack Wolf, whose home was in the back hall and who visited with me under the grand piano in the livingroom. The voice of reading was a place—or places, since each book had its own voice. I do not know how to evoke those voices, only to name them. Although I long ago lost the ability to live in a book, I have kept the earsight of the voices of reading. *Heart of Darkness* is one voice, *The Blithedale* Romance is another, *The Ambassadors* is another, and so on. Reading is a world of sound, only secondarily now one of sight.

All the voices of the old books. One voice is a barrel with a little pig rolling down the hill at dawn. Another begins, "Once upon a time there were four little rabbits, and their names were Flopsy, Mopsy, Cottontail, and Peter. They lived with their mother in a sandbank underneath the roots of a very large fir tree. One day old Mrs. Rabbit said, 'Now my dear, . . .'" I could, I think, go on for quite a while. Oh, the cat with the twitchy tail! Oh, the dampness and the scurrying! Oh, how I became small, small in a gray-green garden. It is impossible to extricate that earliest reading from the word-ocean in which it swam. My grownups all sang, and so I sang—"The Rose of Tralee" and "Onward Christian Soldiers" and "Swing Low, Sweet Chariot" and "Believe Me, If All Those Endearing Young Charms" were as much a part of reading as the stories my grandmother told me about when she was little, and all are mixed with squares of sunlight in the morning falling on the linoleum nursery-rhyme people on my bedroom floor (there were letters, too, which must have been their names) and that thing on my thumb which was wiry and cold and my tongue could go between the spaces of the coils just a little and by and by the bad taste would go away. At the end of the day when my mother would come home from her work at Macy's, she would get out the black notebook and I would tell her things to write, sometimes doings and sometimes, I think, poems. She would write it down and then read it back to me. But I can't remember that; I have only the notebook, archaeology of buried time.

I don't remember learning to read, or even the earliest things I read. I always was reading, and the early reading is washed away under the billowing waves of childhood reading from later on. I would roller-skate to the library, fifteen city blocks away, and skate home reading the topmost of a pile of books, surfacing for street crossings and the bumpiest of the sidewalks. The first stories I told were a kind of reading, since the book, even if invisible, was in my hands when I read to Jack Wolf or to my dolls, or later to my brother. (But I must have been old enough to really read by them, for I am five years older than he.) I would read to him at night, when we were supposed to be going to sleep, reading the words that unscrolled across the mattress of his upper bunk and also across the back of my head inside, unscrolling like a parchment or a road map. I drew pictures before I could read, and I composed before I could write, and I think I never was not reading something, even if it was the sunlight.

Surely when my father read to me he went away and I went away and some other place came there, and Alice was there, not-I'm not-Daddy in that other place that, Gide was right, one went forward to enter.

I have four children less than eighteen months apart because of another book, *The Bastable Children* by E. Nesbit, which created such a powerful world of family that I, who had been small and powerless in a world of large people, who never knew how to talk to other kids unless they passed the secret test of "What books do you like?"—I always knew I would, when I grew up, replicate Oswald and Dora and Dicky and Noel and H.O. and, yes, there was another girl in that family and her name, too, was Alice.

What have I learned, doing this? I retrieved a few memories I thought I had forgotten—I had forgotten that one of the sisters in the Nesbit book was named Alice, until I started writing the sentence. I can trace the links that lead from sentence to sentence, but they are secret, too, Mostly, I realized what a secret, clandestine, ego-centered act it was (and still is). It is as proprietary as eating, as setting out on solitary trips of exploration, as writing. Sometimes it used to be a knowing gesture—because I was lonely and scared, I was a snob, so I belonged to a select circle of other gawky snobs who dealt in books as partly password and partly conversation—fodder—in other words, books were my substitute for a social life for a long time. They were also a good way of shutting out things you didn't want to see or hear,

like calls to dishes. I am still fairly good at WALKING WHILE READ-
ING, but I no longer try to dry dishes while reading. Beth died with
the dish towel in my hand, and I was all hot-faced and throat-hurting
because I wasn't about to let my mother see me cry. Since my reading
was both defense and bolster, I still have divided and strong impulses
about it. I always want to talk about what I'm reading, but there is too
much vested in such talk. Writing is safer—I can arrange it and close
its gaps and control its expression of feeling. I have noticed this summer that I talk about my reading very imperfectly, not at all like the
kind of talk I am capable of when I am teaching—another sign of its
place in my earliest sense of self. And this writing made clear what I
had ascribed to in theory but never realized, that reading and writing
lie very close together for me and always have. It was also interesting
to watch the sentence structures change here, depending on which age
I was recalling as I wrote this. It's hard not to do an imitation of oneself writing, while writing, isn't it? But I tried not to.

AUTOBIOGRAPHY #2

On Reading

I am reading *Tristam Shandy*; it is so funny that last night in bed I had
to suppress my laughter (Jim was sleeping) and it leaked out of my
eyes and ran down my face. I am reading it in a 1957 paperback edition, pages brittle and brown, and whenever I turn a page, it separates
from the spine. It is useful that way (I can find my place today), but by
the time I have finished the book, it will be demolished. I am literally
reading it to pieces, a process that seems especially appropriate for
Tristam Shandy. What is strange is that I read Sterne's novel in a college
survey course and all I remember from that reading is the black page.
Was it a full page? In this edition it is a little rectangle about one inch
by one-and-a-half inches. So maybe I don't remember that. My memory is like the pages of the book; as fast as I finish a day, a doing, it
detaches itself and disappears. Trying to remember my memories is
like rustling old, loose, disordered pages.

   Here, I started to write, "We were a reading family," but memory
immediately modifies. I *thought* of us as a reading family. My grandmother (who lived with us half of every year) read *The Saturday
Evening Post* every week and *The Reader's Digest* every month; my
father bought books on the subjects he was interested in—Pepys's
Diary, Boswell's Journals, Sandburg's *Lincoln*, books on photography

and the history of the movies. He would read snippets aloud to us when something was especially interesting. My mother, who had been an Intellectual in college, owned books but was too busy cleaning and cooking to read much. I did not read her books, although I remember their faces—Robert Frost and *The Winged Horse*, Haredy and Galsworthy. But it was my mother who began the family tradition of always giving books as presents, two for birthdays and two for Christmas; and, as I told you before, I was read to from very young and was taken to the library once a week long before I was old enough to walk the thirteen blocks to get there alone. (So my mother must have been reading, too—surely she didn't walk us there just for children's books. There is a lot about my mother that I have suppressed from those days.)

My reading method was simple. As soon as I was old enough to go to the library by myself, when I found a book I liked, I would read all of that author's other works. My mother bought me a copy of *Little Women*, brought it home from work one day. (She went back to work when my brother, five years younger than I, was four or five. Could I have been ten? Or eleven?) After I had laughed and cried my way through *Little Women*, I read all the Alcott I could find. Two memories branch: the first is, how much children learn from reading without knowing they're learning. I inhaled, from *Joy's Boys* and *Eight Cousins* and *Little Men* and *Little Women*, an entire culture. Perhaps I understood the Victorian world so well because it wasn't entirely different from my own. I was raised in a solitary cosmos. My mother, who was only superficially gregarious, was an only child; my father, who was an introvert, was one of two. None of my aunts and cousins lived near. Both my grandmothers, formidable women who stamped my childhood with their tales, were older than the usual grandmother, not only in years, but in culture. My father's mother, born in 1861, remembered the men coming back from the Civil War; my mother's mother, though twenty years younger, was raised on a farm in North Carolina whose customs, transmitted to me in stories of her girlhood, were those of the early nineteenth century. *Tom Sawyer*, *Huck Finn*, *Little Women*, were home country to me. The puritanism, the conscious do-good, self-sacrificing abnegation of women, the moral rectitude, the large meals, the everyday familiarity with death—those were all as familiar as the smell of my grandmother's ironed aprons. None of those fitted very well with the externals of my life, with air-raid drills in the corridors at school, with the subway, with the crowds of girls my own age whom I didn't understand and who had nothing to say to me. What seems strange to me now is that I didn't think about how those things didn't fit together. In a kind of inversion of what I suppose is most children's experience of their lives, I lived in two worlds of which the outer, daily one was the unreal one, and the inner, imaginative one was the reality. The parlor in Marmee's house, or the one from which Alice went through the looking-glass, are more vivid in memory than the five-room Queens apartment in which I grew up.

Isn't it strange how people make pictures in their minds from their reading? For instance, *Little Women*. I haven't read it since childhood, but I can still see its places. The parlor at the March's house is small and dark and brown; the one at Mr. Laurence's is cooler, full of gray and dark green. Both face me—let us call it a north-south orientation. The March's parlor has no windows, but the one at Laurie's has tall floor-to-ceiling windows with a green view and green draperies. Aunt March's parlor, where Jo didn't get to go to Europe (how I *hated* Aunt March for that!) faced east-west and was closely stuffed with dark furniture over which towered a brass bird-cage for the parrot. The scene of Meg's humiliation at the party (belladonna, pinch your cheeks to make them red, a pale-blue-gray silvery dress) had a tall white wall with a gilded mirror. I understand the place where Jo got her hair cut, because that looked like the barber shop down next to the subway where Daddy went; I don't understand the other places. They were similar in quality to places I was familiar with from our summer visits to the farm (my paternal grandparents' dairy farm in upstate New York) and to "Down South" (my great-aunts' and uncles' homes in Durham, N.C.). All those houses were liberations from the suffocation of our apartment. In the summer I had the freedom of great rambling structures with shadowy stairs (two sets, on the farm) and porches, smell of straw matting and creak of wicker, scratchy feel of sun-warmed wood with peeling paint, stiff slippery horsehair sofas, oilclothed kitchen tables (little patches peeling, showing the fabric underneath), pantries, home-canned tomatoes and home-bottled root beer, singed chicken and blueing in laundry rinse water, warm dapple of sunlight or dank dark smell of piano practicing on wet afternoons. But none of the places in Alcott's books were places I knew. None of the furniture was the same, none of the rooms. Unlike real places, the places in books had no peripheries. They were like the places I see on a rehearsal stage, before the set is in place—sharply detailed just where the actors are, and though potentially present everywhere else, fading out towards the edges. This kind of imaginative construction of vision must go on all the time. My classroom *looks* different with every class that enters. There is always a time at the beginning of the year, before the kids have come, when I stand in my empty room and remember last year's classes and see the room like a kaleidoscope rapidly rearranging itself in its proportions and colors. But I haven't answered for myself the question of where the ingredients come from with which I paint the settings of the books I read. The difference in this respect between my childhood reading and my adult reading is not one of degree, but of attention. I still make images so specific that I could (laboriously) draw them after I read, but I don't enter the places myself in the same way I did as a child. I think we must construct them from a mixture of cues. The words themselves, of course; but they give only a general indication. The rest I think must come from the style—the sound and sequence of the words and sentences, as well as some visual equivalence, surely metaphorical, we infer from and give to characters. I think I even do that in fleeting snatches with every stranger who, however briefly, catches my attention—I have a mental setting for the barber and the lady at the dry cleaners too. How amazing that the mind is always painting from raw materials!

A long way above I said that there two branches to the memories of my childhood reading. The other is the patch that leads to the Jackson Heights Public Library, a two-room brick library building ruled over by an empress with a large bosom inside a buttoned dress. She never left the high counter from behind which she rolled the stamp decisively in the back of my books and peered (I was certain) to make sure that I wasn't taking books from the Adult shelves. (You had to be twelve to borrow from the Adult room, and I was timorously cheating by ten.) What did I read? Fortunately the Victorians wrote big books. I went a long time on Dickens and Thackeray, and another spurt on Kipling. All of Jules Verne, all of Dumas. All of Conan Doyle, and all of Nancy Drew. Poe—bad dreams. Since I had no guidance in my reading, I missed people I wish I had read then; I would have loved George Eliot and Walter Scott. My novel-reading dwindled somewhat after I started high school, but that was when I read a lot of poetry—Browning and Shakespeare's sonnets and more Kipling and Housman. Those were my baby-sitting years, and I entered different kinds of worlds in different young parent's apartments. I read Richard Wright and *Quiet Flows the Sun* at one house (1940s socialists, horn-rimmed glasses, not much furniture, nothing to eat in the refrigerator) and *Gone with the Wind* in another (chintz sofa, a rug, and Coca-Cola—my mother said they were flighty). I read some of the Russians in high school—*Brothers K, Anna Karenina*—and, my senior year, a lot of plays. I can remember laughing out loud at *You Can't Take It With You* on the subway on the way to school. The things I read for school I had either read already (*A Tale of Two Cities*) or didn't enjoy and promptly forgot (*Ivanhoe*) and

Silas Marner). The only thing I read in school that I liked was *The Return of the Native*, and thereafter I read through Hardy. Murder mysteries were my junk-food reading then and later; they got me through all my children's early years, a long period in which I was dormant and depressed—but that's another story. But, lord help me, I have read all of Ngaio Marsh and Dorothy Sayers and John Dickson Carr and Raymond Chandler and so on and on. I forgot to mention *Dracula* and Mark Twain. I read *Tom Sawyer* and *Huck Finn* before I was thirteen, then discovered a whole set of Twain in the attic Down South and read most of them. (How did I know they were funny, long before I was old enough to understand or explain their humor? How did a child understand Twain's laughter at childhood? These kinds of questions make me feel that there is an impassable gulf between me and my students. I didn't learn anything about reading in school, so I don't really know how to teach to others what no one taught to me. Perhaps I was too different for my own experiences to be useful in teaching; or perhaps we have passed a cultural divide too wide to cross. Can a woman who remembers a time before there was frozen orange juice or instant coffee speak to sixteen-year-olds in any meaningful way? What questions could I ask to find out if their reading experiences were like mine? I am patient but mystified when they tell me they don't like to read.) Lots of books come to mind, now. I took *Moby Dick* with me to the hospital four times (something about childbirth and large mammals, I guess), but am ashamed to say I still haven't read it all. But I read *War and Peace* at the sandbox in Riverside Park. And I forgot Jane Austen—I had missed her as a child and read her when my kids were babies; about every four years I read through Austen again. And how could I have forgotten the Oz books? A friend of my parents' gave me all his old ones from when he was a child, and they were wonderful reading when I was about ten. And, oh my, Mary Poppins. And the *Blue Fairy Book* and Hans Christian Andersen—unsettling, chilling. And George MacDonald's *The Princess and Curdie*, and Kingsley's *Water Babies*. And of course, E. Nesbit. The books people write for children now are too limited in vocabulary and ideas. Kids can understand hard words, well before they can define them. All those old books taught me, in ways too subtle for denotation, about what it was like to live in other times. I can't justify that knowledge to my students. It doesn't earn one more money (I am certainly a living example of that), and I would find it hard to demonstrate that it makes one a better person. But I would hate to have to live in only the world of my daily occupations. Somewhere in my memory, more accessible than I thought when I started this writing, are generations and multitudes of worlds—colors, sounds, thoughts, feelings, without which I would feel very two-dimensional indeed.

I still react to libraries and second-hand bookstores the way I did as a kid—I can't believe all that good stuff is there for the taking, like a bargain banquet. (If there is a god and a heaven, he will assign me to an unending second-hand bookstore.) The reading I am doing for school now is in a way a return to my youth, since I am for the first time since then reading all of a novelist in great bites. I have just read through all of George Eliot this summer, crying over *Adam Bede*, wishing there were more. I thought of my father all through Hume and Johnson; my mother just wrote me that she finished *Middlemarch* and enjoyed it. In his fifties, my father, who had not gone past eighth grade, studied theology and was ordained an Episcopal minister; my mother, a former English teacher, was eighty last spring. My daughters all read more or less constantly: Jenny is reading *Zen and the Art of Motor-Cycle Maintenance*, Amy is reading Vonnegut, Alice tells me I should try Richard Hughes. Alice remembers getting her first library card at five years old; they had to bring her a little stool to stand on so she could sign her name to the important and serious pledge that granted the privilege and responsibility of borrowing books. We all talk about books when we are together, comparing our reactions and memories. If I have written as much about my family and my childhood as about my reading, it is because my books and my past and my present are all interwoven.

AUTOBIOGRAPHY #3

Reading Autobiographical Texts

My childhood reading was all autobiographical, as I have indicated in many ways in these writings. The marked impression that Dickens's novels made on me is easy to account for in terms of story; I most strongly identified with David Copperfield because I saw myself as an outcast child at the mercy of half-understood and threatening adult events. The Murdstones made all too much sense. I still react strongly to texts with this mythic pattern, no doubt because it answers unconscious needs. I recently read Sylvia Warner's *The Wide, Wide World* (an 1850s evangelical story of an orphan girl who has to make her way despite an unsympathetic aunt, a radical change of surroundings, etc.) almost as I would have read it as a child—very fast, totally immersed in the story, etc. *Uncle Tom's Cabin* likewise; also *Adam Bede* which tore me apart because the episode of Hetty's wandering and infanticide spoke to deepest fears of maternal abandonment, overlaid now by my own experiences of raising four daughters. What is more interesting to me is the process I don't understand at all, and that is, what was happening when I was ingesting the author's style? In my early reading, this happened entirely unconsciously. It still happens that way now, except that I have the words for it. That is, I know it's happening and I am interested to find out, afterwards, how it has happened. But I have no more idea now than I did then what's going on in my mind while I read. I'll give you a tangential for-instance. The professor of my graduate class just gave us a difficult assignment, a fifty-sentence scrambled essay which we were to arrange back into its original form, making decisions and accounting for them at every step. If I decided that Sentence 4 had to follow Sentence 33, I had to write down why I thought so. I found the assignment enormously frustrating because there was more going on that I could capture in sentences. That is, I could certainly write that the pronoun in Sentence 4 had an antecedent in Sentence 33—but what I couldn't write down was the simultaneous awareness that some whole gestalt was constantly being formed, adjusted, and fine-tuned while I was consciously busy with transitions, pronouns, question-and-answer sets, etc. Most of what helped me arrange the essay was its—its "smell"—some elusive thing that had to do with my almost intuitive grasp of the author's methods, a holistic sense that guided her word choice, choice of example, choice of placement for narrative versus statement, etc. Now certainly part of my understanding has been formed by my prior reading experience— I've learned what to expect from writing by reading a lot. But part of that understanding has been with me from the beginning, as early as I can remember. You ask me, where am I in the places of a book? As a child, I was right inside the main character, of course. My sight of Peggety's (sp.?) Kitchen was David's sight. A good portion of that sight was reconstructed from Dicken's descriptions of the way things looked. But not all. It was scented (if I may use that metaphor to point to something much more elusive than the sight of things) with the unmistakable fragrance of his sentences—not just their rhythms and sounds, but their sequences and their situations in the constantly-changing whole. The closest analogy I can think of is that the book-worlds had the vivid being of those worlds we enter when we dream. Unlike my dreams, which I can make, the writers made their worlds. Each writer's style-world was different. When I wrote above that books enabled me to try on different worlds, it was not only—maybe even not importantly—the world of the character's existential or inter-

personal situations that was most important. It was the totally different, unambiguous but ungraspable world of the rhythms in which he
moved. Today as an adult, this quality in a book is the world I enter.
Because I have a stronger circumference to my own identity, I no
longer reenact the characters' story. That I watch from over their shoulders, as it were. But I am just as much *in* the world of the book as I ever
was. It is a metaworld, an analogical construction that makes a world.
People have painted landscapes for a long time, but Cezanne's world
is not the world of Monet, and the difference is everything. It wasn't
that the rooks cawed over the graveyard—it was that they existed in
their own sound. How the writer does that, and how I recognize it, are
the tantalizing questions I try to answer again and again, all the while
realizing that any answer will be partial and sterile. To give you
another analogy: walk out in the fog of some January thaw. The trees
are flattened gray shapes and you apprehend vividly as never before
the distances between them. Shape and space are made palpable by
impalpability. When I see that, I want to *do* something about it—but
nothing I can do (paint a picture, write a poem) will do more than
clumsily point to the experience that moved me to create. So my experience of books is a physical awareness of my own being in a universe.
By strangeness they isolate some basic principles of being, they skin
the eyeballs of the self. Perhaps the object of my experience is simply
myself, experiencing, far below the mind's reach. For this reason, a
book read aloud is a different thing than a book read to oneself. For
this reason, intrusions of interpretation, commentary, are always
beside the point. A summer night sets up yearnings that no embrace
will answer. Should one teach literature at all? Perhaps one's teaching
should be a kind of Emersonian presentation, a series of disjunctive
metaphors with room for the student to supply the transitions, infer
the context, and be moved to his own contemplation, to his own more
or less beside-the-point, ineluctable, but live-giving action.

REFLECTIVE PAPER ON READING AND TEACHING

Reading and Writing about Reading in My Curriculum

This activity with Wendy has been useful to me because I have had to
think about the relationship between my own reading attitudes and
my teaching practice. Some of what I do is because of my attitudes to
reading; some is in spite of it. Or perhaps it would be more accurate to
say that conflicting reading selves have formed my practice. One is

surely the rebellious, introverted, artistic child who created imaginative reading worlds safer than the dangerous theatre of human inter-
course. The other is the adult who uses that solipsistic reading experience as a still-safe base from which to reach out to the world. It has not
been comfortable to look at either self, or to realize that the conflicts
informing my reading life still play out in my teaching, and I am not
sure that I am ready to take the final step of making plain in writing
what is clear but still sheltered just below consciousness. The fact that
I am working in a system which prescribes much of my students' curriculum both masks and perpetuates these conflicts because, ambiva-
lently working within and pushing against its constraints, I find it difficult to analyze what of the curriculum is Butler County and what is
me. Interesting jump here. Writing these pieces has forced me to see
that much of my curriculum is indeed me, and that therefore I must
shed at least some of my old practice of operating from a stance of sub-
version. In actuality, very little of what goes on in my classroom is
written down in that three-inch-thick curriculum guide gathering dust
on my bookshelf: I haven't looked at it in seven years because I assume
that I know better than the committee who wrote it what eleventh-
graders need to learn. If there were not a county-wide final examina-
tion at the end of the year, I would diverge spaciously indeed from
Butler County's requirements, because mine are much more demanding, at least for my honors-level students. I teach a dual vocabulary
program, SAT preparation, a systematic language-and-usage program,
a program in expository writing, and a program in literature. It is no
wonder that I feel that nothing is done completely. (I should say here,
however, that there is an unwritten curriculum guide behind the fat
book, and that the message English teachers get from the county is that
there is no limit to what we should be doing, and doing thoroughly.)
At any rate, I teach most of the required works of American literature,
drop or skimp some, and curve their final exam, thus silently expressing my contempt for it. My choices of what to deal with fully and what
to skimp are based on my own knowledge and enthusiasm, so in a
course supposed to survey American literature from its beginnings to
Arthur Miller, I am heavy and methodical in antebellum writing and
hasty in the twentieth century. Perhaps when I know more about later
American writing I will readjust this balance. I am not so interested in
product as I am in process—would prefer to "cover" less.

Within these limits, then, I have tried to set up a reading-writing
program that acknowledges the county's demand that college-bound
students learn to analyze works of literature while it allows students
some room to think about their own interactions with texts. This diffi-

cult balancing act is complicated by the fact that most of the kids I teach are not ready to do either of these jobs with the required texts because they have such a hard time understanding them. An honest curriculum would address their reading deficiencies more systematically and earlier; as it is, they are confronted in eleventh grade with complex linguistic structures, having had little preparation for that kind of reading in earlier years. (They do read *Romeo and Juliet* and *Great Expectations* in ninth grade and *Julius Caesar* in tenth grade, but as far as I know there is no organized attempt to teach the reading strategies they need to deal with highly complex writing.) Many of my college-bound students cannot determine the main idea of a highly-modified or qualified sentence. I realize that they have to start somewhere, and that they are learning while they read, but the problematic texts they encounter in eleventh grade just compound their problems. At any rate, my reading-journal assignments attempt to improve their reading skills and to force them to encounter the text at some personal level. The series of assignments moves from personal encounter to analysis. The journals begin in the all with worths self-chosen from a list of American authors edited by me from a county list, move to a work read by all but not taught chapter-by-chapter in class, then are adopted for every required text we study together. At present they are reading *The Scarlet Letter* and writing a fact-inference journal designed to get them to thinking about the underlying meanings of the work since they tend to read unquestioningly. This journal will not be so much a dialogue with me as it will be, I hope, a dialogue with themselves about the meaning of the work. In our joint work on the book, I plan to use the journals as the basis for both small-group discussion and for individual essays.

You ask about their individual responses, to what degree are these at the center of the curriculum, to what degree are they marginal? I guess the answer is, both. The journals are preparatory; I believe you have to engage with the text first before you can analyze it. I suppose here I am recapitulating my own reading history, a long period of unsupervised encounters at the level of emotion and fantasy, overlaid with the kind of analytical thinking I am doing now in graduate school. I still prefer to read a text fast, feeling it, enjoying (or crying over) its story, before I begin to think about it. Since many of my kids don't seem to know how to engage with their reading at a personal level, I try to make them do it (or pretend to do it) in their early journals and in many of their ongoing assignments: write a diary entry or a letter, etc.

I still have a big doubtful area about what the literature teacher should be doing in secondary school. Should I be teaching them how to find the literal meaning of complex sentences? Should I be teaching them that literary texts grow from the writer's engagement with his culture? Should I be teaching them that we can learn about ourselves from thinking about literary characters? Should I be providing texts they might not think to choose themselves, and encouraging them to imaginatively ingest those texts? My own reading experience is no guide. I do not remember anything I read in school, Wendy. I have no idea how texts were taught at the High School of Music and Art in the years 1946–1950, because I either had read the things already or I simply didn't do anything with them in any personal way. I know, for instance, that we read *Silas Marner* and *Ivanhoe*—and yet I came to George Eliot with delighted discovery and still am telling myself I want to read Scott. Reading in school just wasn't reading, that's all. And maybe it shouldn't try to be—maybe it should just be the material from which we teach skills. The trouble with that is, that it denies everything I believe in about literature, everything I have formed myself around. So I am in a muddle and often feel as though I am preaching redemption to the mystified if not resentful unconverted.

You ask a lot of difficult questions. "Why is it important to possess without revealing?" I immediately reword that to, Can you possess what you reveal? Obviously a neurotic response. But my reading was/is a large part of my own identity formation. If we all create fictional texts for our lives, mine is a literary text. My identity is a verbal thing. I am a creature who mediates life with words. To do that, I have to be working out of a reservoir into which I dip and select in order to make public representations—but everything in me says, it's better not to bring it all to the light of day because the creative part, the pattern-information, has to go on underground. Analysis is a necessary death, always partial, always reductive. I do not think that what I have learned about literature improves literature. My own writing about texts is really writing about myself, my thinking processes, my pattern-information; a little bit about how life in a given time in a given mind results in a text; not at all really about what the text "means" because that meaning is a living thing that shouldn't have scalpels taken to it. My writing about texts embodies, emblemizes homage to dead writers (and every writer dies as the text is released to others; if it is a living writer, there is a new birth and death with the next work) and to the idea that they live again in me. The analysis is just the outward form that homage takes, and it is mightily beside the point.

No, books shouldn't be social brokers. I did that as a child because I had no other brokerage facilities that I knew of. Books are personal brokers. They can provide children with other selves, other eyes to help them see how they fit in the world. I suppose that would be useful to adolescents. Perhaps I should say it to them, and not just assume that it's happening.

My mother. I remember discovering Shakespeare's sonnets and rhapsodizing about one to my mother who responded, contemptuously, "Everyone knows that. *I* read those, too." So much for all that. Accounts for my attempts to be a better mother to my kids by giving value to their responses. I am hugely ambivalent about this but haven't been able to change my style much. It's pretty clear why I didn't read her books—and yet it was my mother who gave books as presents, books that I loved and claimed as my own (*Mary Poppins, Little Women*). They didn't have my mother's smell; reading them was like sleeping in the bed someone just got out of. I didn't want to see my mother as someone who had had a childhood or adolescence because I wouldn't have been able to find room for myself by making her an other, my enemy. My teaching sometimes has the flavor of giving presents of books. They are highly personal but safe presents. (Incidentally, my mother just sent me a birthday package; in with the earrings and the padded dress-hangers and the strange cedar blocks from L.L. Bean were some books she said [she always writes directions on her presents] she was clearing out and I might find some use for. Oh, well, I didn't get to finish Virginia Woolf's essays before I sent them to her last year. But you can see the kind of emotional load attached to all of this.)

So my teaching is a dangerous act—approach and run away. Find the emotional meaning, find yourself, retreat into analysis (write a topic sentence, learn to write transitions, all that). I am being a little hard on myself here. Since school isn't all of life, and since English isn't all of school, I have made some choices. One of them is to acknowledge the realm in which literature can touch one's own personality while concentrating on the more analytical, perhaps more appropriate and fruitful realm of language—how do words work? What choices does a writer make? What can one do with words that can't be done in other media? To do that even a little bit is enough; let unconscious activities go on in decent privacy.

APRIL'S AUTOBIOGRAPHICAL WRITING

AUTOBIOGRAPHY #1

I have a theory that those of my students who were read to as children are somehow better readers and writers—or maybe they simply like reading more than their peers. When recalling the experience of being read to, my students describe their favorite stories in vivid outline, discussing the main characteristics of the protagonists and antagonists. They also like to talk about where their parents read to them—usually when they are in their beds, or snuggled next to a parent. Some of the families still read together, especially when they are on vacation; some of the children read their assigned English books with their parents so they can discuss the stories together. I always ask my classes to see if any of their parents have read/memorized *The Rime of the Ancient Mariner* or Portia's "Quality of Mercy" speech, or other famous bits. They find it very exciting to report that "my father knew all of it! He sat there and recited for us over dinner." Many students describe how they now read to a young sibling or baby-sitting charge, and when they discuss reading to another, they slip unconsciously from a sentimental mode to a more analytical one: they compare with one another how "little kids always want to stop and ask all these questions," and how "you kind of have to make up and add to the story, instead of just reading it to them." When they babysit, many of them like to read a book that they enjoyed "as a child." Last year's class had a great affection for Thumbellina, and for weeks after our discussion of reading experiences, they'd recounted Thumbellina's adventures to one another.

Books and bookstores have always held a special, magical attraction for me—My parents were always buying new books to read to us—it may be that in living overseas, we read and were read to more often than my peers who grew up with television—Because books were hard to come by, we belonged to a number of mail-away book-clubs; excitement was when Dad would bring home in his briefcase those thick, stiff cardboard packages of books from America. There were a few good English bookstores in Bangkok, though the books were very expensive. Somehow the expense made books seem all the more precious, and we children knew we had to choose carefully—when we took our family trips to the Penguin bookstore, and everyone was allowed one book. There was something special about being in the shop with other English readers—standing next to adults in the quiet, unhurried atmosphere of the shop. And after I had found my book, I would up and down the aisles of adult books, looking at the pictures on the paperbook novels, flipping through the big cocktail table books.

My sister and I devoured Nancy Drew, the Hardy Boys, and a whole series of English boarding-school stories by Enid Blyton. When we read Blyton's "Adventures of the Famous Five," about four cousins and their dog, we assumed the characters' personalities, speech patterns, and quirks. We created our own stories about Nancy Drew and her boyfriend Ned, and we made dolls to represent characters from different stories (a great tragedy occurred when the nancy doll died mysteriously, her egg-shell head cracked in two pieces). Occasionally on weekends, Dad would take us to his office where we would type up the stories, then bind them into important-looking books, complete with illustrations.

At the same time—from the time I was seven until I was ten—we read comic books voraciously. Every few weeks, mother would take us down to the exchange store where we'd buy or trade large stacks of cheap comic books—Casper the Ghost, Dot, Richie Rich, Superman and Batman, Archie, and G.I. Joe stories—The stack would then be put up in a cabinet until the parents went out for the evening—then a given number of comics would be brought down, to keep us company for the night.

When we were even younger, my parents would read to us. There were all sorts of different books, from Chinese and Japanese fairy tales, with delicate water color pictures, to Grimms's Tales, Winnie the Poor series, and Dr. Seuss books. There are two books that stand out when I think of Mother reading aloud. The first to come to mind, oddly enough, is *Wind in the Willows*. This strikes me as peculiar because at the time we considered the book a failure—Mother kept trying to push it, but the children lost interest, and in the end we never finished the book. But today, I can still clearly envision my favorite character, Mr. Toad. Mr. Toad was one of the few spunky, colorful animals. Something of a cavalier, Toadie was very wealthy and spoiled. He wore a smoking jacket, puffed on cigars, and terrorized the other animals by ripping about in a 1920s roadster. Later Toadie gets thrown in jail and repents all his sins, which I considered grossly unfair.

My other favorite read-aloud was a large book with unusual angular, stylized pictures and tales from Greek myths. I remember pouring over the book and stories with my mother and siblings, as we discussed the characters and their adventures. We were particularly fascinated by the Trojan war and the gods and goddesses who helped the various mortals; Odysseus' adventures seemed frightening and sad to me, and I kept worrying about inconsequential details—the poor Cyclops with the stake in his eye, the men whom Circe turns into swine, and Odysseus' faithful dog . . .

There were also stories. Mother told stories about "Mr. Green-Fish," a wise soul who lives under the bed of a little boy names Timothy; though these stories were exclusively the property of Mother and my younger brother, Anthony, my sister I were allowed to come sit on the bed and listen, if we were quiet. Dad spun numerous bedtime stories about a tricky and skillful "Magic Rabbit." Dad also owned an ancient Chinese "genie bottle," and would tell us tales of the genie; occasionally the genie would bring forth toys and balloons for us, and there was always a story explaining how the genie had come into ownership of these goods. A famous Dad story is "Home for a Gekko," the story, which Dad taped for us, recounts the adventures of a Taiwanese lizard, searching for the right family to live with. We children would play the tape—with authentic gekko noises—when the parents were out at functions, and I remember feeling very comforted to hear my father's voice telling and retelling the story.

As a child, it seemed to me that my parents were always going out; the house seemed impossibly empty and lonely. The three of us would usually spend the evening in our playroom playing with our dolls and toys, with the ayah sitting in the corner. The books, stories, and recounting of stories were a solace. At different times, different ayahs took interest in joining in, and we'd read the "American" books to them, while they in turn told us their stories. From ayahs I learned folk tales, ghost tales, tales of village life and superstition. In Bangkok, we learned the stories of the Ramakien (the Thai version of India's

Ramayana)—we followed the adventures of heroic Rama, his kid-napped wife and loyal brother, and the wily lascivious monkey-god, Hanuman. When we felt very bored, on rainy afternoons after school, my sister and I would amuse ourselves by watching Chinese soap-operas on television—we'd make up elaborate stories to match the action and try to put English words to the Chinese songs.

There are only a few unpleasant stories that have stayed with me from that time in my childhood. One—which all we children still remember sadly—is about a Duck named Ping who lives in the Hongkong Bay and who catches fish for a living. The horrible part was that Ping has a metal ring around his throat which chokes him and made it impossible for him to ever swallow the delicious, fat fish which he catches for his employer. Undoubtedly, Ping's life took a turn for the better, but I hated to think of his life in subjugation.

The other story is one that a nun told me in Religious school. About one hundred and fifty years old, Sister Elizabeth was a crotch-ety, mean-spirited nun who told my class a story about a family that goes on vacation. As they get into their car for the outing, their youngest daughter prays to Jesus that the family will travel safely. But on the highway, a truck swerves into the car, and everyone perishes—except for the youngest daughter, because she remembered to say her prayers. The story panicked me for months after, and I desperately urged my bemused parents to pray before they went on trips.

AUTOBIOGRAPHY #2

During our last mini-vacation, I allowed myself a great luxury—I read a book. A work that had nothing to do with anything, then everything to do with all things. A delicious, sybaritic settling into bed with cof-fee, water, and a bowl of popcorn at my side; pillows propped up and blankets snuggled up, over and tucked about my feet.

Throughout the first chapter, the English Teacher kept intruding on the Reader; she examined the prose critically, noting any overwrit-ing, too-broad strokes of characterization, and awkward use of dia-logue. I stopped at one point and wondered if I couldn't just skim the book then turn my attention to where it belonged—to the stack TO BE READ that I keep next to the bed. But somewhere near the end of that first chapter I was hooked, lured into the realm of Catholic school girls—monastic hallways—brightly lit offertory candles—and the hushed repetition of mummered prayers—the four walls of my bed-room had dissolved.

There's something quietly exciting about coming to realize that yes, this is going to be a good read—a book that will transport me into its own world. Nothing about TV or even a very excellent movie can match it—what is the difference? Maybe it's the control—I love slowing down to savor a particularly evocative passage, racing through exciting parts, and going back to read a passage again and again. I always reach a point in my reading when I look anxiously to see how many pages remain and I wonder if I should "save" the book, space it out over a few days—I look at the clock, and debate whether I should be prudent—one more hour? two? There is a satisfaction that feels slightly illicit when I decide no, this is my indulgence—I'm going to go for it.

On that night, with Antonia White's *Frost in May*, I read until seven in the morning, until my eyes ached and I had to close and rest them at times—but there was nothing about feeling tired, only a wistfulness as I watched the story coming closer to its end. During the next few days I carried the book about with me, picking it back up again to reread—not quite ready to let it go.

That is my reading as a luxury and indulgence, a huge, fat chocolate candy bar. It frustrates me that I seldom have the time to read like that—that it is so difficult to read an entire book through. I listen to my students with envy and some disbelief—these voracious adolescent readers who can devour a book over the weekend, who casually hand back *The Europeans, Pride and Prejudice, Rebecca, Brave New World,* and ask so what else do you have?"

The true reason I had taken that book up to read is because I had promised by students that I would. The day before break, I gave each of my classes a "book talk." I lined my blackboards with all sorts of books, but mainly those that would make for *entertaining* reading—*The Adventures of Sherlock Holmes, Rebecca, The Portrait of Dorian Grey, The Martian Chronicles, Passage to India, The Spoon River Anthology, The Wide Saragasso Sea,* Robert Frost's *Collected Poems, All Creatures Great and Small,* and a number of others. I began by talking at length about *Rebecca* by Daphne Dumaurier—I read the first chapter, and described the overall feeling of the book—the mystery involved, and the romantic/luxurious/ominous/mysterious exciting feel of the story. This was the book I had come up with about a month ago for two girls to read, because their mothers complained to me that they were reading far below their ability—Nancy Drew mysteries, mainly. I told Brooke and Eutbe about *Rebecca* and I promised them that if they read the book, we'd get together to discuss it, and then watch the movie. A number of other girls heard about our "bargain" and asked if they could get in on the deal. After I spoke about *Rebecca* to the class, I turned to the other books and described each briefly—then I left the last ten minutes of class open, so they could mill about, examine the books, and take home any of those that caught their interests. I, in turn, was challenged to read *Frost in May* and to come back and discuss it. I remember thinking "great—where am I going to find the time?" Why is it, loving books as much as I do, that I find it so difficult to find time—? I have another group of girls that meets once a week to read and discuss a novel—right now we are reading *A Brave New World*. (This book, interestingly enough, was their choice; when we decided to read a book together, we each brought in our choice and presented it to the other members—I had tried to steer them toward less difficult reading, but they were intrigued when I told them that they would read BNW in tenth grade, and then adamant that that was the book they would tackle.) I discovered at the last meeting that I was the only one who hadn't gone ahead and read to the end of the book—when do they have the time?

My six bookcases ache with books that I am constantly arranging and rearranging and finding some other window sill or countertop that can take a collection of books so that I can fit a few more into place. But sometimes I look at my books and wonder if I am not just a buyer of books and not a reader of books—. Not only do I not have the time, I don't have the span of attention—I don't have the mental time to commit to a book—my mind is racing off to work that has to be finished or started, projects, letters, notes, papers to be graded.

When I do read it is usually in snippets. That pile next to my bed contains books stuffed with yellow tabs—a chapter on Coleridge, another on creative writing techniques, teaching Shakespeare, language games. There is the last *Shakespeare Quarterly*, *Time*, and *Newsweek*, *Smithsonian*, *English Journal*, and underneath, the O'Keeffe exhibit catalogue, Grebanier's book on Shakespearean actors, Boswell's account of Johnson's trip to the Hebrides, *Folktales from Thailand*, *The Ramakien*. On the bottom—but often surfacing to the top because it is the most manageable, is a file fat with xeroxed articles on myriad subjects. Always close by is a book of poetry—Chinese poetry, Japanese haiku, *Norton's Anthology of Poetry*; it's a great consolation to end my day and a session of reading by flipping through to some undiscovered gem or to the lulling repetition of an old-shoe favorite. The pile is ever changing, growing or shrinking, exciting or oppressive, sometimes neglected, often dusty.

AUTOBIOGRAPHY #3

Okay, fresh start—press the purge buttons on the computer and get rid of the previous faltering attempts to write this third piece ("purge" I like that word; I wonder which sardonic computer wit thought that one up?).

Why "faltering"? I'm not sure exactly, and I'm somewhat intrigued by the difficulty I've experienced in trying to write about high school reading experiences. It is not exactly like Laurie's experience, where she has blocked out completely unhappy memories—but there is something in there—anger, frustration, unhappiness—in my case it has more to do with the "culture shock" of returning to American and maybe American school systems and maybe American school reading systems—I'm not sure.

There *was* something exciting about coming to the United States for high school, in terms of books,—so many books! Vast (it seemed to me) public libraries, with more books than I could have hoped for—that availability is something I always miss when I leave the country—but it isn't what first comes to mind when I think of h.s.—too much baggage in the way, maybe.

The libraries. I remember the sad American embassy library in Kathmandu. Tucked away in an attic room of an obscure administration building in the USAID compound—one small room, packed mainly with crumbling paperbacks or hardbacks with that ugly 1950s feel to them—cheap paper already ruined by the acid of the print—with those stiff plastic covers—mylar?—always dirty, always brittle and torn on the top, so that you'd rip your hands up when you'd try to read, and the only solution would be to cautiously tear off the tape and slip the book out of its cover. There was something mysterious and pleasant about that library—half the time it would be locked and I'd get the key from the manager of the commissary—slip up into the cool, dark room, mingle solitarily amongst the books, load up with an armful before I settled down to browse through, decided which ones to take home. A very sensory reading setting—white plaster walls, cool and dark, with uncomfortable rattan mats, which would leave impressions of their design on my legs if I sat too long. The tables were too high and the wooden chairs too uncomfortable, so usually I'd sit myself at a particular window that overlooked the compound—overlook the broad, thick trees with heavy foliage and armies of Nepalese crows—the irregular red-brick paved courtyard—and the impossibly blue skies and ghosts of Himalayas in the distance. It was a good secret-nook, although I suppose in truth I went there less than I remember, for eighth-grade life does not revolve around a shabby old library.

It's an odd thing about the American library—it was very exciting to me at first—I spent a lot of my time in the first years back at that library—it was named Richard Bard, after the polar explorer, which always struck me as rather horrible and very American (did *he* read books, after all?)—I went to films there, and weekend workshops—walked up and down the stacks and learned about the various reader's guides—the weekly files, microfilm and fiche and so forth. I'd surreptiously browse through the "young adult" section, though rather disgusted to be in a section so branded; I'd thumb through the nonfiction sections of household and cooking and at one point became particularly fascinated with automobile how-tos. I remember feeling extremely embarrassed to check out "classics" like *Gone with the Wind*, feeling it was somehow too corny to be reading such a book.

But there was also something I began to hate—and still hate—about that library and public libraries in general—the air was too thin and gave me a headache; the chairs were uncomfortable, and the books had that same damned stiff plastic covering. The library was habitually unkempt—books vaguely disordered, bathrooms filthy, and librarians stereotypically dowdy, dull, and petty about their tiny kingdom. I went to the main branch of the Montgomery library last weekend and encountered the same thing; though initially I felt a thrill as I walked in the door and looked down the long hall of stacks, there was that same shabby, ugly feeling about the place. No card catalogues, just a mess of microfiche cards strewn about, the machines left on, cards missing, torn, on the floor; same dirty bathrooms and thin air. But I could babble on about libraries—and won't.

High school reading. A few reading experiences stand out vividly. My first English high school class was a chilling introduction to the American system; but then the entire school—with a student body of three thousand, as opposed to my eighth grade class of eight students—was something of a shock. That class was dominated by unruly, loud boys, and kept in shaky control by a mousy middle-aged woman, who broke down and wept in class the second week of school. (I remember that day very clearly—I remember thinking "what an idiot—she'll never regain complete control—I would never let that happen"—a strong negative experience that informed my own teaching, later). I don't remember the full reading list, though I think it included *The Diary of Anne Frank, Catcher in the Rye, Brave New World*, and *Lord of the Flies*.

I do remember *Lord of the Flies*, and the feeling of despair—repulsion—I remember slumped low in the back of the room, watching the boys in front of me rolling a joint, thinking that my worse nightmare would be to be trapped on an island with this English class—wondering who would be killed first (the English teacher and the fat girl with heavy glasses who always had a cold but no handkerchiefs, and then maybe me, unless I could get away). What was that teacher thinking when she chose her book list? What did she title the course—"Alienation and Despair?" The first time I began to think about systems of education was when I came to West High School—how could a school have such extensive modern equipment—science laboratories, the newest books, movies, film strips, records, a fabulous arts studio—and yet be such a demoralizing place of study? What I remember of WHS are long underlit halls, bathrooms stinking of cigarettes, and everything bureaucratized, systematized, regulated—being sent to the principal for my habit of sitting on my knees ("who do you think you are, Pocohantas?"), being caught reading instead of going to the pep rally ("what do you think you come to school for?") . . . but here we go again—Fear and Loathing in Suburban USA; enough.

At the same time I was in that first tenth grade English class (I had taken correspondence for 9th grade overseas), I read voraciously at the public library everything I could find on Indochina and America's "Involvement." Depressing stuff—accounts by P.O.W.'s mostly— I would pour over these books, as though reading pornography—with titillation, horror, and absolute secrecy. The memory of these books, this period, had completely escaped me until recently, when I watched *Hanoi Hilton* and found I knew all about the POW camps—and remembered why. My parents were amazed—and somewhat mystified, dismayed—to hear of this secret obsession.

In the next two years of high school I settled down, learned to work the school's system, discovered some of my best friends in the teachers, and began to explore wonderful books. A course called "World Literature" introduced me to a whole realm of translated material, and, for the first time, fascinating existentialist works—Sartre, Borges, Camus, Beckett. In that class I first discovered Dante, Milton, Tolstoy; in a creative writing class I read Oates, Barth, Gorki, Woolf; in the AP class, Kafka, Conrad, Faulkner. I was immersed in a whole world of reading—and a new world of university libraries. I used to drive an hour out to U.M. to "research" different projects—and find myself instead walking the stacks and collecting armfuls of books.

It was the start of my own library, too. At first (I hate to admit), from books from the school—I'm still slightly horrified that I have so many anthologies stamped "property of WHS department of English,"—although I have tucked into my guilty memory some idea that my favorite English teacher may have permitted these "borrowings" or perhaps gave me books too old to keep? (Doubtful.) In my senior year I discovered the bookstores of D.C., and with a part-time job in the city during holidays was able to spend more time down there, reading and buying.

When I think of it, those later high school years were extremely productive—a time when I discovered many writers and avenues in the writing world. So why is it that the first and strongest memories are of the horrors of high school reading—of that one terrible class and *Lord of the Flies*? And why was this last piece so difficult to write—that time painful to delve back into? I suppose it is, in some ways a typical reaction to teenage years—but Westfield was terrible: my family used to say "someday we'll look back on all of this and admit that it really wasn't bad, we really were happy here—." It hasn't happened yet. Now we ponder that perhaps the gods made us experience Westfield so that we'd appreciate the rest of our lives. Ridiculous as it seems, I still have nightmares about that school; nightmares of being lost in vast, anonymous halls with rows of lockers and faceless people—and a particularly panicked nightmare of trying to find my locker and then trying to remember my combination—. So my memories of high school reading are inextricably woven into the experience of being a teenager, of living in that particular suburb. But when I look back, I think a number of negative experiences from that time continue to inform and influence my teaching now.

FINAL REFLECTIVE PAPER ON READING AND TEACHING

[If we had had the best of all possible worlds, I would have had much more time to acquaint myself with your research and its purpose; more time to meet and consult with you; more time to evaluate my curriculum and to reflect on your responses, and so forth—. I suppose that is a teacher's never-ending wail—if we had time and world enough. But I did want you to know how interesting and worthwhile I have found this study to be. I am only sorry not to have been able to give more, give better, you will have to excuse this final piece, as the circumstances of it's writing were somewhat strained.]

Before this summer and your first general introductory session, I had not been previously acquainted with the theories of reader response. Your discussion and your reading materials fascinated and encouraged me, perhaps because this approach for studying literature seemed to ring true. It articulated and made sense of (and, perhaps, validated?) many of my own inclinations about teaching reading in the secondary school.

I still feel fairly ignorant about reader response—I haven't had enough time or mind-space to proceed what I've read and what we've discussed—I still need to sort out, decipher the jargon, understand and put to use these newly gleaned ideas. But the whole process of this study and thinking in these terms has been enormously helpful; it has—and will continue to—influence and reshape my curriculum.

I am still quite new to teaching; in my first two years, I found— as the Red Queen tells Alice—it took all the running I could to just to keep in one place; I'd have to run twice as fast as that to get somewhere else. Maybe I've finally increased my speed, but happily, in this my third year, I at last have some time to examine what I'm doing—how, and why I'm doing it. At the top of that list of consideration is my reading curriculum. I have never felt comfortable with it, and I feel it is important to me. I suppose I have been fighting toward this all during these three years—and though I feel I am making headway, I'm still frustrated. Last spring I sat down with my department head for two hours, trying to discover the overall SENSE of the reading program, of the books chosen. And though, at the end of this session she had broken the books down into units and categories of "fantasy and exploration," "language and structure," and "exploration of the self," etc., it still seem/ed/s like artificial and arbitrary categorization— imposing sense instead of making sense. Must the book list have to have unity and logic, or can each unit stand on its own? Perhaps I am considering the idea of curriculum too narrowly—I'd be interested to hear what you think.

The curriculum I inherited seemed to be a confused hodge-podge of readings. When questioned, the members of the department admitted that these books were left over from various eighth-grade courses, which had been organized around themes such as Mystery, Adventure, Fantasy. Somehow, these texts remained, but they didn't "hang together" in any way. I particularly objected to *The Good Earth*, which I consider poorly written and racist. When I read this book, additionally, I see Buck perpetrating unhealthy stereotypes about women and to a lesser degree, men: "Good girls" like O-lan make suffering and sacrifice their badge; nobody who has read that book can forget how O-lan delivers her first child with no assistant, then returns to work in the fields two hours later. O-lan is silent, subservient, noble; her one selfish act is to request two pearls from her husband, which of course, he denies her, giving them instead to his mistress. The melodrama is served up fairly thickly in this book. Bad girls show up in the person of that same opium-smoking mistress, and men are shown as having uncontrollable lust (of course, none of the women possess any sexual desires).—The strokes in this book are fairly broad and crude—but that is how the book speaks to me—interpretation right?

It fascinates me how many people in their late fifties extol the virtues of this book—and I have to wonder if their view is not colored by their memory of Louise Rainer in the film. But I have also considered how thirteen-year old girls respond to this book—especially because I remember reading it when I was an adolescent, and loving it; for weeks my sister and I imitated the heavy and sorrowful tones of these characters, speaking as they did: "It is meet that we should do it thus." It was at this point that my sister began to argue vehemently for my grandmother to hold onto her farmland (the land! the land!). And, interestingly, too, I remember my mother was the first to steer me away from Buck by first telling me about, then reading me a short story. In this story, again, the strokes are so broadly drawn—the cruel, bitchy, insensitive white woman who hires a poor, starving Chinaman (who is supporting this many children, a dying wife, etc.). At the end of the story she rejects his work, leaving him to certain death.

What of my students? In the first two years, the department implored me to "at least try it," so I gave in, assigning *The Good Earth* as summer reading. Most students responded to it with enthusiasm— they enjoyed the foreign setting, the elemental-ness of the living-life and death, starvation, floods. Only few were disturbed by the portrayal of the Chinese and the women. When we reread the book later, we took more time to examine the writing and the attitudes of the author. This was successful/not successful. Though in most cases the students felt triumphant to re-evaluate a book and to go beyond and deeper than their first reading, others felt resistant and even resentful—I was ruining their relationship with this book in asking them to view it in a different, more judgmental way.

I suppose that gets back to our discussion of the objective, thinking reader and the pleasure reader, and that whole can of worms. I reject the idea that these two completely separate ways of reading—I think there are cross-overs, and that the two ways of reading can inform one another. And yet—though at first I thought this would be an exciting way of showing students how to re-evaluate a book, reconsider it in a different way, after consideration, I have come to think that there are other, less "violating" ways of accomplishing this same task.

In my first two years, I hear often, "why do we have to analyze *every-thing*? It destroys [a book, a poem]; why can't we just enjoy some of these things?" And I felt particularly responsive to the complaint, because I used to voice it myself. I haven't heard that complaint recently, perhaps because I've been able to guide the students into interpretation and analysis in a manner which is more acceptable to them. (This December we viewed an RSC video called "Interpreting a Character" in which two actors discussed their different portrayals of Shylock. The students took notes and then discussed what they agreed and disagreed with—how they pictured Shylock, which choices they accepted or rejected and why.)

Incidentally, as part of that second-read, I had my students compare *GE* to Maxine Hong-Kingston's *Woman Warrior*. This book, written in 1975 by a Chinese-American woman, explores some of the stereotypes and attitudes about Asians. It is also fairly bitter in its feminist viewpoint—something which the students felt perplexed and irritated about; something which I had not focused upon until they pointed it out—(we spend some time discussing this—their reactions, my nonreaction, etc. It was exciting for me to have them discover something I had "missed.") Despite my best efforts, this book was not well-received, for a number of reasons. Kingston experiments with her writing style freely, mixing fantasy and reality. Her progression is nonlinear. She will establish a truth in one chapter, only to violate it in the next, and come up with a third solution in the following chapter. A number of my students felt completely lost with this book and (interestingly) very angry at the author for these techniques. Some were also overwhelmed by the graphic images—of a strangled fetus, of monkey brains, and other disturbing passages—a crazy woman who is stoned to death by villagers.

So *The Good Earth* and *Woman Warrior* left the curriculum after two years. In the case of the first book, I was relieved; it never made sense to me to teach a book I don't value. I dropped *My Antonia* for similar reasons—I felt I knew so little about the American Midwest that I could not find an approach for the book and therefore could not help my students in reading the book. Of course, it's not to say one shouldn't explore a text that is foreign to one's experience—but I do think that as a teacher I have to make sense of a text, find an approach for it—I think it's dishonest to imagine that a teacher can suspend prejudices or judgments about a text and teach it "objectively." What does that mean? I see little truth in "objective reading"—nonsense, we always react subjectively. I also don't believe that is my task—objectivity—when "teaching" a book, I am necessarily guiding the students to view it a certain way—bringing my interpretation to them—and that interpretation need not be heavy-handed—. But as teachers, we are there to help students see what we see in a particular book—to simply appreciate the story and the prose, the characterization—to help them go further and begin to examine the structure of a book. etc. Aren't we doing much of what our reading parents once did for us in introducing a heavy-handedness as a teacher—with a recognition of our own predispositions, we can also allow room for our students' interpretations—to let them explore their reactions to a text, and not to assume that everyone reads the same. In the case of *Woman Warrior*, I realized that there was much I was responding to that my students did not or could not respond to—that my enjoyment of the text came from an appreciation of writing style which, at this point in their thirteen year old lives, only confused and angered them—and so forth. Considering these reactions after twice teaching the book, I decided this year to let it go—so yes, my students influence the way I handle my curriculum.

This piece has been weaving all about, but before I end, let me make a few notes about what has changed this year, what I hope to change next year. As I began to perceive that my students did a good amount of reading outside the classroom, and that perhaps that might be one area in which I could contribute, I began to look for ways to do this—hence the book talks and occasional journeys up to the library. (I make it a habit to read the middle school over-due lists, which are posted on the bulletin boards, to see what kinds of books they are reading). The book-sharing of this year has been well-received and I am looking for different ways to expand it next year.—This was also in direct reaction to a girl, now in the tenth grade, who had always been a sour, negative student, particularly unwilling to read—who wrote in her comments at the year's end, "I'm a terrible reader, I never read anything, but I see now it's stupid, and I need to start. I wish you had encouraged us more to read books." My aunt, again, has also greatly influenced the way I think of books, pointing out to me that it's not enough to simply give students books—that you have to show them how to read them. Judy rejects the idea that teaching students how to read stops after grade school—it's an on-going process, particularly as students approach more difficult texts. She feels it is important for teachers to help students make transitions in their reading—from personal, intimate family readings to public readings, away from picture books, and so forth. The woman who works on the middle school schedule has agreed to consider creating a reading time once or twice a week, and the seventh-grade English teacher and I have discussed any number of ways we can take advantage of this—with silent reading sessions, browsing sessions, read-alouds, exchange programs with the lower school and kindergarten, etc. We have just recently erected a "reading board" outside my room, where students are encouraged to tack up interesting articles.—And so on. I anticipate continuing to examine my texts and my approaches with those texts, continuing to look for different ways to enrich and expand my students' reading experiences. This study has been a great help—for one thing, it has made me reflect back upon my own reading experiences and consider how that relates to my own teaching, and the experiences I can help create for my own students. I apologize for the haphazard nature of this last piece—and for whatever dreadful generalizations I've made. I hope this summer I will have more time to consider all this, and to work it out in a more logical fashion.

NOTES

INTRODUCTION

1. See Anthony Wilden's "Translator's Introduction to Lacan's *The Language of the Self,*" and Wilden's "Lacan and the Discourse of the Other" in the same text.

2. If fathers increasingly share in the primary caretaking of their children, *parental* representation can replace the *maternal* representations to which Kristeva refers. For the time being, the representation of a child's first relations is most accurately described in terms of "maternal relations" reflecting the situation of mothers in gestation and lactation, and the lengthy history of mothers being primary caretakers in many societies. I have alternated using the personal pronouns "he" and "she" to represent both sexes throughout the text. At times I have relied on "he" when a distinction is needed between the "she" in the sentence who refers to the mother and the child in relation to her.

3. Madeleine Grumet in *Bitter Milk*, p. 20.

4. I learned this autobiographical method from Madeleine Grumet and William Pinar. See *Toward a Poor Curriculum.*

CHAPTER 2

1. See Dorothy Dinnerstein's *The Mermaid and the Minotaur: Sexual Arrangements and Human Malaise.*

2. My discussion builds on the work in gendered parenting and object relations theory of Chodorow, Keller, Bordo, as well as Dinnerstein and Flax.

3. Statistics taken from Ellen Nakashima, in "When It Comes to Tough School Jobs, Women Find It Tough to Get Ahead," *The Washington Post*, April 21, 1996.

4. See Jacques Lacan, *The Language of the Self.*

CHAPTER 3

1. For a thoughtful account of the symbiotic relationship between body and language see John Vernon's *Poetry and the Body.*

CHAPTER 4

1. Twenty years ago Madeleine Grumet introduced me to the philosophy of Merleau-Ponty and his work in the phenomenology of perception through the body. Her excitement about and deep understanding of the body's question inspired her ground-breaking work in theater in education from which my work in theater cannot be separated. See especially her concept of scoring in "Merely Players," and the bodyreader in *Bitter Milk.* Her reference to this concept of Merleau-Ponty's is in *Bitter Milk*, p. 142.

2. Throughout this passage, Merleau-Ponty is quoting Werner in *Untersuching uber Empfindung und Empfinden II.*

3. Carolyn Hill is quoting Derrida in *Writing*, pp. 225–227, in this passage.

CHAPTER 5

1. Unpublished manuscript read at Modern Language Association Annual Conference, New York City, December, 1992.

2. See Daniel Stern in Katherine Nelson's *Narratives from the Crib*, (1989) for recent research on a child's dialogue with herself, patterned after her dialogue with her father who put her to bed.

CHAPTER 6

1. Curriculum theorists may be familiar with Ralph Tyler's *Basic Principles of Curriculum and Instruction.* Giroux, Penna, and Pinar (1981) describe Tyler's rationale as one that weighs "the outcomes of instruction against the

objectives that underlie the essential function of the instructional process." In such a rationale, "the notion of evaluation is tied to measuring changes in students' behavior to see if the latter changes conform to the original objectives designed to modify such behavior via certain predetermined learning experiences" (p. 237). I think this is essentially a curriculum rationale based on confronting students only with what they lack.

2. See "Toward a Unified Theory of Literacy Learning and Instructional Practices," *Phi Delta Kappan*, November, 1989. This constructive model honors students' need for narcissistic protection.

3. See especially the footnote by Freud in his essay, "Beyond the Pleasure Principle," on page 599 of Peter Gay's *The Freud Reader*. In this footnote, Freud relays a true story of a child of eighteen months with whom he was residing at the time, and whom Freud felt "confirmed" his interpretation of how children come to transcend separation through pleasure. Freud writes in the text that the boy was preoccupied with a game in which "What he did was to hold [a] reel by the string and very skillfully throw it over the edge of his curtained cot, so that it disappeared into it, at the same time uttering his expressive, 'o-o-o-o,'" which the mother and Freud had recognized from other encounters as representing the German word, "Fort," meaning "gone." Freud continues, "He then pulled the reel out of the cot again by the string and hailed its reappearance with a joyful 'da,'" meaning "there." In the footnote Freud writes, "One day the child's mother had been away for several hours and on her return was met with the words, 'Baby o-o-o-o!' which was at first incomprehensible. It soon turned out however, that during this long period of solitude the child had found a method of making himself disappear. He had discovered his reflection in a full-length mirror which did not quite reach to the ground, so that by crouching down he could make his mirror-image 'gone.'" In this essay, as well as "The Ego and the Id," in the text, *Group Psychology and the Analysis of the Ego*, Freud interprets the child as conquering the mother by replacing her with his own image and gaining control over it. He will develop this line of thinking in his theory that the child will master his fears about mother by moving toward an ego-ideal or super-ego (Gay 1989, 641).

4. Lacan will focus on how the image in the mirror in Freud's story represents this ego-ideal or super-ego, and he will see it as rivalrous and masculine. Anthony Wilden describes an important aspect of Lacan's view: "For the boy, the specular identification with an ideal, notably with the father, constitutes the subject in the *position* of the real father and thus in an untenable rivalry with him; what the subject must seek is the symbolic identification with the father—that is to say he must take over the *function* of the father in the normalization of the Oedipus complex. This is an identification with a father who is neither Imaginary nor real: what Lacan calls the Symbolic father, the figure of the Law" (Lacan 1968, 164). For Lacan the mirror stage is not an occurrence, but a structural or relational concept (1968, 174). This structure is paternal for Freud, as well. Freud writes (Gay 1989, 639), "This leads us back to the origin

of the ego ideal; for behind it there lies hidden an individual's first and most important identification, his identification with the father in his own personal prehistory." Freud also assumed that the child "cannot have possibly felt his mother's departure as something agreeable or even indifferent" and explains the child's pleasure in repeating the fort-da games as the pleasures of mastery and even revenge (1989, 600); although he has misgivings about how this interpretation can be compatible in a pleasure principle theory. Kristeva will offer the missing and powerful interpretation, to my mind, that the child gradually identifies with the mother's pleasure in going out to seek gratification beyond the child and that the child identifies with her desires and the satisfaction of her desires, and assumes due to narcissism, that these gratifications have something to do with gratifying him as well. These gratifications can be met by father, but certainly not the stern, potentially humiliating and threatening father of guilt and conscience alone. The gratifying father, for Kristeva, is one who refers the child back to his mother and the building up of his world. The mother's sexual relations with the father suit this purpose of conceiving the child, but so could her relationships to other women, work, the community, and the world in which she makes a place for the child.

5. See "Freud and Love: Treatment and Its Discontents" in Kristeva, 1987.

CHAPTER 7

1. The title of this chapter was inspired by Kristeva's insistence that "we are not 'simple knowing subjects' but subjects of desire" (Elliot 1991, 239), which can be transposed in this pedagogical situation to read: "The knowing reader is always a feeling reader."

BIBLIOGRAPHY

Abbs, P. (1974). *Autobiography in education*. London: Heinemann Educational Books.

Alcorn, M. W., Jr. and M. Bracher. (1985). Literature, psychoanalysis, and the re-formation of the self: a new direction for reader-response theory. *Proceedings of the Modern Language Association*, 100: 342–354.

Allport, G. (1942). *The use of personal documents in psychological science*. New York: Social Science Research Council, Bulletin 49.

Anderson, M. and P. Hill Collins, eds. (1992). *Race, class, and gender: an anthology*. Belmont, Cal.: Wadsworth Publishing.

Ashton-Warner, S. (1961). *Teacher*. New York: Simon and Schuster.

Atwell, N. (1987). *In the middle. Reading writing, and learning with adolescents*. Portsmouth, N.H.: Boynton/Cook Publishers.

Atwell, W. (1980). Review of *Subjective criticism*. *Journal of Curriculum Theorizing* 2(1): 248–252.

Auer, B. (1984). Teacher candidates' perceptions of personal and professional growth. Paper presented at the American Educational Research Association, annual conference, New Orleans.

Barthes, R. (1966). Introduction to the structuralist analysis of narratives. In C. Kaplan, ed. *Criticism, the major statements* (2nd ed.), 555–589. New York: St. Martin's Press.

Belenky, M. F., B. M. Clinchy, N. R. Goldberger, and J. M. Tarule. (1986). *Women's ways of knowing: the development of self, voice and mind.* New York: Basic Books.

Benjamin, J. (1988). *The bonds of love.* New York: Pantheon Books.

Bettelheim, B. (1977). *The uses of enchantment.* New York: Vintage Books.

Bleich, D. (1975). *Readings and feelings.* Urbana, Ill.: National Council of Teachers of English.

————. (1978). *Subjective criticism.* Baltimore, Md.: Johns Hopkins University Press.

Bogdan, R. and S. Biklen. (1982). *Qualitative research for education.* Boston, Mass.: Allyn and Bacon.

Bogdan, R. (1977). Voices: First person life histories as a method of studying retardates. Paper presented at the 101st annual convention of the American Association of Mental Retardation, New Orleans.

Bordo, S. (1987). *The flight to objectivity.* Albany, N.Y.: State University of New York Press.

Branscombe, A. (1987). I gave my classroom away. In D. Goswami and P. Stillman, eds. *Reclaiming the classroom: teacher research as an agency for change,* 206–218. Portsmouth, N.H.: Boynton/Cook Publishers.

Bruyn, S. T. (1970). The methodology of participant observation. In W. J. Filstead, ed. *Qualitative Methodology,* 305–327. Chicago, Ill.: Markham.

Butler, L. (1968). *The difficult art of autobiography.* Oxford, England: Clarendon Press.

Butler, R. N. (1968). The life review: an interpretation of reminiscences of the aged. In B. Neugarten, ed. *Middle age and aging: a reader in social psychology,* 486–496. Chicago, Ill.: University of Chicago Press.

Cain, W. E. (1984). *The crisis in criticism, theory, literature, and reform in English studies.* Baltimore, Md.: The Johns Hopkins University Press.

Cameron, D. (1995). *Verbal hygiene.* London and New York: Routledge.

Caughey, J. L. (1979). Introspection in the ethnography of consciousness. Paper presented at the 78th annual meeting of the American Anthropological Association, Cincinnati, Ohio.

Chodorow, N. (1978). *The reproduction of mothering.* Psychoanalysis and the sociology of gender. Berkeley: University of California Press.

————. (1989). *Feminism and psychoanalysis.* New Haven, Conn.: Yale University Press.

Chong, D. (1994). *The concubine's children*. New York: Penguin.

Cixous, H. (1981). The laugh of the medusa. In *New French Feminisms*, ed. and trans. E. Marks and I. de Courtivron. New York: Schocken Books.

Cox, J. M. (1971). Autobiography and America. In J. H. Miller, ed. *Aspects of narrative*, 252–277. New York: Columbia University Press.

deMan, P. (1986). Semiology and rhetoric. In C. Kaplan, ed. *Criticism, the major statements* (2nd ed.), 606–622. New York: St. Martin's Press. (Original work published 1979.)

Derrida, J. (1976). *Of grammatology*. Trans. Gayatria Spivak. Baltimore, Md.: Johns Hopkins University.

———. (1986). Of grammatology. In C. Kaplan, ed. *Criticism, the major statements* (2nd ed.), 590–605. New York: St. Martin's Press. (Original work published 1967.)

Devereaux, G. (1967). *From anxiety to method in the behavioral sciences*. The Hague, Netherlands: Mouton.

Dewey, J. (1944). *Democracy and education*. New York: Free Press.

Dimen-Schein, M. (1977). *The anthropological imagination*. New York: MacGraw-Hill.

Dinnerstein, D. (1976). *The mermaid and the minotaur: sexual arrangements and human malaise*. New York: Harper and Row.

Eagleton, T. (1976). *Marxism and literacy criticism*. Los Angeles, Cal.: University of California Press.

Earle, W. (1972). *The autobiographical consciousness: a philosophical inquiry into existence*. Chicago, Ill.: Quadrangle Books.

Elliot, P. 1991. *From mastery to analysis: theories of gender in psychoanalytic feminism*. Ithaca, N.Y.: Cornell University Press.

Faber, M. (1981). *Culture and consciousness*. New York: Human Sciences Press.

Fairbairn, W. R. D. (1954). *An object relations theory of the personality*. New York: Basic Books.

Filstead, W. J., ed. (1970). *Qualitative methodology*. Chicago, Ill.: Markham.

Fish, S. (1986). Is there a text in this class? In C. Kaplan, ed. *Criticism, the major statements* (2nd ed.), 623–638. New York: St. Martin's Press. (Original work published 1980.)

Flax, J. (1983). Political philosophy and the patriarchal unconscious: psychoanalytic perspectives on epistemology and metaphysics. In S. Harding and M. B. Hintikka, eds. *Discovering Reality*. Holland: Reidel.

Fletcher, J. and A. Benjamin, eds. (1990). *Abjection, melancholia and love: the work of Julia Kristeva*. London and New York: Routledge.

Foreman Peck, L. (1985). Evaluating children's talk about literature: a theoretical perspective. *Children's Literature in Education*, 16(4), 203–218.

Freire, P. (1981). *Pedagogy of the oppressed*. Trans. Myra Bergman Ramos. New York: Continuum.

Freire, P. and D. Macedo. (1987). *Literacy: reading the word and world*. South Hadley, Mass.: Bergin and Garvey.

Freud, S. (1961a). The ego and the id. In J. Strachey, ed. and trans. *The standard edition of the complete psychological works of Sigmund Freud*. Vol. 19, 3–66. London: Hogarth Press. (Original work published 1923.)

———. (1961b). Psychoanalytic notes on an autobiographical account of a case of paranoia. In J. Strachey, ed. and trans. *The standard edition of the complete psychological works of Sigmund Freud*. Vol. 12, 9–82. London: Hogarth Press. (Original work published 1911.)

Frye, N. (1986. The archetypes of literature. In C. Kaplan, ed. *Criticism, the major statements* (2nd ed.), 501–515. New York: St. Martin's Press. (Original work published 1951.)

Gallop, J. (1982). *The daughter's seduction*. Feminism and psychoanalysis. Ithaca, N.Y.: Cornell University Press.

———. (1984). *Reading Lacan*. Ithaca, N.Y.: Cornell University Press.

Gates, H. (1990). Whose canon is it anyway? *The New York Times Book Review*, February 26.

Gay, P. (1989). *The Freud Reader*. New York: W.W. Norton.

Giroux, H., A. Penna, and W. Pinar. (1981). *Curriculum and instruction*. Berkeley, Cal.: McCutcheon Publishing.

Gloversmith, F. (1984). *The theory of reading*. New York: Barnes and Noble.

Goodlad, J. (1984). *A place called school*. New York: McGraw-Hill.

Gottschalk, L., C. Kluckhohn, and R. Angell, eds. (1945). *The use of personal documents in history, anthropology, and sociology*. New York: Social Science Research Council, Bulletin 53.

Green, A. (1978). Potential space in psychoanalysis: the object in the setting. In S. G. Grolnick and L. Barkin, eds. *Between reality and fantasy: transitional objects and phenomena*. New York: Jason Aronson.

Greenacre, P. (1969). *Trauma, growth, and personality*. New York: International Universities Press.

Griffin, G. and S. Barnes. (1986). Using research findings to change school and classroom practice: results of an experimental study. *American Educational Research Journal, 23*(4), 572–587.

Grumet, M. (1978a). Merely Players: curriculum as theater. *Curriculum Inquiry, 8*(1).

———. (1978b). Autobiography and reconceptualization. In Giroux, Penna, and Pinar, eds. *Curriculum and instruction*, 139–146. Berkeley, Cal.: McCutchan Publishing Co.

———. (1989). *Bitter milk: women and teaching*. Amherst, Mass.: University of Massachusetts.

———. (1992). The Language in the Middle: Bridging the Liberal Arts and Teacher Education. *Liberal Education, 78*(3).

Guba, E. G. (1978). Toward a methodology of naturalistic inquiry in educational evaluation. *CSE Monograph Series in Evaluation*. (Serial No. 8).

Habermas, J. (1968). *Knowledge and human interests*. Trans. Jeremy J. Shapiro. Boston, Mass.: Beacon Press.

Harre, R. and P. F. Secord. (1972). *The explanation of social behavior*. Oxford, England: Basil Blackwell and Mott.

Hill, C. (1990). *Writing from the margins: power and pedagogy for teachers of composition*. New York: Oxford University Press.

Hillman, J. (1983). *Healing fiction*. Tarrytown, N.Y.: Station Hill Press.

Holland, N. (1975). *Five readers reading*. New Haven, Conn.: Yale University Press.

Holly, G. (1980). Review of *Subjective Criticism*. *Journal of Curriculum Theorizing, 2*(1), 252–256.

Horner, A. (1984). *Object relations and the developing ego in therapy*. New York: Jason Aronson.

Kaplan, C., ed. (1986). *Criticism, the major statements* (2nd ed.). New York: St. Martin's Press.

Kappeler, S. and R. Bryson. (1983). *Teaching the text*. Boston, Mass.: Routledge and Kegan Paul.

Kaufman-Osborn, T. (1993). Teasing feminist sense from experience. *Hypatia, 8*(2), 124–144.

Kegan, R. (1982) *The evolving self: problem and process in human development*. Cambridge, Mass.: Harvard University Press.

Keller, E. F. (1983). *A feeling for the organism. The life and work of Barbara McClintock*. New York: W. H. Freeman and Co.

——. (1985). Reflections on gender and science. New Haven, Conn.: Yale University Press.

Kristeva, J. (1980). Desire in language: a semiotic approach to literature and art. Trans. L. Roudiz, A. Jardine, and T. Gora. New York: Columbia University Press.

——. (1982). Powers of horror: an essay on abjection. Trans. Leon S. Roudiez. New York: Columbia University Press.

——. (1986). The Kristeva reader. Ed. Toril Moi. New York: Columbia University Press.

——. (1987). Tales of Love. Trans. Leon. S. Roudiez. New York: Columbia University Press.

——. (1988). In the beginning was love: psychoanalysis and faith. Trans. Arthur Goldhammer. New York: Columbia University Press.

——. (1989). Black sun. Trans. Leon Roudiez. New York: Columbia University Press

——. (1991). Strangers to ourselves. Trans. Leon S. Roudiez. New York: Columbia University Press.

Lacan, J. (1968). The language of the self. Trans. Anthony Wilden. New York: Dell Publishing.

Lambert, K. (1981). Analysis, repair, and individuation. London: Academic Press.

Langness, L. L. and G. Frank. (1981). Lives, an anthropological approach to biography. Novato, Cal.: Chandler and Sharp Publishers.

Lauter, P. (1985). Race and gender in the shaping of the American literary canon. In J.L. Newton, ed. Feminist criticism and social change. New York: Metheum.

Layton, L. and B. Schapiro, eds. (1986). Narcissism and the text: studies in literature and the psychology of the self. New York: New York University Press.

Lazerson, M. (1986). Review of "A study of high schools," a dialogue in three parts. Harvard Educational Review, 56(1), 37–48.

Leininger, M. N., ed. (1985). Qualitative research methods in nursing. Orlando, Fla.: Grune and Stratton.

Leverenz, D. (1982). Where children strove at recess: English professors and psychoanalytic criticism. College English, 44(5), 451–458.

MacNeil, R. (1989). Wordstruck. New York: Viking Penguin Press.

Marks, E. and I. deCourtivron. (1981). New French feminisms. New York: Schocken Books.

Mauro, L. (1980). Personal constructs and response to literature: case studies of adolescents reading short stories and poems about death. Unpublished doctoral dissertation, Rutgers University, New Brunswick, New Jersey.

McCuller, C. C. (1984). Teacher perceptions of students and teacher classroom behavior. Paper presented at American Education Research Association annual conference, New Orleans.

Merleau-Ponty, M. (1962) *The phenomenology of perception*. Trans. Colin Wilson. New York: Humanities Press.

Misch, G. (1973). *A history of autobiography in antiquity*. Trans. Dickes. Westport, Conn.: Greenwood Press.

Moruzzi, N. M. (1993). National abjects: Julia Kristeva on the process of political self-identification. In K. Oliver, *Ethics, politics, and difference in Julia Kristeva's writing*. New York: Routledge.

Muller, J. (1986). Light and the wisdom of the dark: aging and the wisdom of desire in the texts of Louise Bogan. In Woodward, K. and Schwartz, M., eds. *Memory and desire*. Bloomington, Ind.: Indiana University Press.

Myers, B. K. & B. Spodek. (1984). An analysis of one teacher's beliefs about events in her classroom. Paper presented at the American Educational Research Association annual conference, New Orleans.

Nakashima, E. (1996). When it comes to tough school jobs, women find it tough to get ahead. *The Washington Post*, April 21.

Nelson, K., ed. (1989). *Narratives from the crib*. Cambridge, Mass.: Harvard University Press.

O'Brien, M. (1981). *The politics of reproduction*. London: Routledge and Kegan Paul.

Oliver, K., ed. (1993a). *Ethics, politics, and difference in Julia Kristeva's writing*. New York: Routledge.

Oliver, K. (1993b). *Reading Kristeva: unraveling the Double-bind*. Bloomington, Ind.: Indiana University Press.

Olney, J. (1980). *Autobiography: essays theoretical and critical*. Princeton, N.J.: Princeton University Press.

Oxford English Dictionary—The Compact Edition. (1961). Oxford: Oxford University Press.

Parker, W. C. and J. J. Gehrke. (1986). Learning activities and teacher's decision-making: some grounded hypotheses. *American Educational Research Journal*, 23(2), 227–242.

Pinar, W. and M. Grumet. (1978). *Toward a poor curriculum*. Dubuque, Ia.: Kendall/Hunt Press.

Peterson, P. L. and C. M. Clark. (1978). Teachers' reports of their cognitive processes during teaching. *American Education Research Journal, 15,* 555–565.

Ransom, J. C. (1986). Criticism as pure speculation. In C. Kaplan, ed. *Criticism, the major statements* (2nd ed.), 450–469. New York: St. Martin's Press. (Original work published 1941.)

Reese, W. L. (1980). *Dictionary of philosophy and religion.* Atlantic Highlands, N.J.: Humanities Press.

Reppen, J. and M. Charney, eds. (1985). *The psychoanalytic study of literature.* Hillsdale, N.J.: The Analytic Press.

Ricoeur, P. (1976). *Interpretation theory.* Fort Worth, Tx.: Texas Christian University Press.

Rorty, R. (1980). *Philosophy and the mirror of nature.* Princeton, N.J.: Princeton University Press.

———. (1982). Nineteenth-century idealism and twentieth-century textualism. In R. Rorty, *Consequences of pragmatism.* Minneapolis, Minn.: University of Minnesota Press.

Rosenblatt, L. (1976). *Literature as exploration.* New York: Noble and Noble. (Original work published 1938.)

Salvio, P. M. (1990). The world, the text, the reader. In Lunsford, Noglen, and Slevin, eds. *The Right to Literacy.* New York: Modern Language Association.

Sartre, J. P. (1964). *The words.* Trans. B. Frechtman. New York: George Braziller.

———. (1986). Why write? In C. Kaplan, ed. *Criticism, the major statements* (2nd ed.), 482–500. New York: St. Martin's Press. (Original work published 1949.)

Schwartz, M. (1975). Where is literature? *College English, 36,* 756–765.

———. (1986). Shakespeare through contemporary psychoanalysis. In C. Kahn and M. Schwartz, eds. *Representing Shakespeare, new psychoanalytic essays.* Baltimore, Md.: The Johns Hopkins University Press.

Sharratt, B. (1982). *Reading relations.* Atlantic Highlands, N.J.: Humanities Press.

Shavelson, R. J. and P. Stern. (1981). Research on teachers' pedagogical thoughts, judgments, decisions, and behavior. *Review of Education Research, 51*(4), 455–498.

Skura, M. (1981). *The literary use of the psychoanalytic process.* New Haven, Conn.: Yale University Press.

Slatoff, W. (1970). *With respect to readers: dimensions of literary response.* Ithaca, N.Y.: Cornell University Press.

Smith, F. (1983). *Essays into literacy.* Portsmouth, N.H.: Heineman.

Stern, D. (1977). *The first relationship: infant and mother.* Cambridge, Mass.: Harvard University Press.

————. (1985). *The interpersonal world of the infant: a view from psychoanalysis.* New York: Basic Books.

————. (1990). *Diary of a Baby.* New York: Basic Books.

Sullivan, H. S. (1953). *The interpersonal theory of psychiatry.* New York: W. W. Norton and Company.

Takaki, R., ed. (1987). *From different shores: perspectives on race and ethnicity in America.* New York: Oxford University Press.

Taylor, D. (1989). Toward a unified theory of literacy, learning and instructional practices. *Phi Delta Kappa, 71*(3), 184–193.

Thomas, D. (1967). Poem in October. In *A Pocket Book of Modern Verse.* Ed. Oscar Williams. New York: Washington Square Press.

Van Manen, M. (1982). Phenomenological pedagogy. *Curriculum Inquiry, 12*(3).

Vernon, J. (1979). *Poetry and the body.* Urbana, Ill.: University of Illinois.

Vygotsky, L. (1962). *Thought and language.* Cambridge, Mass.: MIT Press.

Webster's new world dictionary of the American language, college edition. (1968). Cleveland and New York: The World Publishing Company.

Weilland, S. (1983). Relations stop nowhere: cases and texts, critics and psychoanalysis. *College English, 45,* 705–723.

Westlund, J. (1984). *Shakespeare's reparative comedies.* Chicago, Ill.: The University of Chicago Press.

Winnicott, D. W. (1965). *The maturational processes and the facilitating environment.* New York: International Universities Press.

————. (1971). *Playing and reality.* London: Tavistock Publications.

Wolf, S. (1995). Language in and around the dramatic classroom. *Journal of Curriculum Studies, 27*(2), 117–138.

Woolf, V. (1957). *A room of one's own.* New York: Harbinger.

Wright, E. (1984). *Psychoanalytic criticism: theory in practice*. London: Methuen.

Young, I. (1989). Oppression and abjection: unconscious dynamics of racism, sexism, and homophobia. Unpublished paper presented at the Society for Phenomenology and Existential Philosophy, New York.

———. (1990). *Throwing like a girl and other essays in feminist philosophy and social theory*. Bloomington, Ind.: Indiana University Press.

INDEX